# THE GRUDGE

# THE GRUDGE

*Scotland vs. England, 1990*

TOM ENGLISH

YELLOW JERSEY PRESS
LONDON

Published by Yellow Jersey Press 2010
2 4 6 8 10 9 7 5 3 1

First published in Great Britain in 2010 by
Yellow Jersey Press
Random House, 20 Vauxhall Bridge Road,
London SW1V 2SA

www.rbooks.co.uk

Addresses for companies within The Random House Group Limited can be
found at: www.randomhouse.co.uk/offices.htm

The Random House Group Limited Reg. No. 954009

A CIP catalogue record for this book
is available from the British Library

ISBN 9780224082761

The Random House Group Limited supports The Forest Stewardship Council
(FSC), the leading international forest certification organisation. All our titles
that are printed on Greenpeace approved FSC certified paper carry the FSC logo.
Our paper procurement policy can be found at: www.rbooks.co.uk/environment

Mixed Sources
Product group from well-managed
forests and other controlled sources
www.fsc.org  Cert no. TT-COC-2139
© 1996 Forest Stewardship Council
FSC

Typeset in New Aster by Palimpsest Book Production Limited,
Grangemouth, Stirlingshire
Printed in the UK by
CPI Mackays, Chatham ME5 8TD

For Lynn, Eilidh and Tom Jnr

# CONTENTS

# CAST OF CHARACTERS

Featuring . . .

## FROM SCOTLAND

Jim Telfer, aka Creamy – forwards coach, all-round
ball-breaker

Ian McGeechan, aka Geech – head coach, deep thinker

Gavin Hastings – full-back, class act

Tony Stanger – rookie right wing

Scott Hastings – outside centre, the emotional one of the
family

Sean Lineen – inside centre from Auckland, grandfather from
Stornoway

Iwan Tukalo – veteran left wing from Italian and Ukrainian stock

Craig Chalmers – fly-half, not lacking in confidence

Gary Armstrong – scrum-half, teak-tough

David Sole – loosehead prop, captain, strong and silent type

Kenny Milne – hooker, powerful and out to prove himself

Paul Burnell – tighthead prop, honest journeyman

Chris Gray – second row, based in Nottingham

Damian Cronin, aka Del Boy – lock forward based in Bath,
ducker and diver in the antiques game, character

John Jeffrey, aka JJ – back-row forward, canny operator,
wind-up merchant

Finlay Calder – openside flanker, intense, streetwise

Derek White – laid-back No. 8, primary target of Telfer's thunder

FROM ENGLAND

Simon Hodgkinson – full-back, dead-eye goal-kicker
Simon Halliday – winger, an operator in the City of London
Will Carling – centre, captain, not as cocksure as he lets on
Jerry Guscott – centre, graceful, emerging genius
Rory Underwood – winger, record-breaking try-scorer, flying
   machine
Rob Andrew – fly-half, statesman
Richard Hill – scrum-half, firebrand
Paul Rendall, aka The Judge – veteran prop
Brian Moore, aka Mooro – hooker, pack leader, as thorny as
   they come
Jeff Probyn – prop, driven man
Paul Ackford – formidable lock forward, police inspector
Wade Dooley – giant lock forward, the enforcer of the team
Mick Skinner, aka Skins – blindside flanker, most extrovert
   player in England
Peter Winterbottom – openside flanker, the voice of reason
Mike Teague, aka Iron Mike – No. 8, hard nut
Geoff Cooke – manager, architect of England's boom-time
Roger Uttley – coach, dog of war from his old playing days

AND . . .

Margaret Thatcher, aka That Bloody Woman – Prime Minister,
   scourge of the Scots

# ILLUSTRATIONS

1 The teams: Scotland and England teams before the match on 17 March 1990 (both courtesy of Colorsport)
2 The characters: Scotland: John Jeffrey in action on 17 March 1990 (courtesy of Colorsport), David Sole in 1987 (courtesy of PA Photos), Jim Telfer in 1994 (courtesy of the *Scotsman*) and Ian McGeechan in 1990 (courtesy of Getty Images)
3 The characters: England: a publicity shot of Will Carling in January 1990, Brian Moore in the game against Wales, 17 February 1990 (courtesy of Getty Images), Wade Dooley arriving in Edinburgh the day before the match (courtesy of the *Scotsman*)
4 Margaret Thatcher as depicted by Spitting Image (courtesy of PA Photos); a poll tax demonstration on the streets of Edinburgh in April 1989 (courtesy of the *Scotsman*)
5 England vs. Wales, 17 February 1990 at Twickenham (courtesy of Getty Images); tickets sold out in Edinburgh, a month before the final (courtesy of the *Scotsman*); the Scottish team training on 16 March 1990, the day before the big match (courtesy of PA Photos)
6 The match: David Sole leading his team onto the pitch, the infamous 'slow walk'; England's Jeremy Guscott in a tussle with Tony Stanger and John Jeffrey of Scotland (both courtesy of Getty Images)
7 The match: referee David Bishop awards Tony Stanger's try (courtesy of PA Photos); Damian Cronin of Scotland and Wade Dooley of England both jump for the ball (courtesy of Getty Images)
8 The celebration: the jubilant Scottish team in their dressing room (courtesy of PA Photos); *Scotland on Sunday* headline the following day (courtesy of *Scotland on Sunday*)

# THE FINAL BEASTING

They saw his shadow from across the field, this giant figure coming towards them, his booming voice travelling out of the night and into the pits of their stomachs. That voice they'd heard year after year, belittling them and hypnotising them all at once.

The eight men of the Scottish pack against the lone figure of their coach, Jim Telfer. And, somehow, as Telfer approached, the eight felt outnumbered. There was a reason for that, of course. Bitter experience. They all had previous with him. Every last one of them. They'd all known what it was like to be his target, what it was like to be humiliated, what it was like to have him standing an inch from their noses, spraying them with spit as he told them what a bunch of inadequates they really were. Old school, that was Telfer.

They knew it was coming, this beasting session. With three days to go before Scotland played England for the Calcutta Cup, the Triple Crown, the Five Nations championship and the Grand Slam all rolled into one momentous package, Telfer greeted them with five seconds of familiarity followed by the promise of two hours of terrible punishment. Intensity in training, that was his thing. Nobody did it better.

'We're doing fifty scrums,' he stated, 'and if they're not right, we're doing another fifty and then another fifty. We don't leave until everything is perfect because, boys, this Saturday you have the chance to write your names in history and I won't let you fuck it up by being soft.'

The silhouettes of ten men appeared in the distance, the ten toughest characters that Telfer could lay his hands on. Battle-hardened props, big old locks and back-row forwards not quite good enough to make his final selection but bitter enough to give the chosen ones a test.

Telfer looked at the eight and pointed to the ten. 'This is England you're up against now,' he said. 'That's Brian Moore. That's Wade Dooley. That's Mick Skinner out the back. Are they out tonight in this weather? Are they putting themselves through this? Do they want it as much as you? All this work, all this pain, all this abuse. And for what? To lose in front of your own people? To be robbed of the greatest day of your lives by a mob that think fuck-all of you? Is that the way you want this thing to end?'

And so the beasting began.

He demanded many things that night. He demanded concentrated scrummaging, he demanded controlled explosions in the rucks, he demanded precision in the line-outs and, if it wasn't done to his satisfaction, they'd start all over. Scrums upon scrums, rucks upon rucks, twenty-second breathers and go again. Some nights there was no silencing the boys, no amount of physical exertion that would button John Jeffrey's lip. But this was different. Tonight, even JJ, the most talkative man in Scotland, was too tired to jabber.

'Derek White, where are you?'

'Here, Jim.'

'Right, boys. Derek is going to take this ball up and when he hits the ground I want you to ruck him out of it. He's an Englishman, okay?'

More than anything in the world Derek White wanted to point out at this juncture that he wasn't an Englishman, that he'd been a Scotland international longer than any of them, that nobody could mistake him for Skinner or any of his formidable cronies, no way, no how. But White didn't say anything. In his dreams, yes, he was a militant, a revolutionary storming the gates of his oppressor. But in reality he kept his trap shut because that was what Telfer's forwards were programmed to do, because he knew what would happen if he said something, and it really wasn't worth it.

'He's lying over your ball,' said Telfer. 'He's killing it. Are you going to let him at it or are you going to give him a dose of reality?'

The seven Scottish forwards formed an orderly queue and took turns to ruck their teammate off the ball, knowing that if they skimped Telfer would notice and then they'd be next, down there in the dirt with a hundred stones of driven men raking over the top of them. 'Sorry, Whitey,' said one as the studs came up. 'You know how it is,' said another as his boot came down. 'I don't want to do it, Derek,' said a third, 'but what Telfer wants, Telfer gets, so you're getting shoe, my son, and plenty of it.'

On they went, Telfer reminding them all the while what was at stake on Saturday, how good the English pack were, how many Lions they had. Brian Moore. Wade Dooley. Paul Ackford. Peter Winterbottom. Iron Man Mike Teague, the star of the Lions series in Australia the year before. England had buried everybody so far. They'd battered Ireland 23–0. They'd gone to Paris and put up a record score. They'd doled out such a hiding to the Welsh forwards that the coach walked out, mortified at what had become of his team. The newspaper headlines were paeans to Scotland's opponents. 'Ruthless England turn on the style'; 'Wonderful England's finest hour'; 'Power and glory for irresistible England'.

Telfer sat his pack in a circle after training and began talking. This was his first big address of the week and he'd prepared the words meticulously. Some thought his speeches were off the cuff but they weren't. He rehearsed them, as if acting. In many ways, he *was* an actor. For hours he'd worked on intonation, planning when to raise his voice and when to lower it, planning when to use silence and for how long.

None of his players sat close to him. The spray put them off. The spray and the fear of catching his eye and drawing the heat as a result. They lowered their heads and hoped that for once in his life he'd go easy, for once in his life he'd just throttle back on the invective, but they knew the odds of that. About as likely as a tortoise winning the Derby. Jim Telfer was a creature of habit. He did scrums and line-outs and rucks. He didn't do soft-soaps. He said he wasn't doing this job to be popular and, to the players, that was always a bad sign. That sounded like a Gettysburg Address of viciousness was on its way. They knew the triggers off by heart by now.

He wasn't doing it to be liked or respected, he continued. He didn't give a fuck either way quite frankly. He had his family at home in the Borders and his coterie of friends and that was good enough for him. Didn't need any more. He knew he was cruel and he knew he was brutal but he wasn't asking them to do anything that he hadn't done before them. He'd played for Scotland and played for the Lions. He'd put his body in the path of some bad men from his first days in the Melrose senior team at the age of seventeen and had had it kicked for twenty years. He knew their pain only too well. He had never been a great player, but he was honest and he worked hard and the one principle he lived by was that, however hard his opponent trained, he would train harder, however much the other guy wanted it, he wanted it more.

He coached out of a fear of failure and that feeling was never stronger than it was right now. All through his time in rugby he thought about the worst thing that could happen and then he worked like a dog to make sure it didn't. That was his philosophy. He thought about the worst thing that could happen at Murrayfield in three days' time and this session tonight was the result. His players nodded their understanding.

He liked what he saw: the aggression, the focus, the accuracy.

Not that he admitted it, but he couldn't have asked for more. He'd driven them as hard as could be and yet they soaked it up without complaint.

His team rose to leave. Sore and exhausted, they filed out of the room in silence, save for the odd jaded groan. Telfer watched them go. Concealing his admiration behind a wall of stone, he waited for the last to disappear. 'Jesus, boys,' he said quietly. 'Don't you know I wouldn't abuse you if I didn't think you were worth it?'

# CHAPTER 1

# THERE WAS NONE OF THIS HATE BEFORE

## 17 MARCH 1990

Will Carling, strong and handsome and just twenty-four years old, looked in his bedroom mirror and wondered where the hell he was going to find the right words. How would he address his team just before they left for Murrayfield? What wisdom could a greenhorn like him impart to a pack of forwards that was so hardbitten and cynical?

What could he say to Paul Rendall and Jeff Probyn, survivors of thousands of scrums in hundreds of grounds across their combined sixty-nine years? How could he look Brian Moore in the eye knowing that his rage for victory was so great? How could he understand Peter Winterbottom's motivation, a man who, two years earlier at Murrayfield, after just five minutes of play, was stretchered from the field in near unbearable agony with two ribs sticking out of the side of his chest?

What could he tell Wade Dooley that he didn't already know?

When Carling was fifteen years old and tucked up in private school, Dooley, a policeman, was battling through the night in the front line of the Toxteth riots with a bacon butty stuffed down his pants to keep his gonads warm and a floppy shield in his hand that melted when a rioter's flame flew too close. When Dooley retold the tale of the petrol bombs, the smoke and the destruction, the cars overturned, the shops looted and the smell of a city on fire, and finished with an observation that, typical Scouse, the only things they didn't set alight were the pubs, what was Carling to do? Regale the boys with the day he got detention?

Then there was Mike Teague. Christ almighty, Teague alone was a freak of nature. Carling talked to him about his training regime once and almost passed out with fatigue when told of the things he did to stay in the England team. He did body-building in an abandoned church in the Coney Hill district of his native Gloucester. Salubrious it was not. 'Frankly, it's a shithole,' he told Carling, 'but the company's good.'

'Who'd you train with, Teaguey?' Carling asked and within seconds he wished he hadn't bothered.

'Well, there's a coloured lad called Paddy Robinson. He's a bouncer, a right gym monkey. Then there's big Derek Bottomley, a God-fearing type. Legs and backs one day, shoulders and arms the next day and then repeat it over and over. Every morning, ten a.m. Been doing it for seven year now. But that's just the weights. Then there's the Mad Dogs?'

'The what?'

'Yeah, a group of us go running in the Forest of Dean. Pretty extreme stuff. We cut down trees and put the logs up on our shoulders and yomp up the hills.'

'Jesus!' replied Carling.

'An hour and a half one way, an hour and a half back the same way and then into the club for night-time training, two or three hours of that, couple of hundred sit-ups to finish, a few pints of Severn Cider and home.'

Carling knew that Teague wasn't bullshitting. He'd seen the evidence of his robustness too many times to doubt him. Teague had been named player of the series on the Lions tour of Australia nine months earlier, despite tearing his shoulder tendon off the bone just two weeks before the first Test. He wasn't called Iron Mike for nothing.

So what was Carling going to say on this morning of mornings? Don't give an inch, Teaguey! No backward step, Winters! Take no nonsense, Wade! May as well give the Vatican a ring and remind the Pope to say his prayers at bedtime while he's at it.

Why had the selectors picked him to lead these men? That's what Carling was thinking about. Why was he even playing for England? How the hell had he made it this far?

That guy you saw? That Carling swagger? It was a front, much of it. An act. A big deception. For the cameras he could put on a show of superiority that looked natural and believable, only it was paper-thin. He could convince the Scots into thinking he was in control, but he had the devil's own job convincing himself.

All he wanted to do was go to a clock and wind the hands forward to kick-off time. He'd be okay then. Come the first whistle, he'd be fine. But it was early still, way too early.

'I had to come across as this mega-confident character, this supremely together person,' he said. 'And yet I'd sit in my room and crap myself. I'd get on the bus and crap myself again. I'd sit in the dressing room, changed and ready, and I'd crap myself once more. These doubts would go whirring through my mind. Am I any good? Do I deserve my place? Do the lads believe in me as captain? What are they saying when I'm not there? Honestly, the insecurities!'

There were days when he wanted to go to his heroes for affirmation. Days like this. But he couldn't. He loved Winterbottom and he loved Teague. Unbreakable, the pair of them. Winters and Teaguey were his heroes. He would have killed to have known what they really thought of him.

'In our world, it would have been pathetic to ask. Feeble and sad. If I said, "Teaguey, did you think I was any good today?" he'd have looked at me suspiciously and said, "What the fuck is the matter with you?" I once told Winters that I thought he was brilliant and he said, "Pull yourself together, Carling" and walked off. You didn't bare your soul in that dressing room. You just didn't do it.'

What he did was pretend. He was captain. He needed to get a grip. He looked in the mirror that Saturday morning and gave himself a slap. 'Stop fucking about! Stop it! You're a great player, you're a great captain, you will dominate. Now get your shit together.'

He had time to kill. A couple of hours before the off, a little window before the England team coach pulled up at the front door of the Peebles Hydro Hotel in the Borders and took them to Murrayfield.

What to do, what to do? Chill with the lads, maybe? Nah, no interest, not after he poked his head around the door of the team room and was hit hard between the eyes by Mick Skinner's theatrical performance. 'I'm telling you, girls, this is in the bag,' Skinner was saying. 'IN THE BAG! No way the Sweaties live with us today. Am I right, Mooro?'

'Shut up, Skins,' said Brian Moore.

'I'm guessing fifteen points, maybe twenty,' Skinner continued.

'Shut up, I'm telling you,' Moore demanded.

'Maybe I'll score a try . . .'

If looks could kill Moore's glare would have mowed Skinner down on the spot. 'You know what, Skins? You've an incredible ability to walk into a room, take it over completely and bore the shit out of everybody in it.'

'Too kind, Mr Moore. Too kind,' said Skinner, with a bow.

No, Carling could do without that kind of aggravation. His second thought was for the newspapers.

He'd been reading them all week. Had ploughed through as much battle imagery as he could handle. The coverage had got so out of kilter with reality that he wondered if he should bother wearing his England strip at Murrayfield at all. Maybe a suit of armour would be more appropriate. And a claymore. All the references to bloodbaths past were tiresome. The bastardisation

of the bards, from Robert Burns to William McGonagall, was
rampant in the press, as if a day as incendiary as this needed
any more dynamite attached.

> *Then the Scots charged them with sword in hand,*
> *And made them fly from off their land;*
> *And King Will was amazed at the sight,*
> *And he got wounded in the fight;*
>
> *And he cried, Oh, heaven! England's lost, and I'm undone,*
> *Alas! Alas! Where shall I run?*
> *Then he turned his horse, and rode on afar,*
> *And never halted till he reached Dunbar.*

He had seen tabloid images of his head stuck on the body of
King Edward II, the hapless monarch trounced at the Battle
of Bannockburn, or Butcher Cumberland, the Duke who led the
massacre of the Scots at Culloden, or some other psychotic
sword-wielding English aristocrat who laid waste to half of
Scotland centuries before.

The Scottish air was thick with this stuff. He'd already had
an exchange with a reporter, sitting up front in one of his press
conferences during the week. Carling could tell by the look
of this guy that he hated the ground the English walked on,
particularly the patch of ground that happened to be under the
English captain's feet.

'You know the whole of Scotland detests you, Will,' the
scribbler said. 'How do you feel about that?'

'No problem with it' was Carling's terse reply.

'No problem! Really?' asked the journalist.

'Yeah, it's okay. Honest. I hate the Scots every bit as much as
they hate me. It's mutual loathing.'

'Woah, woah, woah,' went the reporter.

'What's wrong with you?' asked Carling.

'You cannae say that.'

'Oh, right. Why's that then? It was okay for us to come here in the past when we were crap, get our arses kicked and go home again. You were lovely to us then. Soon as we're a threat you're hitting us with anti-English hate. Tell me why that is? '

'Och, years of oppression.'

'Well, I haven't been oppressing you, have I? Yeah, I'm English but, surprisingly, I wasn't around in 17-fucking-whenever. I wasn't exactly leading the charge at Culloden, was I? I'm only twenty-four. Are you not educated or what?'

Carling willed the guy to quote him word for word. 'Put it all in, you prick' was what he wanted to say at the end. 'Stick that in your poxy paper and see how people like it.' But none of it appeared. He checked every line.

He knew what was going on around him. The political back-drop. Margaret Thatcher's second son, that's what the Scottish press did to him. That was the image that resonated with readers. Young and flash and full of money, he was Tory Boy. He was public school, he came from army stock, he was a City type, a capitalist, believed in the greed is good mantra, worshipped at the altar of That Bloody Woman! Like peas in a pod they were.

If only they could see inside his head.

'Bullshit assumptions,' said Carling but nobody was listening. The Scots had their own version of what he was about and they had no intention of changing their minds.

Thatcher had been up a week before. She'd gone on television to trumpet her pride at being the 'prime minister of Scotland'. But Scotland hadn't voted for her. At the general election three years earlier, Thatcher's Scottish MPs were gunned down at the ballot box. When the smoke cleared there were just ten of them left standing, their lowest number since 1910. Labour had fifty. Five times the seats but zero power.

The prime minister thought the reason the Tories were losing the battle north of the border was because people hadn't yet grasped Thatcherism as a concept. Didn't understand it. Weren't

alive to its possibilities. As was written by her critics: 'The Scots
are told that their votes are lying; that they secretly love what
they constantly vote against.' And then she hit them with the
poll tax and hit them with it first, on 1 April 1989, a year before
it came to England. The Scottish newspapers blasted her for
using their country as a testing ground. She tried to explain,
tried to claim that this was myth being sold as fact, tried to get
her message across that she was pro-Scotland, but nothing she
said came out right.

In 1988 there had been none of this hate. Oh sure, there was
a nationalistic fervour on the streets and in the stadium at
Murrayfield, but it wasn't nasty, not like this. There was slagging
then and plenty of it, but there was fun and there was even a
bit of warmth.

Most of all there was drink: drink in the dressing room after
the match, drink on the bus back to the hotel, drink in the lobby,
drink in the elevator going up to the room and coming back
down again, drink at the dinner, drink on the street after the
dinner, drink with fans from both nations.

Carling was no Sir Robin Day but he knew politics was
involved in the shift in atmosphere. It was an ill wind that was
blowing for the Tories. And that's the chill he felt. It was comical
in a way because he had no connection with the Conservatives.
He'd never voted for them. He'd never voted for anybody. The
idea of him going into a polling station and giving his endorse-
ment to one side or another was anathema to him. But there
he was, a convenient target. Very English, very arrogant.
Thatcher's captain.

In his relationships with the Scots, Brian Moore had something
in common with Samuel Johnson. 'The noblest prospect which
a Scotchmen ever sees, is the high road that leads him to
England!' wrote the doctor, and Mooro was not of a mind
to disagree. 'Knowledge was divided among the Scots, like

bread in a besieged town, to every man a mouthful, to no man a bellyful.' Mooro would have endorsed that one, too.

He had first clashed with the Scots in April 1987. First cap, first scrum, the formidable Colin Deans staring him down, Twickenham the venue. England's put-in. Mooro hooks the ball perfectly only it bounces off Jon Hall's knee and shoots back out on the Scotland side. A freak ricochet. Deans, the old dog, flashes Mooro a sardonic smile. 'You've a lot to learn, laddie.' Mooro's response was not that of a man in awe of his famous rival: 'We'll see, you Scottish twat.' He was in awe of nobody, that was his great strength. He was smaller than most hookers, that was a plus too. It shouldn't have been, but he made it work for him. His lack of bulk made him more determined, more obsessed. He looked for slights against his ability and made hay. The faces of the men who suggested he was too small he had in his mind's eye, the words of opponents who'd dissed him he had on the tip of his tongue.

'The Scots don't need much excuse to hate us, do they?' said Mooro. 'Despite the fact that we've paid them a disproportionate amount of money under the Barnett Formula since 19-fucking-whenever.'

His teammates looked at each other. 'What's the Barnett Formula?'

That was another thing about him. He was alive to the world around him. 'I'm like this, you see,' he said, talking to nobody and yet everybody. 'I've studied Scottish history. I tell the Scots when I meet them, "You know Robert the Bruce was French, don't you?"

'They say, "What do you mean he was French?"

'He's French. Your great hero. A Frenchman.'

'No, he wasnae.'

'Yes he fucking was. He was as much French as he was Scottish. And here's another one for you. The famous Act of Union, when Scotland gave up its independence in 17-whenever. Bought and sold for English gold and all that bollocks. I say to them, "Bet you think that the English made you sign that, don't you?" And they go, "Aye". And I say, "No, what happened was you were bankrupt because you tried to colonise some place in Central America and you fucked it up. You lost so much money you were broke. And then we gave you a bribe to sign."

'Aye, you bribed us!'

'Yeah, but you bloody well took it!'

'No we didnae. It was the aristocracy.'

'Well, somebody signed it, didn't they?'

Mooro had worked up a head of steam now.

'I won't have it. They say they never colonised anybody. Well, how is it that when you go around the world, when you fetch up in Tonga or Samoa or Fiji the first person you meet off the plane is called McGregor. It was the British Empire not the English Empire. Their lot colonised as much as we did. There's Scots all over the planet and they all wanted to get out because it's so fucking miserable there.' Mooro was a walking exclamation mark. He was political in a way that Carling could never be. He understood the psyche of the Scottish people better than any of the English players, and, on the subject of Thatcher, he sympathised with them greatly.

He thought the poll tax was appalling. He thought introducing it into Scotland first was grotesquely unfair. If he had been Scottish, quite honestly, he'd probably be carrying a chip on his shoulder about the English, a chip as large as any of the tartan masses heading for Murrayfield. He wouldn't have been able to help himself. That's the way he was. Always railing against something. Always. As targets for Scottish bile, Mooro and Carling were locked together in the bullseye. That's just the way it was.

A little after midday, Carling put on his captain's face and spoke to the troops, reminded them of the devastation they'd caused in the championship already, went through the record books they'd shredded, the landmarks they'd set in their three runaway victories. He'd rehearsed every line and he sold it well for a man who wasn't sure if he belonged there.

Then he picked up his bag and told them that the bus was waiting to take them to Murrayfield. Time to go. And Mooro was first out of the door.

# CHAPTER 2

## PRIVILEGE. I'VE HATED IT SINCE I WAS A LAD

As fate would have it, Jim Telfer's birthday fell on Grand Slam Saturday. He was fifty. They gave him a cake – in the shape of a tackle bag. JJ suggested Derek White present it and, game for a laugh, Derek White obliged. They flicked the lights and out he came, his face illuminated by the glow of the candles, his cheery voice leading the celebration of the man who so often tormented him. Ah, the comedic irony. Telfer saw the humour in it right away. He smiled and he laughed and then, when the fuss died down, he went quiet. 'Fifty years,' he said, softly. 'Fifty years.'

On the night he was born, grey and misty, an RAF torpedo bomber with a nickname of 'The Flying Suitcase' got into trouble southeast of Yetholm in the Scottish Borders and crashed to earth at Windy Gyle in the Cheviot Hills, killing all four servicemen on board, the youngest a nineteen-year-old pilot, the oldest a twenty-six-year-old air gunner.

The explosion happened in Willie Telfer's field, or at least in one of the fields he tended for the Duke of Roxburghe. Telfer, a shepherd all his days, was the first on the scene, the first to see sections of fuselage spread wide across the countryside, the first to raise the alarm.

Years later, when his son was old enough to understand, he would tell him about it. 'You came into the world with a bang, Jim,' he'd say. Well, that just set young Telfer's mind racing. Next chance he got, he nipped out of the cottage, hopped on a bus and then walked to the scene of the tragedy to look for fragments of plane to take home as souvenirs. It was the first recorded example of Jim Telfer's obsession with the breakdown.

He can tell you now that he was in his late teens when he joined the dots of his childhood and became bitter, but even as a boy of eight and ten and twelve years old he knew there was something wrong with the world. He wouldn't say he became a socialist that early in life, but looking back he can see clearly the seeds being sown.

His father, a quiet and determined man, left school when he was fourteen. Didn't matter if Willie Telfer was bright or not. His path was clear. He was going into service for the Duke.

Peggy, Jim's mother, a gentle and bright woman, was a servant in the big house. She, too, had finished school at fourteen, despite showing promise. The pair of them were brought up by parents who were subservient to the landed gentry. 'Yes sir, no sir, three bags full sir'. That was how it was done. It was the way of things.

The way of things grated on Telfer from as early as he can remember. The Duke this and the Duke that, the doffing of the cap and the knowing their place – it wasn't for him. Whenever the landlord paid a visit they were expected to line up to greet him. Telfer could never understand why. 'I'd think, "What's he done that's so great?" I'd wonder, "Why is he being treated like he was special?" I just didn't get it.'

As a young man he got confused when a group of other children suddenly appeared in the fields one Christmas, stayed a while and then disappeared again for months on end. It took him time to work out that these were the landlord's kids, who had parachuted in from boarding school in Edinburgh during the holidays and were then driven back there when the holidays were over. Day trippers to the land, they were. Tourists. These

people with their private educations and their big houses and
their new cars were living it up off the back of his parents' hard
work, his parents who rarely had a day off, who didn't have fancy
things. It wasn't right. It wasn't fair.

'I was a farm worker's son so I was never going to be a farmer.
Had I been a farmer's son it would have been different, but I
wasnae. I was a shepherd's boy, just like my father before me.
Och, my dad was never given a chance. In a way I resented it,
aye. He walked the hills all day. Never got a break. Never had
the chances that others had. Resentment came into my head,
that's true. Privilege. I've hated it since I was a lad trying to make
sense of why some people had so much and some had so little.'

The Dukes and the Lords and the clan chiefs. Telfer thought
the ordinary people of the Borders had been sold down the river
by absentee millionaires. 'They're crafty, they only look after their
own,' he'd tell his mother. 'They're living down in London, living
in luxury, living off the sweat and honesty of people like us.'

Telfer remembers Peggy saying: 'Oh, Jim, don't be talking that
way', but she knew he was right. She knew lots of things. She
knew what she wanted for her son and it didn't involve lambing
or shearing or that lovely job that Willie had to do with the pigs
from time to time: hitting them over the head with a hammer
to stun them before slashing their throats with a butcher's knife.
Peggy wanted her son to make his money sitting down. She
pushed him into education, not that he needed much pushing.
He was clever and inquisitive. The land was never going to hold
him. A job in a bank was nirvana to his mother. Or something
that required a collar and tie and a briefcase, instead of a jumper
and trousers and a shepherd's staff passed down the generations.

In time, Peggy's dream came true. Jim left the farm and went
to college in Edinburgh, took the first steps down the road to a
career as a chemistry teacher.

In the capital he stayed with his aunt and uncle. His daily
route – or the route he chose – took him by George Heriot's, one
of the city's more illustrious private schools. The place oozed

history and opportunity and wealth. And it preyed on his mind. On the footpath outside the school he made his statement, a little message to the people he'd grown to resent, the significance of which was known only to him. When the uniforms walked towards him each day there was no way on earth he was getting out of their way. He would not alter his course to let them past, not by an inch, not by half an inch. He would not break stride to let a boy in a blazer through. If it meant a collision, so be it. In his mind it was a point of principle about the privileged classes.

'When I was making my way I developed a huge fear of failure that was always with me. It drove me on as a player and it drove me on as a coach. I had and still have an inferiority complex. Aye, I do. Coming from the background I came from, I suppose it was inevitable. Raised in an environment where the landlord and the Duke were the kingpins made me feel small, despite me railing against it. It made me a bit of a rebel to be honest with you. I saw that you were judged on what you have rather than what you are and I didn't like that. I didn't like it one little bit.'

The Melrose boys were in the clubhouse at the Greenyards swapping stories, rain hopping off the windows, wind shaking the building. 'Dirty ol' night,' they agreed. Foul as could be. A night for ducks, not for rugby players. Eck Hastie, Wattie Hart, the Chisholms, Derek Brown, Leslie Allan and the rest. They all agreed, agreed unanimously; you'd be pure mad to go out in that.

Leslie Allan, international centre, put his hand to the pane and wiped away a strip of condensation. Through the clearing he could see activity outside. A person running. Togged out and doing laps. Soaked to the skin, for sure, but not stopping. Not this fella.

'Look at this,' he suggested.

'Is it easing off?'

'No, it's down for the night,' said Allan.

'What is it, then?'

'I'm not sure, but I think it's young Jim Telfer.'

The boys went to the window and looked into the bleakness. It was Telfer right enough. They could see him but they couldn't hear him, couldn't hear him reminding himself as he ran that nobody else would be out training on a night as wild as this, that nobody would do the things he was prepared to do to make that Melrose first team.

The thought of his rivals sitting at home or yakking in the clubhouse drove him on. He was seventeen years old and already it was clear in his mind that, while he wasn't and would never be overblessed with talent as a back-row forward, there were two things that he would never, ever lack and that was fitness and desire. He had as much of both as he needed.

The weather gods would test him to the limit. Rain and wind were the least of it. He could train in that all day. But then the snow came. And the sleet. It was like somebody on high was challenging him. 'You want it, do you? Okay, here's a blizzard, let's see what you're fucking made of.'

He went down to Melrose one evening and, apart from snowmen, there wasn't another soul about. The place was a thick blanket of white. Bar the tracks made by the wheels of a car it was an uninterrupted covering. So he ran in the tracks. Sprinted in the gaps and revelled again in his solitary life as the only player in Scotland who'd be out in such weather. And when that was done he would break into the clubhouse. Without a key to the door he'd get in the window, shuggling the latch just so, freeing it up just enough to flip the glass up and slide in through the opening. He'd do weights in there, unsophisticated lumps of things raised above his head for hours. Other times, he'd go to the burn near where he lived at Wester Housebyres and stand in gently lapping water hoisting rocks.

'This one is a bit different,' said Ogilvie Scott one day and, because it was Scott, the tough second row, saying it, everybody paid attention. Scott was a veteran in more ways than one. He'd been around. It was said that his time fighting the Germans in

World War II was a useful trial for all those Border League matches he put himself through.

'What you mean, he's different?' the boys asked.

'I mean I've seen him kicked and raked and spat out of rucks.'

'Aye. We've all been there.'

'Kicked and raked and spat out and then getting up with his jersey torn and his head cut open and all the while smirking at the fellas who did it.'

'Smirking?'

'Smirking.'

'Oh.'

Word got round the Greenyards and soon all of the Borders would know about this kamikaze pilot at Melrose, this young lad who thought nothing of sacrificing himself at the bottom of rucks. Everyone at the club revelled in their discovery, but back home the audience was far harder to please.

'My father, he was a man I could never satisfy in rugby. I would never ask him how he thought I played or anything like that. Oh Christ no, never ever. You didn't have conversations like that. We were a Borders family. There was always that bit of distance between us. I'd want to know, though. It didn't worry me if he thought I was rubbish, but I wanted to know, so I'd say, "What did you think of the game, Dad?" and I'd wait for his answer. He'd never talk you up. Just wouldn't do it. He didn't praise me for passing an exam at school, he didn't praise me for playing well at rugby. He'd say, "Hmm". And that was fine. He wasn't that kind of man and I wasn't the kind of boy who needed the praise, to be honest with you. I never needed it. Praise never spurred me on.'

Privilege did. Although he loved rugby and he loved Melrose, he wasn't blind to the self-importance of some people around him. Sure, the Greenyards had no shortage of working-class boys but he saw it as something of a snob's club that tolerated him and his growing left-wing views just because he was doing a hell of a job for the team.

In 1964, the Scotland selectors decided they needed Telfer's grit in the national team. It was the first of twenty-five caps for his country. He loved the game itself, but some of the people who ran it just got his back up. The sport, in his opinion, was overloaded with the upper classes. The SRU, RFU, WRU and the IRFU all got by with the old school tie. Throughout his playing years he'd be at banquets after internationals and losing the will to live while listening to the blazerati drone on in their pompous and patronising ways.

In 1965 Mike Campbell-Lamerton was his captain with Scotland. As far as Telfer was concerned there was a lot of good in him, a lot of the right stuff. Campbell-Lamerton had come close to death more than once in his early life and that kind of thing earned him respect. He survived getting speared by a javelin at school, escaped without a scratch after he trod on a landmine in Korea during national service and lived to tell the tale after he fell out of a helicopter sixty feet above ground while pursuing Cypriot terrorists.

He was a good bloke and they got on, but Campbell-Lamerton was one of them, he was the son of a lieutenant-commander, later he'd become a colonel, later still a bursar at Balliol College, Oxford. 'These people have never been in an ordinary house in their lives,' Telfer would tell himself.

'These men had balls in their mouth when they spoke. Some of the most embarrassing team talks I've ever heard were from people from public schools who tried to bring the language down to the ordinary man. The swear words just don't come out right. Mike was a great fella but he didn't live on the same planet as me. He was "army this" and "army that", using the f-word and the c-word, but he couldn't pull it off.'

Telfer could. And the summer of 1966 helped him. It was a period that shaped not just the way he played the game but also had a profound impact on the way he would coach it years later. That driven man on the training ground in March 1990 was influenced by many things: his parents, the landlords, the Duke, the injustice of society. That's where his determination came from. But his rugby beliefs? They came from another place, far, far away.

## FRASER PARK, TIMARU, WEDNESDAY 15 JUNE 1966

'Look at them,' said Brian Price of Newport.

'They don't look much,' said Ronnie Lamont of Instonians.

'Wiry little devils,' said Jim Telfer of Melrose.

It was a sunny afternoon on New Zealand's South Island and Mike Campbell-Lamerton's Lions were lining up for their tenth match on tour. Down the other end, a combined side drawn from South and Mid Canterbury and North Otago. Farmers mostly. A side that the Lions respected but hardly feared. If appearances counted for anything, the visitors, towering over their opposite numbers, would have won in a hack canter, instead of a hard-fought slog.

It took Telfer precisely two minutes to figure out that size is not everything on the rugby field, the time it took for the wiry little devils to go to work on a Lion. Roger Young, a dental student from Belfast, was the first one to get it. Young made a break and was hauled to the ground by an openside flanker by the name of Vercoe. Young was on the deck, isolated. He would have looked to see where his teammates were but he was pre-occupied by the sight of the opposing pack coming for him, a tight and terrifying unit, bent low and with their backs parallel to the floor. They swept over him in an apocalyptic blur, their boots firing him away from the ball as if he'd been shot out of a cannon, studs connecting with his head and back and legs. By the time the Lions reached him, the ball was gone and Young was semi-conscious.

Telfer was concerned for his injured teammate but also fascinated by the men who had done the damage. Props who were only skin and bone, little blokes in the second row up to the shoulders of his own second rows, flankers who were small and lean and not particularly impressive physical specimens. Their technique was what stunned him. Their leg speed, their body positions entering the ruck, the timing that allowed them to hit with devastating force despite their absence of real bulk.

And their ruthlessness. Jesus, they took no prisoners, these lads. If you were lying on their ball you either got off it quick or they'd drive over the top of you, kicking you out of the way without a second's hesitation.

'That was the day that made me think,' said Telfer. 'That was the moment that changed me.'

Telfer was used to hard rucking in the Borders. Or thought he was. But this was rucking of a different order and it was the brainchild of a man sitting in the stand in Timaru, a man by the name of Vic Cavanagh.

Cavanagh was the oracle of New Zealand rugby. He was gone from the front line of coaching by then, but after what he did at Otago nobody could deny him a place in New Zealand rugby history.

In the 1930s and 1940s he was in charge of unfashionable Otago, previously a bit-part player in the race for the coveted Ranfurly Shield. Traditionally, that prize was for the big boys – the Canterburys, the Hawke's Bays, the Aucklands. Cavanagh knew that his side would never be a physical match for those teams, so he had to find another way of succeeding. He knew his major opponents would always have more talent, so he had to be cleverer than them, had to hit on an idea that levelled the field.

Reinventing the ruck was his Eureka! moment. Previously it had been a loose affair, an ill-defined scrap for the ball. Under Cavanagh, it became a science. Otago won multiple shields and his doctrine spread across the country as a result, to Wairarapa and Wanganui, to Poverty Bay and Bay of Plenty and to places like Fraser Park, Timaru.

It was said of Cavanagh that all he needed was fifteen fit

boneheads who had the mental capacity to follow orders and he'd win the game. His coaching was thunderous, his language harsh, his team talks by turns intimidating and inspirational. He was respected by his players but never popular. But that didn't matter to him. All that mattered was victory. In Otago it was often written that Cavanagh was unique, that his blend of gifts could never be repeated by another person. But they were wrong.

In 1974 Telfer decided enough was enough and hung up his playing boots after two Lions tours, twenty-five Scotland caps and 317 appearances for Melrose. To fill the gap between teaching hours, he turned to coaching. And he suffered for it. Melrose, Scotland B and Scotland were the foundations for his ascent to the highest office as Lions coach. It was 1983 and he was heading back to New Zealand. He thought he was ready. Thought his knowledge was sufficient now to go head-to-head with the modern day Vic Cavanaghs.

He was never more wrong about anything in his life. The Lions were routed 4–0 in the Tests. Telfer was humiliated. The fourth and final Test was in Auckland and the Lions lost 38–6, a landslide to beat all landslides. Telfer was asked what he would do next. He answered the question with a question. 'Is there life after death?'

He was asked another. 'Are you worried about the reception you're going to get from the Scottish people when you go home?'

'The Scottish people?' he responded. 'I'm worried about the reception I'm going to get from the Selkirk people, never mind the rest of Scotland.'

On the long journey home he gave serious thought to jacking it all in. Did he really need this disappointment in his life? Did he have the heart to keep going on with the late nights at training and the hours of planning and the ups and the downs?

He was deputy head of a high school now, he had two children, aged twelve and thirteen. There was no shortage of calls on his time. The SRU wanted him back for the 1984 season but he wasn't sure. Eventually, he said he'd chance one training session and see how he felt. He felt good. Felt invigorated. Felt like his old self.

On his forty-fourth birthday, his Scotland team, playing the rucking game plucked straight from Fraser Park, Timaru, beat France at Murrayfield and won the Grand Slam. It was the nation's first since 1925. Telfer was the toast of the land. The shepherd's boy had made it big.

And then he walked. At the peak of his coaching powers, he gave it up. He was offered a job as head of Hawick High School and he took it. For four years the only time he spent on the rugby field was with the first, second and third years at school. That was it. The quiet life fulfilled him.

Then, in the early autumn of 1988, a familiar voice came on the phone. It was Finlay Calder, twin brother of Jim, the man who had scored the winning try in the Grand Slam decider four years earlier. Finlay and Telfer spoke the same kind of language. They were both to-the-point rugby men. There was mutual respect there. Calder requested a meeting. Could he and Iain Paxton and Iain 'The Bear' Milne meet him for a chat? Telfer thought too much of these guys to turn them down. The players wanted Telfer to come out of retirement. They reckoned they had a good squad again, a real shot at something special down the line. Ian McGeechan had just been promoted to the Scotland job. A few seasons as number two showed him to be an imaginative thinker and an exciting choice as head coach but, the way the players saw it, a combination of Geech and Telfer was a dream ticket. Telfer didn't know about that, but he knew about Geech. Not much, but enough. Enough to say yes to the players' plea and return to the mainstream once more.

# CHAPTER 3

# STEEL IN HIS EYE, I'D PICK IT OUT WITH TWEEZERS

Geech is in his office in London, sitting forward in his chair, hunched over a laptop that is relaying images of 1990. Scotland are walking out. Slowly. David Sole, a picture of intensity, is leading them. Behind him, Kenny Milne, looking like he's going to hit somebody. There's JJ and Whitey and Finlay Calder.

The noise is rising, the flags are waving and Bill McLaren's voice is trembling. 'I've never quite heard a reception like this at Murrayfield in all my years,' he says, admitting later that the pause at the end of the sentence wasn't so much for effect but for necessity. Dear old Bill, the professional to beat all professionals, was close to tears.

The eye is drawn to Scott Hastings. 'Jesus, look at him,' says Geech. 'He's out of it. He's in another world. Look at the emotion on that face!' Later, the camera pans to the coaches, to Geech and Telfer; Geech smiling and shaking somebody's hand as he takes his seat, Telfer unsmiling and oblivious to every last person in the stadium bar the thirty players on the pitch, the three officials and his jovial mate sitting alongside him.

We stop it there, the picture paused with Geech and Telfer in the middle of the frame.

'You look at ease.'

'I wouldn't say that,' says Geech.

'You look like this is just another day.'

'Appearances can be deceptive, believe me,' he replies.

'You're not uptight, not like Telfer.'

'Nobody in the world is like Jim Telfer.'

'He wouldn't agree with you on that.'

'No?'

'No. He says you two are alike in some ways.'

'He said that?'

'He said that you've made the most passionate speeches about Scotland and Scottishness that he's ever heard.'

'That's nice.'

'Even though you hardly ever lived there.'

'Hardly ever.'

'He said that your passion was as great as his, only you showed it differently.'

'That's interesting.'

'He said it was something to do with your father.'

'Yeah.'

'And the kind of man he was.'

'It's true.'

'He says you really never spoke about it much.'

'Well, you don't, do you? You don't talk about things like that.'

You can't know Ian until you know Bob. You can't understand the forces that continually drove the son 220 miles up the road from his home in Leeds for training sessions and meetings and matches and hassle and 220 miles back down again until you've heard his father's story. Can't understand why Geech would put his teaching career in jeopardy and his family life on hold to serve Scotland's cause until you know the background.

Reared in Govan, Bob McGeechan was Glaswegian to his bootlaces, a handy boxer and an even handier footballer. He stood just five foot six inches tall but he was quick and elusive and good enough to catch the eye of Glasgow Rangers as a boy.

He played for them at youth level and dreamed of going all the way, wondered all the time what it would be like to run-out at Ibrox with the noise of a full house ringing in his ears.

His football life came to an early end, brought to a conclusion by the outbreak of war. Bob joined up before his twentieth birthday, placed a glengarry on his head and officially entered the ranks of the Argyll and Sutherland Highlanders as a stretcher-bearer in the medical corps. This is where the story gets a little sketchy because whatever happened to him in the Highlanders he was always slow to talk about it when his children pressed him for details years later. Occasionally he spoke about his pal Ginger. They were in the north African desert. Bob was in a jeep with Ginger alongside. They travelled together always. He remembered the cry from up ahead in the convoy, remembered his pals jumping out of their vehicles and scrambling underneath. A low-flying Messerschmitt tended to have that effect.

One of the chief fighter planes of the Luftwaffe, the Messerschmitt Bf 110C was painfully familiar to the boys. It had two wing-mounted cannon and four machine guns that between them could fire off more than four thousand rounds and it seemed that day the Germans were determined to cut loose with every last one. Bob and Ginger bailed out as soon as the enemy launched the attack.

Bob leaped from the jeep and took cover to the right, Ginger to the left. When the gunfire eventually ceased Bob crawled round the other side and found Ginger lying dead, a bullet through his head.

'Dad would talk sometimes about how lucky he was to survive the war and he'd mention Ginger then,' says Geech. 'If he'd jumped left instead of right it would have been him that got it and he never forgot that.'

Bob was destined for Crete. His ship landed at Tymbaki and he joined the rest of the Infantry Brigade at Heraklion. The following evening it all started, thousands of German paratroopers dropping out of the sky and laying siege to Bob and his mates.

The German units broke through the defences but only after appalling casualties. They lost thousands of men but they kept coming. Indecision and misunderstanding among the Allied commanders led to seismic tactical blunders and they lost hold of vital airfields as a result. The Nazis poured into Crete. More than 1,700 British troops were killed in little more than a week and 1,900 were wounded. Another 12,000 were taken prisoner. The Allies called a halt to the fighting and the dramatic evacuation of Crete began to the sound of constant bombing. Ships came under attack, some survived, some were blown up and sunk. Bob's own escape was a lucky one.

His vessel took a hit from a German fighter. Bob was close enough to the explosion to suffer severe burns to his body. Later, invalided home, he was taken to a military hospital in Headingley to recover. There the wounded Argyll was put in the care of a nurse called Hilda Shearer; she would soon become his wife and eventually the mother of his children.

Young Ian was born English but Bob had plenty of Scottishness to go around. There were nine in his family: four boys and five girls, most of them dotted around the outskirts of Glasgow. In Hilda's there was just herself, a young Yorkshire girl amid a vast Scottish clan.

Bob shaped his son's life in the most subtle ways, possibly without ever knowing it. 'One of the clearest memories I have of him when I was a child was sitting on his knee when he came home from work. He was an engineer. He'd be working with metal a lot. He'd come home and he'd have tiny fragments of steel in his eye because they had no goggles in those days. Health and Safety wasn't heard of back then.

'He'd sit me on his knee and I'd have this pair of tweezers and I'd go and pick the steel out of his eye. I was seven or eight maybe. He'd hold his eye open and in I'd go. God, I remember that like it was yesterday.'

Geech got his secondary education at Moor Grange County, a regular school in a regular area. Out of school, he joined

Headingley Rugby Club. Everybody said it was the only move he could make, given his talent with a rugby ball. His teachers, his coaches, his friends, his opponents; all of them said it was the obvious thing to do.

Headingley was a formidable club. To Geech, it was a club of grammar school lads and public school boys, a club of money and privilege. He wasn't sure he'd fit in there but he did. He loved it. There weren't the airs and graces he'd feared. Almost from the start he felt he belonged.

'After games we'd have a few beers and Dad would put money in my pocket so I could buy my round. He'd give me a few quid so I wasn't embarrassed and I was grateful. It was only after he died that I found out what he was doing. He'd give me a few quid so I wouldn't be shown up in front of the lads and then he'd walk to work. He'd walk to work because he'd no more money. He was dead and gone before I found this out. That was the sort of man he was.'

Bob died of lung cancer in 1969 at the age of forty-eight. He survived to see Geech marry Judy just a few months before, but not long enough to see his son's rugby career flourish. He was in desperate pain for a long time but said nothing, just kept working until he couldn't physically do it any more. Geech never heard him complain about his fate.

It's fair to say that Geech took to Scotland a lot quicker than Scotland took to Geech.

Take Reg Prophit. He was a real ball-breaker. He was the doyen of the *Edinburgh Evening News*, the long-standing rugby correspondent with very black and white views on the way things should be in the game. The way he saw it, Scotland didn't need Geech. Not with him born and raised in Leeds and going around with that Yorkshire accent, not when there were so many home-grown boys vying for a place in the national team, good Edinburgh and Borders lads to pick from. 'Why would we choose an Englishman?' he asked.

'Why don't you go to hell?' Geech replied. Or wanted to.

Geech's family story didn't wash with Reg. At least, that's how he felt. Didn't matter that this was a boy who had turned down a trial with England before the SRU ever gave him a chance to ·shine. Saying 'thanks but no thanks' to the all-powerful RFU was a good enough loyalty statement for most people, but not for everybody.

'Throughout my early years I was utterly convinced that I had to be not just a little bit better but a lot better than everybody else in my position, because I was seen as English by people like Reg Prophit.'

Geech and Jim Telfer clapped eyes on one another for the first time at the Langholm Sevens in early summer 1968. Telfer remembers it better than Geech because Geech was hard to miss. Playing in the centre for Headingley he had long, flowing hair and looked like he really fancied himself. 'He looked like a right poncey devil,' says Telfer.

Later in the year they met again, at a Scotland trial. Geech was playing fly-half for the Whites, Telfer was captain of the Blues. The first words he ever heard Telfer utter were to his back-row teammate, Roger Arneil. He looked at Arneil and pointed at Geech. 'Get that little bastard!' said Telfer. Geech looked as the two men stared him down – and didn't stop running for the entire match.

He wasn't picked for Scotland that year, which was a tragedy, because by the time the next one came around Bob was dead. If anything, his death made Geech all the more determined to represent his country. His desire to wear the Scotland jersey was as profound as his infuriation at the likes of Reg Prophit questioning his right to do so.

Trials came and went and still there was no cap. Geech was a contender at 10, 12 and 13 but there was a logjam in each position. John Frame, Ian Robertson, Jock Turner, Chris Rea, Jim Renwick, Colin Telfer. They were all ahead of him; 1968 became 1969 became 1970, 1971 and 1972. Time and again the Five Nations took place without him.

The All Blacks toured in the autumn of 1972. They were scheduled to play Scotland in mid-December but Geech wasn't holding his breath at that point. Frame and Colin Telfer were ruled out of contention through injury. The Scotland selectors were running out of options but still they were slow to look to Headingley.

A blazer in despair phoned Christopher William Wallace Rea to ask his advice. Rea was clearly a man the old boys could trust. He'd retired from international rugby the year before but he kept an eye on things in the meantime and his opinion was still respected at Murrayfield. 'We're thinking of going with McGeechan against the All Blacks,' said the man from the SRU. Rea sighed down the phone. 'McGeechan? Hmm. I'm not sure,' he replied. 'He's a good club player but he'll never make it at international level. He's a bit diffident, a bit frail. I'd go for some-body else if I were you.'

That was the point. There wasn't anybody else.

'They told me I'd been picked to play against the All Blacks. I was starting at fly-half. You can imagine the emotion of the moment. It was a huge thing in my life. Massive. My father and all the rest of it. He was dead three years which was no time at all, really. Then they said the president of the SRU wanted to see me. Two committee men escorted me through to see him. Alf Wilson was his name. He was sitting there like a member of the royal family. Should I bow? Should I genuflect? I didn't know what to do.'

The president started speaking, calling Geech by his surname at all times. 'This is a great honour for you,' he said. 'You won't let us down now, will you, McGeechan?'

Geech said he'd try not to and that was that. He was taken away by the president's men and a few days later he represented his country at Murrayfield. In the *Evening News* Reg Prophit wrote of the pressure McGeechan was under 'to prove himself'.

The night before the game he took a drive down Leith way, got out of the car and went for a walk. He remembers looking up at the night sky by the waterfront and thinking that the next time the sun came up he'd be a Scotland player. It was a hell of a good feeling.

He must have done okay against New Zealand. Scotland lost 14-9 but old Reg didn't have much bad to say about Geech after that. Not often, anyway.

Occasionally he'd mention the 'Englishman playing for Scotland' but his sniping faded to half-nothing as Geech made his way. He went on to play thirty-two games for his country and was capped eight times for the Lions, playing every minute of the immortal 1974 series in South Africa. He buttoned Prophit's lip for good that summer.

Geech was thirty-three when he finished playing. Part of him wanted to go on and on but his troublesome knee was telling him it was time to quit. So he packed it in. Left rugby behind – for about five minutes.

In 1980 Headingley were stuck for a coach and, Geech being Geech, he couldn't help himself. He said he'd give them a hand and, ah, if they needed him to play the odd match he'd give it a lash. The knee was bound to stand up to the occasional run-out. He broke the news to Judy with a promise: 'Honestly, it's a short-term thing. A few weeks and then I'm out of it.'

He believed it and Judy believed he believed it, but she knew him too well to believe it herself. A few weeks? Yeah, that'll be right. The following year he was still at the coaching, first with the Scotland U-21s, then with the Anglo Scots and the Scotland B team. In 1986 he became the number two in the senior team behind Derrick Grant so his few weeks had by then become six years.

They were a good team, Grant and Geech, and they produced some notable victories in their two seasons together before Geech stepped up to the top job and Telfer reappeared on the horizon. Some notable victories and some bitter defeats. In the Five Nations of 1988, a cranky England team beat the Scots 9–6 at Murrayfield in one of the worst championship games ever seen.

It was Grant's last match in charge and he and Geech were like a pair of anti-Christs in the aftermath. There had been sixty-seven minutes of stoppages in the game, most of them for England time-wasting, or so the boys felt anyway. They pulled up short of saying that England cheated but Grant said that even at the age of fifty he wouldn't have been out of place in the visitors' backline, for all the action he'd have seen.

'England is the birthplace of rugby,' he said. 'But they also know how to kill it stone dead.'

Geech never lost his rag, no matter how bad things got, but this was an exception. 'The trouble with international rugby is England,' he complained. They knew England were under terrible pressure to win but even so they saw their negative tactics, their unending cynicism, as an affront to the game.

'We were fuming because England didn't play any rugby at all. It was awful. The crowd were booing. It was the worst atmosphere I'd ever witnessed. They had all the ball, all the control and just refused to play any rugby.'

England were unapologetic. Roger Uttley, the coach, went to the Scottish dressing room for the traditional thank you to the hosts. Geoff Cooke, the manager, advised him against it, said no good would come of it. 'Rog, seriously, I've heard them roaring in there. I wouldn't do that if I were you.'

Uttley carried on regardless. He poked his head around the door and Geech, stone-faced, just nodded at him. Grant, standing with his shirtsleeves rolled up, shot him a look of fury. Uttley had addressed hundreds of dressing rooms in his time but this one was about as icy as they came. 'Cheers, boys,' he said. 'It was tough out there. Thanks for the game.'

The Englishman didn't quite catch Grant's response at first but thought it sounded something like 'ugghh!' followed by a rhetorical question: 'You call that a game?'

Later that night, as the disappointment was taking hold of

him, Geech's mind was racing. 'I decided that if we had to beat England in the future by playing negative rugby, by creating organised chaos on the field, then we would do it and we wouldn't apologise for it. No way. Not a chance. Not after '88. Their justification was that they were desperate for a win. Well, we were all desperate for a win.'

# CHAPTER 4

# CAN YOU IMAGINE? DYING IN SCOTLAND!

England still had a distance to travel to elevate themselves above a laughing stock, but the win at Murrayfield in '88 proved to Mooro that at least there was an acceptance of change in the ranks now. And to him the awakening came like manna from heaven.

A few years earlier, they wouldn't have had the wit to mess Scotland around the way they had in Edinburgh. He knew that only too well. They'd have just rolled over and beaten an all too familiar retreat. And they'd have done it on autopilot because that was pretty much what they'd been doing for most of the decade.

Mooro had heard all the stories about the drinking and the fighting and the carrying-on, the insanity that was the national rugby team. He knew about the grim episodes from before he was capped and he had plenty more tales of woe from his own time to go with them. He'd only been an England player since April 1987 but a lot of stuff had happened in those twelve months.

Some of the yarns made him laugh, some made him angry, others managed to do both at the same time because they were so mortifying. Like the one about the Great North Run a few years earlier. That was a beauty. As Wade Dooley recalled, the England forwards of the day had entered and the joke went that they'd been beaten home by a man dressed as a seven-foot banana. By the time the cream of the English pack came panting and wheezing over the finishing line the banana had received his medal, downed a couple of pints and was halfway home on the bus.

If Mooro sat down and compiled a list of the low points of English rugby over the last three years he'd be there for a month whittling down the contenders. But there were some stand-out candidates.

## THE TRAVEL LODGE, GISBORNE, NEW ZEALAND, 22 MAY 1985

Before Mooro's time, but he got every sorry chapter and verse from Wade Dooley. It was Dooley's first season in the international team, his first senior tour and his first exposure to the drinking culture in the England team.

It was a dank old night on the North Island and the players were in the mood to party. Never mind that they were crap: abandon all gloom about their lowly place in the world order and ignore the statistic that had them winning only 29 per cent of their Tests in the five years since their now retired captain, Bill Beaumont, had led them to a Grand Slam. Jesus, those days seemed a long, long time ago to the lads.

England had lost ten of their previous fifteen matches and had failed to score a single try in nearly sixty per cent of their games going back two and a half years. But that very night in Gisborne they'd put forty-five points on the second-raters of Poverty Bay and the duty free was getting attacked as a result.

'And this was when?' asked Mooro of Dooley.

'The Wednesday night.'

'And when were you playing New Zealand?'

'The Saturday.'

'Fuck me.'

The squad assembled in the team room, each of them clink-clanking their way in toting bags of cheap booze. They laid it all out on a table and pulled two high stools alongside. Steve Brain, the Coventry hooker whose drinking credentials were world class, sat on one of them and Dooley lowered himself onto the other.

Brainer didn't think anybody could outdrink him and not many ever tried. He was a legend, after all. Dooley was new and keen to prove himself to his teammates in any way he could, so he raised his hand and said, 'I'll have a go', and the night's entertainment was set.

The boys were allowed to go to the toilet, but only with an escort for fear they'd jam their fingers down their throats and make themselves sick. Bang out of order, that. Unsportsmanlike. If they needed a piss but didn't want an escort, well, there was always the cactus plant in the corner. They'd be given every spirit under the sun and the first man to fall off his stool was the loser.

They were at it a good two hours. Absurd amounts of drink had been put away with indecent haste and Dooley was swaying, barely able to focus on his adversary opposite, unclear as to what state the great Brainer was in. Muhammad Ali versus Joe Frazier it was not.

Brainer wobbled, straightened, wobbled again and came crashing down on top of the drink-laden table like a falling plank, bottles spinning in the air, glass breaking, his body flailing and his eyes rolling. Martin Green, the coach, walked in as six of his players were hauling Brainer out of his drunken devastation and as a seventh, big Wade Dooley, was holding his arms aloft, declaring himself champ.

## SCOTLAND VS. ENGLAND, MURRAYFIELD, 15 FEBRUARY 1986

As the boys recounted the details of England's record defeat in Edinburgh, Mooro would just shake his head and wonder how in the name of God they could lose 33–6 to Scotland. Even with all the drinking, how was that possible? He had asked the guys left remaining in the squad: Winters, Dooley, Rob Andrew, Simon Halliday and Paul Rendall, known forever as The Judge.

The Judge was half-English, half-Irish. Came from a family
of Arsenal supporters on his father's side and a family of builders
from Killarney on his mother's. Mostly, though, he was north
London. He wasn't the right shape for football so he gave prop-
ping a go. He was handy. Got himself in an England squad in
1979 and eventually got capped, 'when all the others had either
retired, emigrated or died', in 1984, at the age of thirty. Everybody loved The Judge. Loved him for his down-to-earth wisdom
and his honesty and his funny way of looking at things.

Mooro would say, 'What were you lot playing at, getting
hammered by that mob?'

And The Judge would reply: 'They weren't a bad old crew, to
be fair. The thing you're forgetting is that Scotland were streetwise. JJ and Finlay, them two were unbelievable. Big Dooley
would stick a finger over the offside line and he'd get pinged
and the two boys would be fucking ten yards off and getting
away with it.'

'Cheatin' bastards,' said Mooro in admiration.

'Top boys,' said The Judge.

'Who were you up against?' asked Mooro.

'Iain Milne. The Bear. I was told he was an operator and I was
told right. Left myself high in a scrum one time and he did me.
Put me up in the air and made me look like a right muppet. Said
to myself, "I won't be doing that again". I kept my nose to the
ground after that. First twenty minutes the scrums were going
great for us. I was going to Brainer "it's not bad this, for a change".
Then we twigged. Soon as we fed the ball in JJ and Finlay fucked
off from the back of the scrum looking for Rob Andrew. While
they were taking the head off him we was still pushing against six
men. We hadn't a clue. It was freezing cold that day and all.
Weather's always at the top end up there, innit? It was a hurricane.
Half-time I wanted to go and get two cartons of chips to stick me
feet in. We all just wanted to get on the plane and go home.'

Some of them wished they'd never got on the plane in the
first place. Dooley spent the night before trying to stop the

snoring of his room-mate Maurice Colclough. When old Maurice inhaled the walls shook and the windows rattled and the receptionist phoned from three floors below wondering if there was a wild boar knocking about up there somewhere.

Dooley shouted at him, poked him and belted him with pillows. He considered tipping him on to the floor but thought better of it. In the end he made up a bed in the bath.

He was feeling ropey come kick-off. Tired and narky. Then John Beattie, the Scotland No. 8, clouted him in the face and his eye started to swell and close. He couldn't see properly for half the game. 'Lucky you,' said The Judge later on.

To find the epitome of misery all you had to do was take a look at the weary Dooley. Or the stunned Simon Halliday.

When Scotland scored their third try close to the end, Halliday spotted Stuart Barnes, a substitute, leaning against the posts awaiting the conversion. Barnes said he was metaphorically smoking a fag, 'pondering this existential nightmare' he had just walked into when Hallers approached.

'All right, Barnesy, didn't know you were on,' Hallers sighed. 'When'd you arrive?'

'Eight minutes and sixteen points ago, Hallers,' Barnes replied, looking at the big clock and counting time.

Ah, the glamour of playing for England.

Their own fans subjected them to ridicule and ripped apart the last vestiges of their dignity. To ease the pain the brave England boys turned to drink. It was the one area of rugby life where they remained in a league of their own.

## WALES VS. ENGLAND, CARDIFF ARMS PARK, 7 MARCH 1987

Before the Scots became England's mortal enemy, before Murrayfield became the place they all hated the most, it was Cardiff and the Welsh that raised the hackles of the English.

The Arms Park was the hellhole of the earth to some of

them. Not to Mooro (yet) but to Dooley and certainly to Richard
Hill. As a Bath player, Hill, the England captain, was used to
crossing the Severn Bridge and playing the Pontypools and the
Pontypridds and the Bridgends and the Maestegs. Wet Wednesday
nights fighting the hard men of the Valleys. Rugby Armageddon.

Hill stoked the fires earlier in the week. He revealed that his
wife was heavily pregnant. He said that she wasn't going to the
match for fear she'd go into labour. Hilly didn't want a child of
his born in the Principality. No chance.

If there was any prospect of peace on the Saturday, that blew
a hole in it right there. The way Hilly saw it, and the way he
explained it to the rest of them, it was high time England started
standing up for themselves. For years they'd been bullied by
champion liberty takers like the Scots and the Welsh. Their pack
hadn't fronted up in the physical stakes. They hadn't won in
Wales in twenty-four years. How was that possible?

He saw 7 March as the turning point, the drawing of the line
in the sand.

They went on to the pitch on the Saturday for their warm-up
and got spat on by a group of Welsh fans gathered at the tunnel.
They trotted back in and got spat on again. Hilly had all the
ammunition he needed now for his final rallying cry.

Mooro was on the bench but he heard the first part of Hilly's
speech and thought his captain was going to spontaneously
combust such was his rage, his anti-Welsh thunder. Hilly thought
he was ensuring that his team didn't take a backward step. What
he actually ended up doing was ensuring they took many forward
steps, at pace and with fists flying.

England emerged from the dressing room psyched up to the
high heavens and found the Welsh snarling at them. Mayhem
followed.

After six minutes of pressure cooker rugby, both teams
blew their tops. Welsh flanker Bob Norster lashed out at Steve
Bainbridge with an elbow but instead caught his teammate
Steve Sutton square in the face and smashed his nose to bits.

The Arms Park reacted to Sutton lying prostrate on the ground, assuming it was an Englishman who'd done it. The place went mental.

Play carried on. Phil Davies threw his arm around Jon Hall in the tackle and to Dooley it looked like a cheap shot. He came trundling in and drove a fist into Davies' face with gruesome force. The Welshman was carted off to hospital with a hairline fracture of his cheekbone and the madness carried on from there. The ball was in play for fourteen minutes and forty-one seconds and the penalty count was off the charts.

It ended with a Welsh victory and claret everywhere, but Hilly could see the upside quite clearly. He came in afterwards and he was buzzing. 'Fucking brilliant, boys.' For once England hadn't backed down from the challenge and he was proud of his team. What's more, he said, Green, the coach, and Mike Weston, the chairman of selectors, were proud, too.

The reaction in the media was seismic. *The Times* called it 'The match that betrayed rugby'. The great Gerald Davies began his piece: 'The spirit of rugby football died a little on Saturday.' The *Rugby World & Post* headlined it 'Sickening!' on the front cover. Every newspaper slaughtered England and put the lion's share of the blame at their door. Don Rutherford, the embattled technical administrator of the RFU, said he was going to burn the video of the game. 'I never want to see it,' he said.

The RFU had to act. They banned Hilly and he missed the inaugural World Cup in New Zealand and Australia as a result. Green phoned him and said: 'Look, mate, the hierarchy heard all about your pre-match speech and they're disgusted. It's either you or me for the World Cup. And, frankly, I'm looking forward to seeing the Great Barrier Reef.' Dooley also got dumped, but only for one game. He was too important to ban for long. Gareth Chilcott was thrown out but was forgiven quickly but Graham Dawe lost his place and never won it back again, save for two caps in the following eight years. Even though he hadn't taken much, if any, part in the violence in Cardiff, Dawe was the one who suffered the most. For waiting in the wings was a hungry replacement, a pitbull of a hooker gagging for his chance.

Mooro had led an eventful life from day one. He was born to an unmarried teacher from Birmingham and given up for adoption at two weeks old. At a few months a couple from Halifax, Ralph and Dorothy Moore, took him from his foster parents and duly became his mum and dad.

He could not have found a more gentle or caring home. Ralph was a teacher of mentally and physically handicapped children, Dorothy a school secretary. They met through church and their Methodist faith was at the core of their lives. They had two daughters and then Mooro and, following Mooro, came two more adopted children. These were good people.

Their boy was a double handful. When people said how amazing it was that they had a son who played for England, Ralph and Dorothy would smile and say the really amazing thing was that they had a son who hadn't managed to do himself permanent physical harm long before he ever played for England.

When he was six he almost electrocuted himself when he stuck a metal screwdriver into a live power point. Thanks to his father, who moved him away from the socket in the nick of time, he escaped with burns only to his hand and wrist.

A few years later he was within a foot of being run over by a bus. The family were en route to the Shetland Islands and Mooro ran out on to the road at a stop-off in Aberdeen. 'I still recall the bus driver's face. He was white with shock. He managed to stop just inches short of my nose. If he'd been doing forty miles an hour instead of thirty I would have been dead. Jesus, can you imagine? Dying in Scotland!'

At ten, he fell out of a tree and landed on his back, injured and in shock, but not crippled, fortunately. Years later, as a young man on his travels in Canada, he was held up by an armed robber at a drive-in movie joint where he was working.

A guy comes around the corner in a green poncho and a

sock on his head. Mooro bursts out laughing and asks the fella, 'Who the fuck have you come as?' The robber tells him to fill up his bag with cash, then a gun is produced and Mooro's ordered to turn around and kneel on the floor. Now he's worried.

'I was praying. "Christ almighty, he's going to shoot me in the head". I'm telling him, "Just go, mate, just run, eh?"' He says the sound of the guy running away was the sweetest sound he's ever heard. 'I just keeled over with relief. Two weeks later a bloke at a local 7-Eleven got shot dead for fifty dollars.'

Mooro was a deep thinker and a logical man. If something didn't make sense he didn't want to know. Parents, teachers, coaches, they were all the same. If they told him to do something and Mooro couldn't see the point of it, he'd just sit on his hands and say no. It's why he said he wouldn't have lasted half a minute in the army. Soon as some officer barked at him to march, he'd be asking why, what would it achieve?

He took an A-level in Religious Education and quickly lost faith in the teachings of the Church. It just didn't stack up as far as he could see. He reckoned that parts of the Bible were propagandist, touched up selectively to validate the message. Him leaving the Church was hard for his parents to take, but that was the way it had to be. Belligerence was in his DNA. He found that out years later when he met his natural mother. She was an argumentative sort, too. Mooro seemed to have more energy than anybody else. His teammates would conduct spoof searches for his missing thyroid. 'It's gotta be on the floor somewhere, Mooro. It's sure as fuck not where it should be.'

He was a loose cannon from his earliest days, a madman at times. When he took to rugby, his determination to succeed was frightening. Everybody could see it. At Crossley and Porter School, at his first club, Old Crossleyans, and then on to Roundhay, there were people telling him he needed to calm down for his own good, but Mooro never listened.

He was a dirty player. He punched and kicked players and showed little respect to anybody on the field. His teammates had to watch him all the time, waiting for the red mist to descend. It didn't take much to bring it down. In hindsight, he says he needed someone to teach him a lesson but they never did.

'I was terrible, absolutely terrible. I was seventeen, eighteen, nineteen and twenty and I was a lunatic. Somebody should have put me up against the wall and said, "Look, you little shit, you keep going the way you are and we're going to put you away permanently". Maybe they did say it, but it didn't get through. If they tried to sort me out, I suppose I'd have brushed it off anyway. That was the kind of person I was.'

On one occasion, he shoed an opponent in the head. It was a blatant act. He didn't get sent off but he should have been. He should have been sent off a lot. The committee at Roundhay told him that if he'd done that on the street he'd be doing time within a week. He sat down and thought about it awhile and was ashamed of himself. 'It wasn't even brave, was it? It was a cheap shot. A horrible thing to do. The guy wasn't hurt but he could have been. He could have been badly hurt.'

When the time came Mooro decided to study law at Nottingham University, partly because he liked watching the soap opera *Crown Court* on television, partly because his mates encouraged him to. 'It's all about arguing with people. You're perfect for it.' At Nottingham Rugby Club they knew he was coming. The coach, Alan Davies, had got word from Roundhay: 'He'll be great', they said. 'If you can only control him.'

Mooro spotted an unfamiliar face at training with Nottingham one evening and asked Alan Davies who he was.

'Oh, he's new,' said the coach. 'A hooker from Zimbabwe. He's supposed to be good.'

'A hooker?' replied Mooro.

'Yeah, a hooker. He's decent, I think.'

Mooro walked off to resume training. Things were going fine until a melee broke out suddenly. At the heart of it was the Zimbabwean, flinging digs at Mooro, only missing. Mooro may have landed with a few counterpunches but Davies can't quite recall. What he remembers clearly is the Zimbabwean walking out of the club that night, still hopping mad, and never returning.

'What happened, Mooro?' Davies asked.

'Dunno.'

'Did you provoke him?'

'Might have done. If he can't take it he's no good to us, is he?'

Not for the first time he'd seen off a rival for his place in the first team.

Davies loved Mooro and the feeling was mutual. The coach had never before come across a player who was as passionate talking about his politics, his literature and his history as he was his rugby and he'd sure as hell not seen one as focused on getting to the top. He took a lot of handling, but he was worth it. Mooro got himself and the club into desperate trouble with his lack of discipline but he helped them get results, too.

Mooro had a punch-up with Brainer when Nottingham played Coventry, mainly because Brainer was the England incumbent at the time. Then Mooro would go to Bath and it would kick off with Dawe because Dawe was another rival for the national team.

The Nottingham boys would lap it up, this stand-off between these stubborn men. 'You'd hear them in the scrum,' said Nottingham and Scotland lock Chris Gray. 'They'd be fucking each other out of it. There'd be all sorts of things said. These were the only words they said to each other for about eight years even though they were in the same England squad. That would have been Mooro's doing.'

When Dawe got banned following the debacle in Cardiff, Mooro's time had come. He rang up Davies on the night he found out he had been picked.

'Alan, I want to come and see you,' he said.

'But Mooro, it's two in the morning,' Davies replied.

'I'm coming round.'

Davies opened his door and Mooro jumped on him, ecstatic

at getting his break and grateful for his mentor's help. 'He gave me what I'm sure he thought was a kiss,' said Davies, 'but it was actually a nibble, just below my neck. His lovely teeth – 'the kind you get from a DIY shop and hammer in yourself,' said The Judge – had left their mark. When I told the missus that I'd got my love bite from a hooker it took a fair bit of explaining.'

When England arrived in Australia for the 1987 World Cup, two of the first team got off the plane in Sydney wearing Reagan and Gorbachev masks. When they departed, after a loss to the Welsh that the normally mild-mannered Winterbottom called a disgrace and an embarrassment to the nation, some of those on the England bench felt like standing up and applauding and thanked the man above that they were finally going home.

It all started to change in the months that followed, when Geoff Cooke became England manager and Roger Uttley became coach. Cooke and Uttley found their players riddled with insecurities. They'd been crucified in the press for years, they'd been dropped from the team, reinstated and dropped again, rarely, if ever, being told the reasons why. Psychologically they were basket cases, reluctant to express themselves in word or deed. Cooke and Uttley had a mountain to climb.

'The RFU were peculiarly ambivalent at the time,' said Cooke. 'They wanted the team to be successful but they didn't want to be seen trying too hard. Anything that smacked in the slightest of professionalism was frowned upon. We used to meet on a Thursday for international matches and I told them I wanted to change it to Wednesday. Oh, my God, the fuss and bother! Professionalism in rugby was being talked about more and more and they were frightened to death of it.'

Dudley Wood, secretary of the Rugby Football Union at Twickenham, was King Canute, holding back the tide of pay for play. They'd say to him, 'Dudley, there's already professionalism in English rugby', and Dudley would choke a little.

'What do you mean? That's impossible!'

'Take Wade Dooley and Dean Richards. They're going to be with England for up to sixty days a year soon and somebody is paying them for their time. It just happens that it's not the RFU, it's their employers, the police force. But they're being paid.'

'But that's not the same.'

'Yes, it is. What's the difference between the police paying them and you paying them?'

Tom McNab remembers having that conversation with Wood. He had it many times but dear old Dudley never relented. McNab was a Glaswegian. A former triple jumper and a high-achiever. He was the UK athletics coach in the 1960s and 1970s, then he became a best-selling novelist, a scriptwriter, a lecturer and a technical director on the film *Chariots of Fire*.

He was also Cooke's fitness coach and broke the backs of the England team for fun.

He was fifty years old and fitter than most of the players now in his charge. A drastic lack of self-belief was one problem but a catastrophic shortage of conditioning was quite another. McNab couldn't believe what these guys were getting up to – the amount of booze they were putting away, the crap food they were eating, the minuscule amount of training they were doing. There was a story – and McNab believed every word of it – that one of his props keeled over blind drunk in a restaurant one night and fell into a salad trolley. All the boys said it was the closest he'd ever come to healthy eating. Any time McNab applied the pressure and pushed them hard they'd empty their stomachs in front of him. Their idea of rest and recovery was having just the ten pints and calling it a night at 2 a.m. They were a dismal lot. He drew up a fitness programme that demanded commitment and discipline. Instead, the boys would play drinking games and eat fast food. That was the culture he and Cooke and Uttley were trying to change. There was militancy but it was short-lived. Brainer said he had a Friday night routine that he followed like clockwork: curry, pub, nightclub. As a concession to the new order he

was prepared to knock the curry on the head. And maybe the
nightclub. But the pints were non-negotiable. Brainer didn't
last very long.

Maurice Colclough retired on the high stool at about four
o'clock one morning at a squad weekend. He was tired and
emotional, worn out from McNab's bleep tests and his training
exercises with stupid names, the Jelly Jaw and the Sergeant
Jump. What was wrong with laps all of a sudden? One by one
the players either walked or adapted.

McNab told the boys that playing international rugby was like
running a marathon, but instead of getting a cup of water along
the way they'd get a punch in the head. He started hitting them
with buzz phrases. 'Technique is freedom,' he'd say. He got that
one from Martha Graham, the dancer. 'Fatigue makes fools of
us all,' he'd tell them. That belonged to legendary American football coach Vince Lombardi. The favourite was his own creation.
'You can't fire a cannon from a canoe.' Once he explained that
there was no way they could fire on all cylinders as players unless
they had a solid fitness foundation he started winning them over.
And having Mooro as a disciple did no harm.

Mooro cottoned on to the fitness revolution quicker than
anybody. 'You can't fire a cannon from a canoe.' That became
his mantra. When Mooro upped the pace in training some of
the old guard would tell him to take a pull and he'd tell them
where to go. He wasn't getting dragged down by the refuseniks.
When McNab called the hooker 'an evil little bastard' he said it
with a smile, for they got on just fine. 'He had no great ability
as an athlete,' said McNab, 'but he was willing to work his balls
off to stay in the team. He was incredibly bright and unbelievably spiky and hard to get to know. He smiled with difficulty.
He was the only man I'd ever met that had clenched hair. There
was a good fella lurking underneath the surface but he was kept
well hidden. For all that, I really liked the guy.'

*     *     *

In the bowels of the Parc des Princes, Roger Uttley led his forwards out of the tiny visitors' dressing room and into a hallway and told them to pair up and knock themselves about a bit. It was the first game of Cooke and Uttley's new era and the Parc, a bearpit of a place, was expecting a rout.

Eight starting forwards and three subs left an odd man out. It was Mooro. Uttley said 'come here with me' and so coach and hooker sparred as the clock ticked down to kick-off. The rest of the players took it easy, tempering their aggression with the realisation that the real enemy lay elsewhere. Mooro was a little different. He had the scariest eyes, almost French-like in their intensity. He drove at Uttley and stuck his shoulder in the coach's chest with one heavy thud followed by another. It was later that night when Uttley started to feel the pain. He woke at four in the morning. 'Mooro had battered me sternum. I could hardly move. He was a right short-arse but, Jesus Christ, he packed a punch. I never did that exercise again. Or if I did, I avoided Mooro like the bubonic plague.'

Mooro was in a bit of a state himself by that point. At the Parc his opposite number was French captain Daniel Dubroca. A hero of Agen, Dubroca had been a Test player for nine years, a veteran of twenty-nine Tests. But, at thirty-four, he was coming to the end of a tumultuous career. Dubroca had much of the same badness about him as some of his more notorious team-mates, but he was cuter than most. When he took somebody out, he tended to do it under the referee's radar.

It was a nasty game – as if there was any other type in Paris. At one scrum, the French wheeled and drove and England couldn't stay on their feet. They folded under the shove and Mooro was left stranded on the floor, his two dishevelled props lying across him. Dubroca shuffled on to the scene and the last thing Mooro saw before he turned his face away was the sole of the Frenchman's boot descending on him. He got cut open, but didn't want treatment. That would have been a sign of weak-ness in his book. He waited five minutes and, not wanting to give Dubroca the pleasure of knowing he'd hit the target, he pretended he'd taken an accidental dunt at a line-out. The doctor said he needed stitches.

'Do 'em here,' said Mooro.

'We'll have to go to the dressing room, Brian,' said the doc.

'The dressing room's ten fucking minutes there and back. Stitch it now.'

The doc got out the needle and thread and went to work. 'I went back on to the field absolutely hyper. I said, "Right, where the fuck's Dubroca?" I went after him the whole game but never got him.'

England lost 10–9. The performance was hailed as a break-through, a sign that maybe things were turning. Mooro was only convinced of that when they won that debacle at Murrayfield seven weeks later.

What was also becoming obvious was the need for a new captain. The job had bounced around the dressing room for some time and had brought the incumbent nothing but misery. During Mooro's first year in the side, Mike Harrison had it and then got dropped and never reappeared. Nigel Melville had it for two games and got injured and never played for England again. John Orwin had it for three games also and was so out of his depth it was embarrassing. That was the last England saw of Orwin. Then Richard Harding had it for one game against Fiji, his twelfth and last cap.

Cooke needed a man who ticked all the boxes. He had to be assured of his place, had to have presence, the ability to inspire and the doggedness to fight. He needed somebody far removed from the old way of things and to Mooro that narrowed the field down considerably. Winters was brilliant but he was quiet. Wade Dooley was tainted by Cardiff and a propensity towards occa-sional outbursts of violence and Rob Andrew was troubled by inconsistency. You couldn't give it to The Judge unless you planned to put a big top over Twickenham. The Judge was a great ringleader but he was no captain.

In Mooro's mind that left one person. Himself. He'd captained England B, he'd led the fitness revolution, he was certain of his place and he had more passion and devilment than any of them. It had to be him. Just had to be.

# CHAPTER 5

# I HAD TO PUT UP THE MASK

Mick Skinner came through the door with a clatter. He'd arrived in the River Room at the Petersham Hotel in Richmond via the bar at Harlequins Rugby Club and he was excited. It was just before 7 p.m. on a Saturday in late October 1988 and the England squad had gathered at their team base to find out the identity of their new captain

'All right, ladies,' he said.

'Wotcha, Skins,' replied The Judge, the only one in the England haven to answer.

'What's the brief then, eh?' Skins wondered. 'We finding out who the Pope is today or what?'

Mooro was still hoping for the best but deep down he knew it wasn't him. He could read the tea leaves. Nobody had written, nobody had phoned, nobody had bothered consulting him in any way. He was impatient and gloomy. A little hurt and a little angry. He was in the dark and he didn't like it. But he had company. Rob Andrew had his supporters for the gig but he was going around shrugging his shoulders. If he was the chosen one, he was a damn good liar. Winters and Dean Richards said they'd heard nothing. Big Wade and Paul Ackford were coppers but they hadn't come up with a single lead. The morning paper had brought a story about Simon Halliday having a chance but

Hallers was a straight shooter so when he said he'd heard nothing and was expecting nothing then everybody believed him.

Through it all, one man was keeping his head down as if transfixed by the floor. He was examining the weave on the River Room rug as if it contained the solutions to all the great mysteries of the world. He didn't make eye contact with anybody for fear of getting drawn into a discussion he had no desire to be a part of.

Geoff Cooke came in and started talking. He mentioned the tour of Australia in the summer, a disastrous expedition that had undone a lot of the good work from Murrayfield in the spring. John Orwin had led the team Down Under but he was never a long-term bet for the captaincy. Not after two soul-destroying defeats by the Wallabies and some rancour in the camp.

The new guy was here for the long haul, said Cooke. He was the standout. The unanimous choice. He neglected to mention the utter bewilderment among his selectors when he put forward the name in the first place, but that hardly mattered now. He'd convinced them that there was only one man for the job, and it wasn't Mooro or Hallers or Andrew or any of the other established names.

'I have to say I was spoilt for choice,' Cooke began. 'There's a lot of big characters in this room. A lot of leaders. I've picked somebody you all respect. A terrific player and a born winner. I know you'll give him everything you've got. Boys, our new captain is Will Carling.'

Carling didn't take his eyes off the rug. But his ears? In that moment he was Mr Spock. He could hear everything.

Skinner was going, 'Well, fuck me, good on you, Bum Face.'

Probyn was saying, 'Is this wise?'

Deano and Winters and most of the rest were silent and it was the quietness that got to Carling particularly. Cooke announced his name and there was a stunned hush in the room. The boys looked to Mooro for a reaction, expecting some kind of thermonuclear explosion. But Mooro was too astonished to protest, too flabbergasted to rail against a decision he saw as both baffling and unjust.

At twenty-two, Carling was the youngest England captain in fifty-seven years but the landmarks didn't end there. As far as his teammates were concerned this was the first time Mooro had been left speechless by anything in his entire life. Even the guy who pulled a shooter on him in Canada hadn't subdued him the way this bombshell had. The image of Mooro sitting in his chair lost in his own furious thoughts was not one any of them were ever likely to forget.

Carling picked up the phone and called Nigel Melville, one of his predecessors in the job. 'They've made me captain, mate,' he told Melville. 'What do I do?' His tone was anxious. And that struck Melville as odd because everything he'd heard about Carling, everything he'd read in the newspapers, led him to believe that he was not lacking in self-confidence. But this was a different person he was talking to; a little tense, a little lost. Not many people saw this other side to him. Cooke saw it regularly and worked hard to reassure his new captain that he was worthy of the accolade. Paul Ackford saw it, too, because he and Carling were club-mates at Harlequins and they had made their England debuts together in Paris. There was a bond there. For a while after the announcement they went for curries and talked things through. Carling wanted to know how he should talk to the forwards; what were they saying about him, did they rate him, did they not?

He had been an England player for ten months and from day one he felt like he belonged. In the beginning, there was no edge to his relationship with anybody, no complications. He had some of the trappings of fame – a nice job in marketing, a Renault 5 Turbo, all the female company he wanted – but none of the hassle. He enjoyed socialising but he also liked being on his own, just him and his sketch pad lost in the countryside. If rugby was his passion it always had a rival in his love of art.

Carling appreciated the simplicity of it all. He could do daft things and nobody judged him. In Scotland, after his third cap, he drank with abandon just like the rest of them, got involved in a food fight, got his trousers covered in grub and then went in search of the hotel laundry. In the bowels of the Carlton Highland he found it, chucked his clothes in for a wash and then crawled into an industrial-sized tumble dryer for a sleep. Recounting the story endeared him to the rest of the players. In his first seven caps all he had to worry about was his game. He didn't fret about speeches, didn't worry what was being said behind his back, didn't have running battles with the press. All that came later.

Now that he was captain, things changed. He gained a lot, but he lost a lot, too. His profile increased and he revelled in it. But there were nights when he pined for an easier existence, when he was alone in his bedroom keeping a distance from his players as they lowered pints in the hotel bar below. When there was drink to be had now, Mooro would drain it with Probyn and The Judge, Dooley and Skinner and, later, with a phenomenon called Guscott. Carling would rarely get stuck in with them. Didn't see it as his place any more.

'I was captain, yeah. Stuck in my own room. Pretty fucking lonely actually. The boys were out for a good time. Well, I couldn't be involved. I couldn't be Jack the Lad one minute and dis-passionate the next. I couldn't be the one demanding we push on to another level if I was up half the night getting pissed, could I? I had to keep my distance. I had to put up the mask. I had a bit of practice at that and I was pretty good at it.'

Consider the back story. A matter-of-fact army dad and a mum he describes as not the earth mother type. His parents led the nomadic life of military people. His father was a lieutenant colonel in the Air Corps and the family moved about, from Hong Kong to Germany to Northern Ireland, where the Carlings did three separate tours of duty. They moved home year after year, never settling in one place long enough to lay down roots or make lasting friendships. Carling took the mickey out of himself as 'the boy who never knew where he lived' but there was a grain of truth in it all the same. As his parents saw it, the only way to bring a bit of stability to their boy's life was to send him away to school. 'And what was I going to say? "Hey, Dad, change your whole world around because it really doesn't suit me"? No, that wasn't an option.'

Carling arrived at Terra Nova prep school in Cheshire at the age of seven, and became something of a loner. Some of his earliest memories are of him wanting to be on his own, him playing rugby by himself, him walking out of a room when others walked in.

Becoming a boarder at such a young age taught him to 'get rid of any feelings for anything'. That might sound dramatic but it's the way it was. He remembers upbraiding himself for being weak, for missing his parents and crying himself to sleep at night in a dorm with eleven others. Then lying about his tears because he didn't want to appear soft.

'I had to sort myself out because nobody else was going to do it for me. That sense of being on my own, that sink or swim thing, had a massive impact on me. Massive. For the worst, to be honest. It didn't do me any good. I closed off. The shutters came down. I didn't let a lot of people anywhere near me. Superficially, yeah. On the surface, no problem. I could laugh and joke just like anybody else. But properly? Nah. That thing of putting on a front started when I was seven years old.'

At twelve, he went to school in Sedbergh on the Yorkshire Moors, a venerable institution founded in 1525, set in the kind of rural landscape that only adults can fully appreciate. As a boy, the rolling hills and smells of the country gave him a feeling of isolation – not surprising since Sedbergh truly was slap bang in the middle of nowhere.

Carling progressed quickly there, though. Almost too quickly. He was big for his age and powerful. He started playing rugby and found it easy. Pick up the ball, run, batter some small fry out of the way and score. Simple. He was more physical than any of his peers. Faster and more dynamic. He stood out a mile.

The coaches said he was good enough to step up a level, so they pitched him in with the older boys. He liked the ego boost but didn't appreciate the fallout. 'It marked me out as different and I didn't want to be different. I wanted to blend in. The kids my own age were saying, "Look at him, he must think the sun shines out of his own arse" and the older kids went, "Who the fuck does this guy think he is?" I was in a no-man's-land.'

Sedbergh developed him as a rugby player and Durham University, where he studied psychology with the help of an army scholarship, did the same. But as a person? He was a complex mix of things. To those who met him fleetingly he could seem supremely confident to the point of arrogance, aloof to the point of rudeness. To those who knew him well, he was all and none of those things. He was conceited and yet terribly unsure of himself; he was distant and yet the life and soul of the party.

Carling graduated from Durham in the summer of 1988, but he resigned from the army just a few months later. The way he saw it, it was a straight choice between being a soldier and being a rugby player. He came to realise that doing both was impossible. It cost £8,000 to buy himself out, but it was a fair price, he said. Rugby was his priority, ahead of everything, ahead of family and relationships. The one constant in his life. It was his default setting.

Trouble with his studies? Play more rugby. Missing home? Play more rugby. Problems with a girl? Play more rugby. His relationships with women were where the cracks started to appear for all to see. This was later on, of course. When the full glare of the media was shining bright in his face, when the tabloids were camped in his garden and banging on his door. That's when the façade started to crack. And when it all came apart there was a certain inevitability about it.

Mooro once defined tragedy not as tree falls on man but tree falls on man because man has a habitual tendency to walk under trees, when he shouldn't. He was actually talking about Carling at the time, about the break-up of his marriage to Julia, his friendship with Princess Diana, and the split from Ali Cockayne and their baby son – an event latched on to by the tabloids and one that almost ruined him.

'You see what I mean?' asked Mooro. 'The tragedy is the inevitability of the downfall of man because of character traits which he can do nothing about. Boarding school at seven? Fucking hell. It must define your character, mustn't it? It must.'

It did, says Carling. 'My personal life just bumped along for years,' he says. 'It carried on down all sorts of wrong avenues. I drifted. I'd find myself heading down a road in a relationship and I'd think, "Oh, hang on, I don't want to go there", but I never said anything. I just bottled things up, I put on a front that looked like emotional attachment but actually wasn't and I got myself in all sorts of trouble.

'I was weak. I was. In certain areas of my life I was a weak man. You start going down a path and you think, "I'm not sure about this", but you keep going because you don't want to hurt someone and then eventually you get to the stage where you say I can't do this any more and then you really hurt them. Very clever, eh? Very grown up. My way was, "Ah, play more rugby and it'll all work out somehow". I'd think sometimes how could I be England captain and be comfortable playing in front of sixty and seventy thousand people while at the same time be so bloody insecure. I'm not sure I ever figured that one out.'

In the River Room of the Petersham Hotel he stood up for the first time to address his troops as captain. Only the troops didn't want to be addressed.

The Judge was telling a joke.

Jeff Probyn was reading a newspaper.

Mick Skinner was recounting the story of a recent escapade.

Dean Richards was playing pool.

Thirty seconds on his feet. A minute. A minute and a half.

The Judge finished his joke.

Jeff Probyn put down his paper.

Mick Skinner fell silent.

But still Deano played pool.

Deano was like the Godfather in this crew. He was laid back and cool. He moved when he wanted to move, listened when he wanted to listen. He was a bit like Winters; he didn't say a whole lot but when he did the place would fall quiet because they knew he had a brilliant brain for rugby. He had a liberal attitude to training but that was okay. Because he was Deano. He was a talent. He was revered. By Carling more than anybody.

Carling said nothing until Deano potted the eight ball and slowly took his seat. Only then did the new captain say his piece. To some in that room the young man showed balls of steel. Ackford reckoned it took some amount of courage to stand there in such an intimidating environment and wait it out until the room was under control, took some amount of guts for him to stay on his feet until all these senior players, these gnarled forwards who'd been around the block a time or two, paid attention to him.

'You've got some bottle, son,' Ackford said quietly. 'You've got, what, seven caps? And you're not intimidated by this lot? You're playing to a tough crowd, kid, and you look like a natural.'

In a way, Will was back at boarding school now. The lessons of Terra Nova returned. He was the seven-year-old again trying to be brave, trying to hide his true feelings, trying to sell a more assured version of his real self.

'The God's honest truth is that I was so fucking scared I couldn't talk.'

He can't remember what he said but he recalls that nobody laughed and that was good enough. Maybe he touched on the calamity in Australia and the need to refocus; maybe he referred to Stuart Barnes walking out of the squad in a strop and asked for dedication; maybe he looked to the senior heads in the room and looked for support. Many things concerned him and high on the list was Mooro.

In his brief time as an England player, Carling had never struck up much of a relationship with Mooro, but then he didn't have to. A hooker and a centre didn't need to communicate. They could live in their parallel worlds and it wouldn't have mattered a damn.

Carling getting the captaincy brought them into conflict and it was always weird after that. Part of it was jealousy on Mooro's part. He could have been captain. He reckoned he should have been captain. He found Carling selfish and secretive and impossible to get to know.

Mooro felt he should have been consulted more on team affairs, on the technical aspects of forward play, but it didn't happen all that often. He was the leader of a pack that was beginning to show wrecking ball tendencies but Mooro rarely got the impression he was in the loop when the key decisions were being made at management level. Cooke and Carling were tight and nobody else really got much of a look-in.

They'd talk. Sure they would. But the conversation rarely lasted more than five sentences. It was about all either of them could stand. Carling had tried to win Mooro over. But Mooro can't remember much of that. Took him out for lunches and dinners, apparently, but found that the barriers were up and there was no breaking them down.

'With Mooro, it was a case of, "You're silver spoon and I'm other side of the tracks". We didn't get beyond that. He had this chip on his shoulder that could not be shifted. He didn't want it shifted. He needed it there. In his mind he was the underdog. He was like, "I'll prove you all wrong, you fucking see if I don't". But prove us wrong about what, Mooro? We all thought he was a total fucking warrior.'

The elephant in the room was the captaincy. Carling knew how big a deal that was to Mooro. He knew how much missing out on it wounded him. 'Mooro had a desperate desire to be The

Man. It was such a point to him that he never captained England. I was always painfully aware that he didn't like me and under-pinning it all was the absolute fact that I had something he wanted and never got.'

Carling tells a story of a row from later in their careers that sums up their relationship. It was not long after the 1993 Lions tour, an unsuccessful trek to New Zealand, particularly so for Carling who had a poor time of it and only played in one of the four Tests.

After the series was over one of the English Lions put a Test jersey up for auction at a charity bash and a nice few quid was raised for a worthy cause. At England training the next season it was suggested by one of the boys that Carling do likewise with his Lions top. Quick as a flash Mooro pipes up: 'He only got one. And he was fucking lucky to get it.'

Carling came back sharply: 'Fair call, Mooro. Fair call. I tell you what, though. Maybe you could auction off one of your England shirts from when you were captain. Oh, fuck, hang on. You haven't done that, have you?'

The way Carling tells it, Mooro was across to him in a millisecond, telling him what a bastard he was. 'I said to him, "Hey, Mooro, you hand it out, you fucking take it". He went bonkers. You needed the mind of a psychologist to understand him.'

But you'd have needed a room full of psychologists to get an angle on Carling's complexities.

On the day of his first Test as captain, Cooke noticed how anxious his new leader was. Nothing unusual there. Not for a twenty-two-year-old. Cooke sought him out and reassured him that all would be well, that he believed in him and that the lads believed in him, too. Carling nodded quietly. Cooke wasn't sure if his soothing words had done the job or not but time ticked on and soon the moment of truth had arrived for the captain.

They were in the dressing room waiting for his speech. A room full of famous heads turned to look at him. And Carling stared

each one down as if he had been doing it all his life. There wasn't
a trace of doubt, not an iota of nerves. He laid down the law
like a veteran and then led them on to the field.

Things went so well for him it was almost corny. England had
the game won by the time Carling started feeling the effects of
an injury and went off. His last act before leaving the field was
to set up the cherry-on-top try that brought the Australians to
their knees and the old stadium to its feet.

He was the darling of Twickenham that day. The Captain
Fantastic they'd waited eight years to find. From the autumn
through to the spring of the following year the press and the
public couldn't get enough of him. England entered the 1989
Five Nations on a wave of optimism. Waiting for them in the
first game? Scotland.

# CHAPTER 6

## IT TAKES A STRONG MAN TO DEFEND THE BORDER

Nigel Starmer-Smith was in his car heading for John Jeffrey's place, trying to remember the complex directions JJ had given him. 'Starmers, listen up,' JJ had said. 'We're a bit out of the way here. You'll need to keep your wits about you.'

'Okay, talk me through it.'

'Well, you want to follow the signs for Hawick and Jedburgh. Then you want to bypass Kelso, okay? Then it's the first left for Morebattle and Yetholm. Then it's the first right. Drive on for two miles and you'll come into a wood. Go straight through it, down the hill, up the other side. You'll eventually see a small gatepost on your left if you're concentrating. That's me.'

Starmer-Smith followed the instructions perfectly and pulled up at JJ's farmhouse with his camera crew in tow. They were there to do some Calcutta Cup filming, to get the thoughts of the man they called The White Shark.

'Starmers, welcome,' smiled JJ. 'You're in God's country now.'

The former England scrum-half and presenter of BBC's *Rugby Special* stood outside JJ's front door and took in the scenery. He saw the Cheviot Hills in the distance and the Bowmont Valley below on one side and the Kale Valley on the other. It was one of the most beautiful landscapes he'd ever set eyes on.

He rolled the cameras and got JJ talking about his sense of place.

'JJ, I can't imagine what it's like waking up to this view every morning.'

'You're right. I feel blessed. I open the curtains in the morning and I swear I can see the colours changing in front of my eyes through the day.'

'You've been here your whole life?'

'Aye. My parents moved in when my mother was five months pregnant with me. It's in the blood. But there's a problem. See that hill over there? That big one?'

'Yes, I see it.'

'Well, the border runs along the top of that hill. Big Cheviot, it's called. See that bit there? That's not Scotland any more.'

'Oh, right. And how is that a problem?'

'That's England, Starmers. The problem is that I can see England from here.'

Starmer-Smith went quiet. 'It was like I hit him with a right hook,' said JJ. 'He didn't know if I was serious or not.' He wasn't, but he enjoyed pretending he was. For a second, as he looked at his interviewer's jaw dropping to the floor, he thought about saying, 'Ah, I'm only kidding you on', but instead his mischievous side took over and he decided to let it ride. That was JJ's thing. He was a ferocious wind-up merchant, a champion of the mind game.

The BBC ran the interview a week later and his comments reverberated around the game. He was anti-English now. Official. He was Scotland's answer to Mooro. McPitbull. If the England players didn't see the interview in real time then they heard all about it later on. Some brushed it off, some didn't.

'Some people took it literally,' said JJ. 'And, in fairness, I wasn't the type to dampen their indignation. If they thought I was serious, well, so what? I thought it was great that they were upset. I wanted to piss them off. The more English people I wound up, the better. They were saying to me, "JJ, you've got to put that chip on the shoulder stuff out of the road once and for all". I said, "Are you for real? How do we ever beat England? It's by revelling in our status as the put-upon underdog". I fed off that stuff. Put it out of the road? Fuck off.'

JJ played on the image of the arrogant English just as Mooro used the chestnut of the whingeing Scot. He stoked the fires any chance he got. From time to time he'd be seen in a pub by some tourists from the south and they'd go over to him and because he was sociable he'd be welcoming and have them charmed in seconds.

'JJ, you live in Kelso, right?' they'd say.

'That's right, boys. And a day out of Kelso is a day wasted.'

'You're on England's doorstep?'

'I am.'

'So if you hate England so much how come you live so close to the border?'

'Because it takes a strong man to defend the border.'

His attitude towards the English went a bit deeper than gentle mocking. He made a joke of it but there was a bit more to it than that. JJ had a difficulty with the Sassenachs and he never denied it. He never denied that his hostility towards some types of English people might have been driven by the little nation syndrome.

He always said that Scotland as a country would be better off if the Scots didn't obsess about the English so much. They tended to blame England for things that went wrong at home and he knew that culture wasn't fair on the English and wasn't healthy for the Scots. But, hey, he wasn't a social commentator. He wasn't a chin-stroker who thought about the intricacies of the Scots' relationship with their neighbours all that much. He was a rugby player and as a rugby player preparing to go and face Will Carling's team it suited him to see them as an arrogant crowd who belittled his people. This mentality made him a more focused animal.

The one thing he hated in life was arrogance and he found

plenty of that down south. He'd go to Twickenham and the
Scotland bus would pull into the West Car Park and he would
look out of the window at the posh folk lifting their picnic baskets
from the backs of their Range Rovers and sniffing as he walked
by. 'Haven't done a proper day's work in their lives, this lot. Up
their own arses.'

Then he'd watch the England footballers string a few passes
together and all of a sudden they were talked about as World
Cup winners. And the cricketers? He loved his cricket. He was
actually an England cricket fan. But the hype over an Ashes win!
You'd swear they were after finding the cure for cancer the way
their media went on.

'I'm a great believer in humility but when the English have a
bit of sporting success there isn't a lot of humility knocking
about. There's a lot of self-importance. Nobody else matters. They
strut. They puff themselves up. Their media goes mental and
that just got my back up and fed my prejudice. And the way I
saw it, that was good. I had a chip on my shoulder and I used
it to my advantage. People used to say to me, "As a nation we
need to remove the chip", and I said, "Yep, I absolutely see your
point and you're probably right, but mine is staying right where
it is, thanks very much".'

When the Starmer-Smith interview was aired, Mooro was
watching. 'Chippy fucker,' said the hooker, as JJ dropped the
bomb about seeing England from the border.

'It's funny,' Mooro said. 'JJ says stuff about England and everybody thinks it's a great laugh and when I say the same about
Scotland there's a riot. Armed neutrality, that's the relationship
I have with JJ. We don't get on and neither of us feels it's a
particular loss in our lives. He's too proud a Scotsman and I'm
too proud an Englishman. As a player? A total nuisance. I'll give
him that much; John Jeffrey is a warrior.'

Nothing better explains JJ's popularity in Scotland than the
shenanigans of '88. He was on the bench for that bitter Calcutta

Cup but that didn't stop him leading the charge into oblivion. The players from both sides decided there was only one way to forget the horror of the game and that was to drink it from the memory bank.

Scotland's rehydration session consisted of a miniature Drambuie, handed to them as they took their seats on the bus. After that, as JJ recalls, Fin Calder pulled a bottle of Orkney malt out of his kitbag and those who didn't mix it with the Drambuie to make a Rusty Nail just drank it neat. The night descended into a drunken blur.

JJ and Deano got chatting and hit on an idea. They took the Calcutta Cup off its stand, filled it with champagne, tipped it over Mooro's head and ran.

They jumped in a taxi and hit the Guildford Arms, then the Café Royal and after that it was on to the Mount Royal Hotel. Just the two boys, a whole load of fans and the Calcutta Cup, the cherished prize dating back to 1878. The cup bounced around from pub to pub that night. Some eyewitnesses claimed they saw Deano kicking it down Rose Street. One lady said she watched as JJ bowled it against a wall. Others say it was simply dropped.

'I don't know where I was at the time,' says JJ, 'but I took a look at it and immediately I sobered up. It was a mess. I said to Deano, "I know the manageress in Buster Brown's nightclub; we'll take it there and see if she can straighten it out". The bouncer had a look, but he gave up. He said if we tried to force it back into place it would come apart in his hands. Deano and me, we looked at each other. "We're in trouble here, mate".'

They went back to the hotel and JJ handed the Calcutta Cup to the night porter. 'I said, "This is a valued piece of rugby history. Look after it". Then I went to bed a worried man. Next morning there was a knock on the door. I didn't need to be Sherlock Holmes to figure out what it was about.'

When the SRU banned him for five months the letters pages

of the newspapers were full of support for JJ. Sure, he shouldn't have done it, but five months! Deano had got one game.

The Union decided to put the battered Calcutta Cup on display to the public and spoke of the repair work that needed to be done, but still the sympathy for JJ tumbled in. The SRU were trying to humiliate him, that's what the letter writers were saying. The country was overwhelmingly on his side.

Exiled from rugby, JJ returned to the farm and counted the days until he could play again.

JJ should never really have been there in 1990. His father didn't want him to play rugby and neither did his father's father. Both of them sat him down and told him that he had to prioritise. Work had to come before rugby.

There was always a secret fear in the Jeffrey household that he was going to get injured. Badly injured. The way he played, the sheer bloody-mindedness of the way he approached every single match, they felt sure that something awful was going to happen to him sooner or later. A broken arm. A broken leg. Something that would stop him doing his duty on the farm.

Around the Borders there were any number of examples of young men who'd suffered injury on the rugby field and had made their parents' lives difficult as a result. In the Jeffreys' bridge club there was one such case. Charlie Stewart had snapped his leg in his early twenties and was rendered useless for close to a year.

'No son of mine will play rugby,' said JJ's dad.

'His place is on the farm,' said JJ's dad's dad.

But when the bug bit, there was no stopping him.

'My parents let me go in the end and they'd come and watch me play because they knew my heart was in it. Grandfather never came. He claimed he never even watched me on television, but I know he did. He just didn't want to let on. The thing was, he would have known people who failed on the farm for one reason or another and he felt my place was by my father's side. He frowned every time I went out of the door with my kit bag. "You should be on the land on a Saturday", he'd say. But I'd like to think he was proud of me at the same time.'

Other things were against JJ. He had asthma, for a start. He wasn't a chronic case but for a player whose success centred around his phenomenal workrate – his suicidal brilliance, as John Beattie called it – it was something he had to watch closely. An inhaler in his pocket was as important to him some days as a jersey on his back.

He had knee problems but he said little about them. In his final year at school he had some cartilage removed and as time went on bone started to rub on bone and cortisone injections became as regular to him as team talks.

He was The White Shark, though. He could handle the pain.

That was another thing. The nickname. He delighted in the image but chuckled at the interpretation. On his rugby travels he cheerily posed for pictures with the carcases of great whites and hammed it up as the shark of the Scotland back row but his moniker had nothing to do with his predatory instincts nor his shock of blond hair.

It was Kenny Macaulay of Gala who came up with it. A gang of Borders lads were in Barbados in the early 1980s and were sunning themselves on the beach when JJ emerged from the water, his pallid body drawing hoots of derision among his pals, bronzed gods by comparison.

'Look out, boys,' shouted Macaulay, 'here comes The White Shark!'

And from that day on he was branded.

JJ did nothing to dispel the myths around him. He got a name for being skilful but he never thought of himself that way. It was always written that he'd a soft pair of hands capable of giving beautifully subtle passes, but he thought of them more as shovels. He was lethal as a try-scoring force, but he always said that he'd have scored twice as many if he hadn't dropped the ball with the line in his sight.

His opponents would complain about his law-breaking, but taking liberties with the rules was essential to his make-up. That and his bravery. 'I pushed referees all I could. I played to the limit of the law and if refs gave me an inch, I took another inch until they told me to stop. If they didn't tell me to stop, I went again. I pushed the boundaries because I was desperate to get to the ball ahead of everybody else. Now, it cost me. I killed ball in games and I've still got the scars to prove it. That was part and parcel of what I was about. I was a disciple of Jim Telfer. I didn't care who kicked me as long as we won.'

People looked at JJ and they could see a young Telfer. The courage, the big engine, the love of the game. The veterans in the Borders would spot the similarities a mile off. They'd tell one tale about JJ that made them smile because it reminded them so much of the 1960s when Telfer was that fearless young buck blasting off the back of the Melrose scrum.

When a hard snow fell one week in Kelso it looked like curtains for the top of the table clash between JJ's beloved Kelso and the peerless men of Hawick. Kelso fancied their chances but their Poynder Park ground was under three feet of snow – useless as a training pitch early in the week and doubtful as a match venue on the Saturday.

JJ sorted it. He chased the cattle out of one of his barns, shovelled the manure up against the walls and created an indoor training facility for the boys. Then on game day he arrived early with spades to rid the pitch of snow. Later, in a tumultuous match, JJ's ceaseless running steered Kelso to a famous victory.

If some of the old guard were thinking of the past and how JJ's determination was reminiscent of Telfer's, most people were thinking of the future. Scotland's team was taking shape. They had a pack of forwards that looked a match for most sides, promising young half-backs and some bits of class in behind.

But it wasn't just on the rugby field where things were changing.

# CHAPTER 7

# OHHH, YOU MEAN THE TESTING GROUND?

Jim Telfer often said that if he'd been knocking about in the 1930s he'd have been a communist. He knew what he was talking about, for he had one in the family. His stepfather-in-law, Ken Harrington, might have been a little too far to the left for Telfer's liking but they still spent many happy hours in each other's company.

Ken had a brilliant brain. He was Cambridge University, but one of the good guys. He ran rings around Telfer intellectually but Jim loved listening to him. He even let Ken take his boy, Mark, on a trip to Russia once.

They discussed politics and the state of society. Telfer was a Labour man but he wasn't impressed with the leadership of the party. He thought Michael Foot had been a clown and Neil Kinnock a vacuous showman.

'Full of wind and piss, that Kinnock,' Telfer would say.

'Wedgwood Benn is the best of them,' Ken would reply. 'A man you can trust.'

In the late 1980s Scottish nationalism was on the rise but Telfer didn't much like the people in charge of the SNP either. There was a growing tide of anti-English sentiment washing about the place, but Telfer had no truck with that.

'Things were festering, aye. Around the country people were saying, "Oh, we're Scottish and we hate the English", but if anybody had cause to hate the English it was us here in the Borders. We fought them for hundreds of years. We're the reason we have a Scotland. Roxburghe Castle down the road was sacked and burned down so often by English raiders in the olden times that we said, "Bugger it, we're nae rebuilding the bloody thing again", so we left it in ruins. Aye. Three or four hundred years ago that was. We burned our own crops so that the English couldn't feed off them when they came up. So if anybody is entitled to hate them it's Borders people but we get on quite well. All that anti-English stuff was stoked up by the politicians and the media.'

Still, Telfer could see where the hate was coming from. Tory rule had angered Scots in their millions. It angered him, too, if truth be told. 'I'd sooner be dead than vote Tory,' he said. 'I had no time for Margaret Thatcher.'

The satirical puppet show *Spitting Image* produced a sketch that cut to the heart of how Scots saw The Iron Lady.

*Douglas Hurd* (Home Secretary): Prime Minister, I think the reason no one voted Tory in Scotland is that they felt neglected by the government.
*Margaret Thatcher*: Nonsense, nonsense, Hurd. What is Scotland?
*Lord Young* (Secretary of State for Trade and Industry): It's that island off the Falklands, isn't it?
*Geoffrey Howe* (Foreign Secretary): I thought it was a shoe shop.
*Hurd*: No, no, no. Scotland, it's that place up north.
*Thatcher*: North? North? Refresh my memory, Hurd.
*Hurd* (pointing to a map): Here!
Thatcher: Ohhh, you mean the testing ground!
*Hurd*: Testing ground?
(The scene changes to a science laboratory)

*Thatcher*: Yes, we've got to have somewhere to test things out. Somewhere – a long way from my house.

*Norman Fowler* (Secretary of State for Employment): So we chose this . . .

*Hurd*: Scotland.

*Thatcher*: Yes, we've been doing it for years now, first with Lena Zavaroni and now Ridley here is testing his Poll Tax on them.

*Nick Ridley* (Secretary of State for the Environment, struggling with a rat dressed in tartan): You never know, it might work.

*Hurd*: What if it doesn't?

*Thatcher*: No harm done, they would have voted Labour anyway.

*Young*: And then there's our new reciprocal fuel experi-ment. We take their oil, they take our nuclear waste. Very successful.

*Thatcher*: Then we're going to try out national service, the repeal of the Safety at Work Act and hanging.

*Hurd*: For what offences?

*Thatcher*: Isn't being Scottish enough?

'God Save The Queen' was the official anthem of the Scotland rugby team. But it was becoming a problem. As soon as the first strains were heard at Murrayfield there was booing in the grandstands and red faces in the committee box. Scottish Rugby Union officials sitting with the cherished patron of the sport north of the border, the Princess Royal, were mortified.

After the 1989 championship, the SRU decided that some-thing had to be done. They needed a new song.

They had choices. 'Highland Cathedral', a haunting bagpipe melody, always went down well with supporters. 'Scotland The Brave' was already the anthem of the national football team and of the Commonwealth Games squad and would have been a popular choice. 'Scots Wha Hae', written by Rabbie Burns

in the eighteenth century and based on his idea of the eve of
battle speech Robert the Bruce may have given at Bannockburn had for years been the unofficial song of Scotland. 'Cale-
donia,' a moving number about an exiled Scot dreaming of
home, pressed all the right buttons emotionally. Another of
Burns' most famous works, 'A Man's a Man for A' That', was
also well liked.

None of these were chosen, though. The SRU, normally a
deeply conservative organisation, opted for the most contentious
song of the lot. A battle cry against the English.

> *O Flower of Scotland*
> *When will we see*
> *Your like again,*
> *That fought and died for*
> *Your wee bit Hill and Glen*
> *And stood against him*
> *Proud Edward's Army,*
> *And sent him homeward*
> *Tae think again.*

Written in the 1960s by Roy Williamson of the folk band The
Corries, it celebrated Robert the Bruce's routing of Edward II at
Bannockburn in 1314. The rugby team had had it as their own
song before it ever became the official anthem, singing it on the
bus to matches, singing it in the changing room afterwards,
singing it again at the post-game knees-up.

With his rebellious spirit, JJ used to sing 'Flower of Scotland' to himself when 'God Save The Queen' was being played.
He'd nothing against Her Majesty and he held the Princess
Royal in the highest regard, but he wanted something that
got his juices flowing. This piece spoke of Scottish pride in
their most famous victory and finished with a verse of pure
defiance:

*Those days are past now*
*And in the past they must remain*
*But we can still rise now*
*And be the nation again*
*That stood against him*
*Proud Edward's Army*
*And sent him homeward,*
*Tae think again.*

'Edward's Army' was indeed in the past, but English oppression was back. Margaret Thatcher wielded no sword but she was more reviled than any prime minister before her.

It was a measure of the way things were that by March 1990 an unwitting twenty-four-year-old rugby player was deemed to be one of her great supporters. Rebranded her blue-eyed boy by the Scottish media purely because he was quintessentially English, Will Carling felt that the Scots truly hated him.

'I was sitting there reading some of this stuff,' said Carling, 'and I'm thinking, "There's some serious political shit going on here that I'm in the middle of but know absolutely nothing about".'

JJ had a theory about the anti-Englishness that swept around Edinburgh in Grand Slam week 1990, and the hostility that followed in the years after. It goes back to football and Scotland's annual meeting with the Auld Enemy.

Seven months before the 1990 Five Nations began, the annual international football fixture was abandoned. On 27 May 1989, in the hours before Scotland met England at Hampden Park, the streets of Glasgow were overrun by hooligans. Stuart Jones of *The Times* reported that the centre of the city 'was turned into a cesspit of obscenity and violence by tribal gangs purporting to be supporters of both nations'.

There were running battles and hundreds of arrests. It was the biggest ever security operation at a domestic football match.

'Mayhem!' was the headline in the following day's *Sunday Mail*. They put the blame mostly on the visiting English, 'armed with bottles and clubs and committing mindless indiscriminate attacks'.

The Scottish newspapers spent the week castigating English hooligans and calling for their national football team to be banned, just like their club sides. Ever since 1872 the Auld Enemy had played each other every season, the cycle of matches only being broken by two world wars. In 1989 the plug was pulled for good.

'There was a vacuum there,' said JJ. 'The Calcutta Cup was now the only time that Scotland faced England in a sporting context. The game assumed a profile and a harshness it didn't have previously. It attracted people that might not otherwise have been that interested before. I'm not talking about hooligans. I'm talking about ordinary people with chips on their shoulders about the English and what Margaret Thatcher was doing to Scotland, who used sporting contests as an opportunity to release some of that resentment. I'm also talking about the tabloid media. It was football-obsessed. Before the match was cancelled, it didn't matter what us rugby players were doing. If the soccer lads broke a nail it was a headline in the red tops. But now the tabloids with their readers in the hundreds of thousands suddenly had an interest in rugby. In the week of the England game they were leading the charge, firing people up, taking it into another dimension, making it political.'

The irony was that the target of their opprobrium, Thatcher, was once welcomed in Scotland like a film star. She stopped traffic the day she first visited the country as the new leader of the Conservative Party, 22 February 1975. In Edinburgh, a crowd three thousand strong turned out to catch a glimpse of her. Three women fainted. Some people were squashed in the ruck of bodies and had to be guided clear of danger. The euphoria was unprecedented for a politician in Scotland.

In Glasgow later that day the scenes were repeated. Cars were halted on George Square as she made her way through the city, more than 1,800 smiling locals following her every step. One of her officials observed the happy chaos and beamed: 'I think the Tory party suddenly has a new problem in Scotland,' he said. 'It's called crowd control.'

The next day's *Daily Record*, a staunchly Labour paper, put her picture on the front page and called her 'Mrs Supercool' in the headline.

Mrs Supercool said she'd had an exhilarating day and that she'd be back. And she was true to her word. Two months later she spoke to a Conservative rally in Helensburgh. 'Here I am again,' she began. 'I'm being selfish. I like coming to Scotland!'

In fact, she wouldn't stay away. By the time she became prime minister in May 1979 she'd already visited Scotland on thirteen occasions. Her first public speech as prime minister was at the Scottish Conservative Party Conference in Perth, and her first holiday as PM was on the Isle of Islay. 'I go there for pleasure, too. Not just for work,' she said, as her husband loaded the golf clubs into the back of the car.

Thatcher inherited a basket case of an economy on both sides of the border and took little time in sending out her uncompromising message. Scotland's socialist ideology had made the people dependent on the state, she said. It had robbed them of their enterprising spirit and their individual responsibility which she was convinced they had, down deep, where Labour had buried it.

To cure the ailing economy with socialism, she argued, was like trying to cure leukaemia with leeches. 'Mr "Wedgwood" Benn says that the "forces of socialism in Britain cannot be stopped." They can be and they will be. We shall stop them.'

At a time when nationalist sentiment was on the increase, she sought to quash it. 'The utter irrelevance and folly of the Scottish Nationalists is at long last being exposed . . . No wonder the Nationalists are known in Westminster as the Rice Krispie

Party. There is a good deal of snap and crackle but at the end of it all – they go pop!'

Her policies needed to be dramatic to get a grip on the disastrous economy – and they were. She put a squeeze on spending that made the eyes water. No more bailouts of faltering industries, no more backing down to the unions, no more throwing good money after bad.

Within a few months of her victory at the polls, 28,000 jobs went in Scotland alone. The Singer Sewing Machine plant in Clydebank folded, leaving 4,500 people on the dole, and they were joined by thousands more from the Monsanto textiles industry in Ayrshire, Pye TMC telecommunciations at Livingston, Wiggins Teape paper company in Fort William, the clothing outfit VF Corporation in Greenock, Massey Ferguson, the agricultural machinery giant, in Kilmarnock.

In 1981 the Peugeot-Citroën car factory at Linwood went under, followed into extinction by the British Leyland plant at Bathgate. In 1982 Scotland's oldest manufacturing company, Carron, in existence since 1759, went into receivership. Scotland had now lost 20 per cent of its industrial employment in three years of Thatcher's government. Resentment grew. Unemployment in Scotland hit a historic high: 15 per cent of the population was out of work.

The perception was that Thatcher was personally responsible for all these people getting laid off. She wasn't, of course. Some of these companies were decidedly rust-bucket and would have collapsed regardless of who was running the country.

The feeling that she had a problem with the Scots started to grow, however. The woman was harsh and unforgiving. Maybe she needed to be to undo the disasters of the previous regime but her manner was cold, her sensitivity 'aggressively absent', as Sir Ian Gilmour, the late Conservative cabinet minister, remarked.

To prove the point, when Sir Ian expressed his reservations about her brutal streak, she fired him.

'We have never until now had a government so determined to

unpick the very fabric of Scottish life and make it over into something quite different,' wrote William McIlvanney. 'Under the government it is not only the quality of our individual lives that is threatened. It is our communal sense of our own identity . . . For Margaret Thatcher is not just a perpetrator of bad policies. She is a cultural vandal.'

The dole queues lengthened by the day. The people saw her as a dog-eat-dog woman, a survival of the fittest type. 'You do not get anywhere by blaming your own lack of progress on others,' she. stated dispassionately. Her key lieutenants backed her up with incendiary pronouncements. At the Tory conference in 1981 Norman Tebbit held court. 'I grew up in the thirties with an unemployed father,' he declared. 'He didn't riot. He got on his bike and looked for work, and he kept looking 'til he found it.'

Tebbit was responding to a young Tory who said that civil unrest was the result of unemployment, but to the unemployed everywhere it was taken as a personal attack. The fact was that they could have got on their bikes and pedalled for days and they still might not have found a job. That truth was lost on Tebbit and many of his contemporaries.

John Junor, the Scottish-born editor of the *Sunday Express*, was a Thatcher loyalist. 'If there is a dislike of Margaret Thatcher among the Scots, it's for two or three reasons,' he told the journalist Kenneth Roy in *Conversations in a Small Country*. 'One is that the Scots are a male chauvinist race, and not any longer particularly intelligent because most of the best people have left Scotland. They are also a whingeing people, which they never used to be. And they have made a mess of industry. They've buggered up shipbuilding, they've buggered up the motor car industry. Margaret Thatcher's too damned good for you all. And you resent her because she's got this upper class or simulated upper class Edinburgh accent. And you resent also the fact that she's pulling you out of the shit that you've put yourself into over so many years.'

\*   \*   \*

Thatcher continued to visit Scotland more than any other part of the UK. 'But she was damned if she did and damned if she didn't,' said David Torrance in *'We in Scotland': Thatcherism in a Cold Climate*. 'The more she visited, the more Scots seemed to resent her interference in Scottish affairs and if she stayed away she was accused of neglecting Scotland.'

She visited a factory in Cumnock in Ayrshire and a thousand people turned up to heckle her. In 1982 a dozen extreme nationalists, a bunch of desperadoes wearing leather jerkins and Tammies and kilts to the ankles and calling themselves Siol nan Gaidheal (Seed of the Gaels), charged at her as she was coming out of the Tory conference in Perth. Chanting madly as they galloped down the street, the protestors were only narrowly foiled, as the police bundled the prime minister into the back of a car before the gang reached her. Her security in Scotland was stepped up from that point on.

To many Scots, Margaret Thatcher's second government had all the hallmarks of an alien force. The south-east of England came out of the recession a lot earlier than Scotland and enjoyed a period of great prosperity. Yuppies came into evidence and the mantra greed is good was pervasive.

Thatcher herself seemed to be legitimising selfishness. The poor felt disenfranchised – told to snap out of it, to pull their socks up. And in Scotland, as in many other places in the UK, things remained grim.

At the 1987 election Scotland sent her a message. Thatcher lost 11 of her 21 seats. In every single constituency the Tory vote dropped. They now had just 10 Scottish MPs out of a total of 72. Labour had 40 more seats and 16 per cent more votes. The morning after the front page of the *Daily Record* ran a picture of the woman they had once called Mrs Supercool under a big bold headline: Scotland Says No!

Tory rhetoric on Scotland turned nasty. Nigel Lawson was seen as anti-Scottish even by some of his fellow ministers. The chancellor thought the Scots were incredibly thin-skinned,

forever looking for insults to rail against. A prickly race. He
referred to Scotland's 'culture of dependency' and criticised the
Scots spongers who were supposedly happy living off state
handouts. 'There is still a barrier along Scotland's road to prosperity,' said Lawson. 'That barrier is the pervasive presence of a
hostile attitude to enterprise and wealth creation.'

The *Sun* reported his comments the next day as: 'Will ye
stop your snivelling, Jock?'

Other Tories followed suit. Sir Ian McGregor, one of Thatcher's
favourite businessmen, was a Scot, born in Kinlochleven. But
he was an exiled Scot, a John Junor type. 'Scots,' he said bitterly,
'have become like drug addicts dependent on state support.'

The words came out of the mouths of Lawson and McGregor
and others but in Scotland they were effectively attributed to
Thatcher, proof that she didn't care. Tory canvassers in local elec-
tions were constantly met with hostility on doorsteps in all areas,
rich and poor. Thatcher had long since alienated the working
class but now the middle class were leaving her, too. Doctors
and lawyers and landowners were starting to speak out.

Scots were telling her they didn't want her but she smiled back
at them and told them, 'Scotland is working.' Thatcher talked of
a nation being transformed. 'The Scottish miracle', she called it.
The Tories published statistics showing that, of all the regions in
the United Kingdom only the south-east did better out of the
government per head of population than Scotland. But all of that
was largely ignored. Thatcher was getting filleted on a daily basis
by the Scottish press. She was That Bloody Woman, The Iron
Lady who had destroyed Scotland's manufacturing industry and
who used Scots as laboratory rats for her experiments.

Nothing reinforced that view more than a piece of local government legislation that was soon to be heading Scotland's way,
the most disastrous domestic policy in half a century. Officially
called the Community Charge, everybody came to know it as the
poll tax.

A flat rate of tax paid by every adult regardless of income or value of property was deemed political cyanide by some in her own party, most notably the chancellor, but Thatcher didn't listen. The obvious flaws were pointed out to her, that a king in his castle would end up paying the same as a pauper in his hovel, but she drove it through regardless.

'She made a famous reference to the poll tax as "the flagship of the Thatcher fleet",' recorded Michael Portillo, one of her staunchest supporters in Westminster. 'Thatcher's "flagship", with its vague reference back to her victory in the Falklands, was a big mistake, one that would return to haunt her, because now, personally, she was linked to it. It had become Thatcher's poll tax.'

The ridiculous truth was the poll tax was actually invented by a Scot, Douglas Mason of St Andrews University, and that the idea of bringing it into Scotland before the rest of the UK also belonged to Scots. This coterie of Tories believed profoundly that it was a fairer local taxation system than the old rates and that Scotland would benefit from a prompt introduction.

At every stage of its passage through parliament warning lights were flashing. But Thatcher had the blinkers on. She was in a phase of her premiership when she'd all but ceased listening to those offering an alternative view. Senior ministers in her own government were now coming around to Scotland's view of her as a bully.

'Mrs Thatcher sees Scotland as her scientific laboratory where experiments and trial runs can be carried out before they are inflicted on the rest of us,' announced Liberal Democrat leader Paddy Ashdown. 'Vivisection is her game and the Scots are her subjects ... How can it be, as she frequently tells us, that the views of 1,500 Falkland Islanders in the South Atlantic must always and ever be paramount, while the view of five million Scots must be demeaned, insulted and ignored?'

Prominent Scottish clergymen delivered an anti-poll tax petition to Downing Street in February 1989, signed by 300,000

Scots. Thirty thousand people attended a demonstration in Edinburgh on the day the poll tax was introduced, April Fool's Day 1989. But none of it did any good.

By brazening it out, Thatcher achieved something the Scots didn't think was possible. She managed to make herself even more loathed than she had been before.

Thatcher politicised rugby in Scotland. It wasn't just the miners and the shipyard workers who rose up against her, it was large chunks of the public sector, people who had been profoundly hurt by her policies.

'A great change has come over Scotland,' wrote Arnold Kemp, editor of the *Herald* in the 1980s and early 1990s. 'The football team is a dull affair and Scotland's national passion is now paraded at Murrayfield where the crowd sings "Flower of Scotland" and reviles the English . . . Its limping lines make even some nationalists wince.'

Murrayfield, said Kemp, was bourgeois Scotland's temple. 'Here is wealth, here is comfort, here is entrenched Unionism. Why, then, do they sing "Flower of Scotland" with such passion and is there anything more peculiar than the sight of some perjink Edinburgh insurance broker, Unionist to his fingertips, unleashing a volley of abuse at the English and all its works?'

Kemp was right. These were strange days indeed.

# CHAPTER 8

# AN ENGLISHMAN IS NOT ALLOWED TO SAY THOSE THINGS

On the Lions tour of Australia in the summer of 1989 Brian Moore and Finlay Calder became mates. They talked about things that others didn't talk about; national identity and the difference between the English and the Scots. They'd sit next to each other on flights across Australia and chat about where they came from.

Calder's view, according to Mooro, was that the English had a contempt for the Scots and saw them as a nation of whingeing savages. Mooro would say, 'Ah, no, not really', but privately he suspected Calder was right. He was right about a lot of things in Mooro's opinion. The Scot said that Englishmen were anally retentive, that he was always underwhelmed by their lack of passion. The ghost town of Twickenham being an example. Where was the heart and soul in that place? Where was the celebration of Englishness? Mooro had sometimes wondered about that, too.

This was one of Mooro's favourite subjects and one that used to drive him mad. When the Scots got patriotic they were celebrated. When the English did the same they were arrogant. How the hell was that fair?

'There are certain words you don't see used on their own,' he said. 'Poverty is one of them. You never see poverty on its own. It's always "grinding" poverty. English is another. It's always "arrogant" English. Think about all the sports songs there's ever been and the only one that says we're going to win anything is "We're on the march with Ally's Army", that fucking disaster in Argentina in 1978. A Scottish song. *And we'll really shake 'em up when we win the World Cup, coz Scotland is the greatest football team.*

'Er, no, you're not actually. You couldn't even beat Iran. But, you see, an Englishman is not allowed to say those things. It's a cross we have to bear. We say we're the best – and we get fucked for it.'

Scottish nationalism was acceptable, said Mooro, but English nationalism conjured up a different set of images. 'I used to get letters from the British National Party. "Dear Brian, you're a proud Englishman . . ." I said to them, "If you ever – ever! – associate me with the BNP I will sue you".

'I was asked several times by the *Sun* to pose for a picture draped in the flag of St George and I said, "I'm not doing it".

'They said, "But why not? You're proud to play for England . . ."

'I said, "Yes, but what will happen? I'll get a reputation for being a fascist. These fuckwits at the BNP will see it and I'll become an icon to these people". The *Sun* was bemused but it was the truth. In my position I had to be aware of my nationalism and the way it was interpreted.'

Calder understood Mooro. In some ways they were alike. In terms of intensity there wasn't a whole lot between them at all. If anything, Calder was the more forceful of the two. That's what Mooro felt anyway.

He knew the Scot was a bit different even before they left for Australia. At the first Lions get-together, at London Irish, the players were put through a battery of fitness drills and Mooro came out as the most in-shape forward. Calder went up to him later and said how impressed he was with Mooro's results.

Mooro was surprised. Sure, Calder was the Lions captain, and building the morale of his players was part of his gig. But he'd served under plenty of England captains and none of them had ever said anything like that to him. With England, you'd have been waiting a bloody long time for a captain or a teammate to compliment you on your fitness.

There was always respect for Calder among the English boys. They knew all about his twin brother, Jim, a remorseless flanker who scored the try that won the Grand Slam for Scotland in 1984. Finlay was made of the same stern stuff.

Each year when the Calcutta Cup came around Calder would be one of the focal points of England's preparation. They used to think that if they didn't stop Finlay, then Finlay would stop them. He'd slow down their ball and cause mayhem. He'd sledge to his heart's content. Him and JJ, forever yapping. His competitive ruthlessness took some quelling, but that's what they felt they had to do more than anything else when he was on the other side.

'Finlay Calder looks like an athlete carved by primitive man,' wrote Simon Barnes in *The Times* just before the tour departed for Australia. 'He is all rough edges with a haircut of iron filings.'

Mooro enjoyed having him as a teammate for once. 'I'd never met a person whose world was more black and white. In Finlay's world, you were either in or you were out. You knew where you stood with him. He was honest. I mean, brutally honest. He was stark. And I respected him for it. You might not like the lack of diplomacy occasionally but you knew when you were in the trenches he'd do anything for you. In rugby and in life. Anything. If Finlay couldn't do it, the chances are it couldn't be done. I have a lot of time for that man. He's the sort of person who would give you his last pound and he'd hand it over with a good heart. If you were in a hole, the first person you'd ring would be Finlay Calder.'

The Lions tour party was dominated by the English and the Scots, picked in record numbers by the coach Ian McGeechan and his assistant, Roger Uttley. There were seven England forwards and four England backs, four Scottish forwards and five Scottish backs. All the marquee names were present bar Will

Carling, who might well have captained the party ahead of Calder had he not been at home suffering from shin splints.

There were thirty guys in the original squad but Mooro was only bothered about one of them. In the months leading up to the tour all he ever heard – or allowed himself to hear – was how Steve Smith of Ballymena and Ireland was the shoo-in for the No. 2 jersey in the Test series.

Smith was a fine player and a hardy customer. He had a decent throwing arm, was a good scrummager and was energetic in the loose. The Lions, it was accepted, needed a beast at hooker in order to handle the unrivalled power of Tom Lawton. At eighteen and a half stone and with thirty-eight Tests to his name, Lawton was the full package. In the newspapers he wasn't just plain old Tom, he was The Hulk, The Strong Man, The Colossus.

Everybody was saying that brute force was required to handle Lawton. Mooro was just fourteen stone, Smith was seventeen stone. It was obvious who the front-runner was. Mooro wanted to say, 'Hang on, what about Twickenham? And what about Lansdowne Road?' England had done a number on the Wallabies in the autumn at HQ and Lawton hadn't got any change out of Mooro that day. Also, in the Five Nations, Mooro had met Smith twice, both times in Dublin, and Ireland hadn't got within ten points. All that stuff seemed to be forgotten, though. That's what it felt like. He was written off on account of his size. Again.

Back in Nottingham he had set about the task of 'hunting Steve Smith'. He had trained twice a day for two months, in his local gym and on the Astroturf pitches at Nottingham University. When he'd got into the Lions camp and Calder had singled him out for praise, that just made him go even harder.

When the other players had finished training, Mooro stayed on for extras. And he made sure everybody saw him. Geech, Uttley, Calder, the media and, above all, Steve Smith. He made a conscious decision not to talk to the Irishman, which suited Smith because he was shy at the best of times. They got by with an occasional and imperceptible nod of the head.

There was nobody more adept at that psychological game than Mooro. He'd played it with Brainer and Graham Dawe and he'd seen off the pair of them. Now it was Smith's turn to try his luck in Mooro's cold war.

At training, Roger Uttley took the forwards out on to the park and explained the kind of game that was required Down Under.

'The maul is key, boys,' he began. 'We take it into contact, drive in with the shoulder, take a big, wide stance and wait for your teammates to take you forward. We don't go to ground if we can help it.'

Calder had a different idea.

'We shouldn't be mauling, we should be rucking. Hit the Australians head-on, go to ground, drive on through and clean 'em out.'

So even before they left London there was a frisson between the big mauling England pack and the hard-rucking Scots.

'It was fascinating watching them,' said Donal Lenihan, the Corkman charged with captaining the midweek team. 'The Scots used to love to roar and shout and beat the shite out of themselves in the dressing room before a game. JJ and Finlay were always at it. Scott Hastings was possibly worse. He was completely mad. The English boys were calm and collected. Mooro was intense but he was controlled. You'd think a really hard man like Dooley would go crazy beforehand but he was quiet. When I was captaining, he'd come up to me when the Scots were going ballistic and say, "Look, I'm going over there to do my own thing". I always felt that the Scots were a product of Jim Telfer. If he told them to jump through hoops of fire they'd have done it without question. They were coming from a background where they were afraid of Telfer. That's how they got motivated – partly through a fear of letting him down.'

Uttley was caught in the middle of all this fervour. He was a Lions veteran of 1974, but in coaching terms he was a relative rookie, certainly at that level, at that intensity.

There was a falling out – between Uttley and Calder primarily, with little pockets of unrest opening up elsewhere from time to time – but there was always a focus on what was really important. When the games came around there was a ferocious unity among them, no matter where they came from and what style of game they felt they should be playing. They ended playing a hybrid of the two. But as a team, when they needed to be, they were as one.

Uttley took a small step backwards, accepting that the senior forwards were going to thrash this thing out between them. He became more of a manager than a coach. And he became suspicious.

'I got it into my head that they thought I was scum English. I had a gut feeling that among some of them there was a rabid anti-Englishness going on. I suspected that there was a little cabal there; Finlay, JJ and David Sole. A few things rankled. I think back now and I suspect I was oversensitive. I'd say that maybe I took things too much to heart. I've met the boys over the years since. Good lads. Finlay, in particular, is a fantastic bloke. Couldn't meet a nicer fella. But I didn't necessarily think that at the time.'

The bond between Mooro and Calder grew deeper despite the hooker's antennae picking up some Scottish disquiet towards Uttley. Mooro thought they were being unfairly dismissive of the coach and said so, but he couldn't spend his time worrying about that.

He was winning his battle with Smith, everybody could see it. Smith was quietly effective on the pitch but Mooro was a bloody pest. Not only was he playing well but he was noising up the Australians with his patter. Very quickly he became a key man.

But, equally, everybody could see that Calder was struggling. He'd damaged his hamstring just before the start of the tour and he'd picked up some extra injuries, niggly little things, after he arrived that left him subdued on the field and testy off it.

Calder was giving the impression that he hated the burden of captaincy. 'It's torture,' he told the press boys. 'I'm wound up. This is a short tour, one short moment in our lives. For many of us it won't come again and we aren't coming off second-best. There's nothing to be relaxed about. We know that if we lose, the public at home will hang us; we mustn't provide the rope.'

As the tour progressed there were two main talking points: the gathering violence of the matches and the diminishing influence of the captain.

Early in the tour the possibility of Calder getting dropped for the first Test was being mooted in the British press. In the *Daily Telegraph*, John Reason was talking about 'awkward and unpleasant decisions' facing the Lions management. He was referring to Calder. The Lions had six wins from six games but still there was an air of foreboding heading to the Sydney Football Stadium for the opening Test.

Mooro was right behind Calder. On those journeys around the country he told him so. He emphasised his support. To the press, Mooro advised caution before penning their next column questioning Calder's ability to find his best form. It's only when the pressure is truly on that you see what's inside a player's soul, said the hooker. Mooro was sure that Calder's time had come.

He was wrong. The Lions got pulverised 30–12.

'Captaincy is weighing heavily on the broad shoulders of Finlay Calder,' reported the *Independent*. 'He never thought it would be quite as bad as this.'

'The forwards, sour to a man, were devoid of any thought,' wrote Frank Keating in the *Guardian*. 'If Plan A hasn't worked, let's change to, er, crumbs, well, er, Plan A, I suppose. We expected more of Finlay Calder.'

At the press conference, Calder and Geech, Uttley and the manager, Clive Rowlands, looked traumatised. They did their best to sound defiant but the truth was they were in shock. 'Rugby is rather like life,' said the captain. 'It has a habit of kicking you in the groin.'

After the nightmare had been talked through *ad nauseam* with

the writers, the radio guys and the blokes from the telly, Calder
went to his hotel room and closed the door. He took out a notepad
and wrote a letter to his wife at home in Edinburgh. The raw-
ness of his emotions and the depth of his disappointment came
spilling out as he told her he was giving up the game. 'I never
felt so down in my life as when we lost the first Test,' he said.

At that point, there didn't look as if there was a way back.


Geech was forty-two, a head coach for just fifteen months and
he was in trouble. He didn't know what flak felt like until now.
Real flak, that is. The doubt of four nations coming at him in
waves.

He'd thought he'd ticked every box in the lead-up to Sydney.
He'd been meticulous in his research about the Aussie behemoths
up front – Lawton and Steve Cutler and Steve Tuynman – and
reckoned he'd figured out a way of stopping their principal rapiers
in the backline – David Campese, Nick Farr-Jones and Michael
Lynagh.

Geech had been obsessive about mood. One of the main
objectives he had going out there was the need for good karma.
He'd learned all about vibe from Telfer's stories of the nightmare
of '83. He thought he'd done all of that, but his work was undone
with contemptuous ease.

He made changes for the second Test. He had to. Mike Teague,
injured for the first Test, had declared himself fit to play and
Derek White dropped out to make room for him at blindside.
Dooley had all along been considered second choice to Bob
Norster but the Englishman now swung into favour like a giant
wrecking ball.

The rookie Craig Chalmers was omitted in favour of the
experienced Rob Andrew and both centres disappeared, too. Scott
Hastings and Jerry Guscott came in for Mike Hall and Brendan
Mullin.

Calder stayed where he was: openside flanker and leader.

A monstrous pack of forwards featuring five Englishmen, two

Scots in Calder and Sole, and the Welshman Dai Young took the field – and they smashed Australia into submission.

Where Australia dominated the line-out in the first Test, Dooley took control of it in the second. Where the Wallabies bossed the physical encounters in Sydney, the Lions were on top in Brisbane. It was attritional stuff. A bloodbath in places. There was stamping and punching and any amount of shoe.

Everything was coming together. There was added wit in the backline in the shape of Guscott, a guy Geech had raved about to Calder months before. Geech had said the Bath centre was destined for greatness. After his audacious and decisive score in the closing minutes of the second Test, Calder was in agreement. 'I see what you mean about Jerry,' said the captain.

Calder, suddenly, had a smile on his face again. He'd put in a monstrous shift in Brisbane just when he needed it and in the process he lifted an almighty burden from his shoulders.

'It is now obvious,' wrote Robert Armstrong in the *Guardian*, 'that although Calder may have mislaid his sense of humour on the tour he has not lost the most important attribute in a Lions captain: the iron will to overcome adversity.'

Calder admitted writing the letter to his wife and said he wouldn't mind if somebody, somewhere, intercepted it en route to Scotland and tore it up. He wasn't going into retirement after all. Instead, he was going back to Sydney for the final Test.

The Lions won with another display of extreme physicality that was enough – by a solitary point – to beat the Wallabies. It was the first time in history that the Lions had come from behind to win a series.

It all turned on a Campese blunder on his own line, pounced upon by Ieuan Evans. But there was another moment in the match that Mooro wanted recorded. It was an Aussie scrum, five metres from the visitors' try line. A time when the Lions eight had to be strong.

Farr-Jones fed it in and the Lions dipped low. Lawton stopped the ball with his foot but before he could tap it behind him the Lions hammered through and ransacked them of possession. Mooro stood back from the vanquished Lawton and all of a sudden felt like the biggest man in Australia. There was only one word for it, he said. Vindication.

Calder knew where he was coming from. Again the captain fronted up. Despite his knocks, physical and mental, he dug deep inside himself and pulled out a performance. He finished the series shattered, relieved and delighted all at the same time. For Calder, it had been a brutal summer. But an unforgettable one.

Picking a man who towered over the others was hard, but everyone decided that Mike Teague deserved the honour. No matter the demands, Teague refused to break. He was as unyielding as the walls he built in Gloucester.

They called him The Iron Man. One day, Teague dropped a ball in training and JJ, out of the picture for the Tests, remarked, 'The Iron Man is getting rusty.' The comment seemed to smack of frustration and bitterness. After all, JJ didn't have the tour he'd imagined in his dreams.

But he and Teague, they understood each other.

'People say we didn't get on,' said Teague. 'We did. There was a definite edge between the Scots and Roger [Uttley] but as players we bonded just fine. JJ was supportive when I got in the team and fair play to him because I'm not sure I'd have been the same way with him. Actually, no chance. I'd have been a complete nightmare. When the final whistle went in the third Test I've gone and jumped on the ball, haven't I? I've nearly killed a ballboy to nab it. I wanted it as a souvenir. I'm walking off and there's a million people around and I hear JJ going, "Teaguey, Teaguey, give us the ball, somebody'll grab it on you, I'll mind it". So I give it him and he minds it and he gives it me back later. I wouldn't have given it to just any bloke. But I gave it to JJ.'

Donal Lenihan spoke at the post-match jamboree and referred to the big men in the Lions squad, the warriors. He mentioned the 'healthy tension' between the English and the Scottish forwards and their shared mania for victory and suggested that the next time they opposed each other on the rugby field there'd be holy war.

Geech was thinking about that, too.

Mooro, Dooley, Ackford and Teague would be the nucleus of the England pack in 1990. Guscott was the rising star of the world game and he'd be playing alongside Will Carling in the midfield, with Rob Andrew at 10 and Rory Underwood out wide. They were looking formidable already.

On the back of the Lions tour, England became favourites, along with France, to take the Five Nations and knowing these men so well now Geech couldn't argue with that. 'You'd have to say that England are going to be special in 1990,' said Geech.

'And what about Scotland?' he was asked.

'Oh,' he said quietly. 'We'll be there or thereabouts.'

# CHAPTER 9

# IT'S GOT FOUR HEADS

Late one evening in the autumn of 1989 Geech gathered up his video cassettes and settled down in front of the television. To hand, he had recent footage of all Scotland's Five Nations competitors, a big notebook and a pen. He looked at the spine of each tape and took out the one marked *France–Australia, Trophée des Bicentenaires, Lille, 11 November* and put it on.

Up on the screen came images from Stade Nord: the unmistakable step of Philippe Sella, the craft of Franck Mesnel, the burning pace of Patrice Lagisquet. Geech flipped the top off his biro and started writing.

He began by noting how often Lagisquet came in off his wing undetected, how he ghosted into the picture on Mesnel's shoulder and was through a gap before the Wallabies knew what was happening. He scribbled something about Scotland's midfield defence and carried on watching.

As the game unfolded the picture quality began to fade and the sound crackled and then stopped. A big black line appeared across the middle of the screen. Geech took out the tape, blew some dust off it and put it back in the VCR again. Same story. He paused the frame in an effort to pick up the numbers on the French players' backs but the picture went into spasm. Just after midnight, he gave up. He put down his pen, switched off the video, turned off the lights and went to bed. He had work in the morning.

Geech was the most talked about coach in the world and among the most admired. He was successful in Australia partly because of his work in front of the video, his hours spent analysing opponents. But now his machine was wonky. Binning it and getting a new one was the obvious thing to do but that was easier said than done. He didn't know how much it was going to cost to replace but he knew these things didn't come cheap.

'Wouldn't the SRU pay for it?' a friend asked.

'Eh, no,' replied Geech. The very idea of him asking the SRU for a replacement brought a smile to his face. The committee men at Murrayfield would have had a fit.

In the end, the convulsions of his old VCR got the better of Geech and he splashed out and bought a shiny silver thing with all the mod cons. The man in the shop said it had four heads. Geech wasn't sure what that meant but he knew his old one only had two, so four sounded good to him.

He went home and connected it to the telly. When the kids were asleep, he popped in a tape – and a bright new world opened up to him. The clarity of the picture was exhilarating. No problem identifying players or set moves or line-out tactics now. All of a sudden Geech was ready for the 1990s.

'I was teaching full time and had a young family. Rob was eleven, Heather was six. We spent a big sum of money on that video and we didn't have a lot. I was driving an old Ford Capri that had about 120,000 miles on it. We didn't have luxuries. Judy, my wife, was studying for a degree during the day and in evening time she'd go out and serve food in the university halls of residence. I'd come home from school and she'd head out to work. And that was the difference between us being able to pay the mortgage and not. I'd put the kids to bed and then get my clipboard out and watch videos. I'd be there until one a.m. usually, studying other teams, taking notes, soaking in anything and everything.'

Geech was a geograpy and PE teacher at Fir Tree Middle School in Leeds. It was a job he loved. Good colleagues and great kids. They all embraced rugby and it was a fun place to be.

Over the years he had worked under two different head-masters and both of them had played the game. When he needed time to head up the road and coach then they scrambled their resources and got by. They never gave him a guilt trip about time off. After all, Geech was bringing some kudos to Fir Tree. When he did interviews he made a point of mentioning the school and how grateful he was for their support. It reflected well on Fir Tree to have such a high-prolife man on the staff.

Things started to change at the turn of the decade. Going into 1990 a new head was in place at Fir Tree. Geech was doing what he always did: eating up the road to Scotland in his tired Ford Capri. But from the boss he was now sensing unease.

As Scotland readied themselves for the beginning of the 1990 championship Geech was growing concerned. 'It was a younger headmaster we had now. The two previous ones were wonderful. They made a big thing of the rugby. We even had assemblies on the international game at times. The place was just buzzing. The new head felt my absence was having a detrimental impact on the kids. He said I was away too often, that maybe I was going to have to make a decision soon about what I wanted to do – teach or coach.

'At home, we were pretty close to the breadline. We talked about it, me and Judy. How long could we go on like this? We knew that sometime soon we were going to have to make a fairly profound family decision. The way things were going, doing the two just didn't look possible any more.'

In the meantime, he stayed up late and did his research. With a remote control in one hand and a pen in the other, he prepared for 1990.

# CHAPTER 10

# IT'S THE JOCKS I'M WORRIED ABOUT

England got out of town early in the new year, headed off to Lanzarote for five days, touched down at a special sports retreat called Club La Santa and enjoyed themselves.

Oh sure, there was training. Plenty of it. Tom McNab was on the trip and he didn't spare the rod. Before the squad unpacked they were brought on to the track for some fitness tests. But this was about bonding as much as running. It was about forging the team spirit ahead of their opening match of the Five Nations, against Ireland at Twickenham, just a fortnight away.

The last time they'd been together was in November and they'd put fifty-eight points on Fiji at Twickenham. Admittedly, Fiji were no great shakes. They were only threatening in a bloodlust sense. Some bad men had made the trip from the Pacific islands and as the tries flew in – five for Rory Underwood alone – the mood of the visitors darkened to the colour of night.

'Was it one or two guys Fiji had sent off?' asked Mooro.

'Two,' replied Wade Dooley.

'Should have been three,' said Paul Ackford. 'Their prop whacked me from behind.'

'You're a bit of a southern softie though, Ackers.'

'Thanks, Wade. How are things at your club anyway? What's it you call yourselves again? The Preston Horsecrappers?'

'It's the Grasshoppers, actually. And we're doing well.'

'In Division Nineteen,' chirped The Judge.

The boys were having beers on the verandah. As the night went on more players joined the party and the conversation turned to the Five Nations. No reason why they couldn't win it this year, they said. They had Ireland and Wales at home, France and Scotland away. The away matches would decide it.

England hadn't won at the Parc des Princes in eight years. Peter Winterbottom was the last man standing from that team.

'So how is it done, Winters?' asked Mooro.

'To be honest, fellas, it's the Jocks I'm worried about,' said Winters. 'They've got something. Reasonable front five, bloody good back row, confident young half-backs, good defence, Gavin Hastings at full-back. Home advantage as well.'

'Geech will have 'em organised,' said Jerry Guscott.

'Telfer will have 'em fired up,' said Dooley.

'Fair enough,' said The Judge, 'but if we do our bit then no fucker should beat us, right?'

Good old Judgie, cutting to the chase as usual.

The hotel complex was a favourite destination for athletes and some big names were milling about the place, Merlene Ottey, the famous Jamaican sprinter, among them. Ottey was in a room next to John Olver, the Harlequins hooker, and Mark Linnett, the prop from Moseley. The boys went out on their balcony and spotted Ottey's running gear hanging on the line. For two of England's principal wiseguys it was an opportunity too good to miss. They hopped over the dividing wall and squeezed themselves into her leotards.

Then they hit the bar.

They flounced in as the boys were earnestly discussing the legalities of JJ and Calder at the breakdown, the seventeen-stone prop leading the way in bright pink. Well, that killed all talk of the Calcutta Cup. As Linnett and Olver sashayed around in the gentle evening breeze, their teammates almost wept with laughter.

As bonding sessions went, this was just about perfect.

The Scots weren't so lucky. They didn't have the sun on their backs, they had Jim Telfer. While England were preparing in the heat of the Canary Islands, their counterparts were enduring a trial match at Murrayfield; the first-choice Blues versus the second-choice Reds for a place in Scotland's Five Nations squad.

Geech and Telfer put the teams together. David Sole, their new captain, would lead the Blues but it was their choice of skipper for the second string that caused surprise. It was Finlay Calder. And, what was more, JJ was alongside him in the back row.

Dropping the captain of the Lions and the best-loved player in the country was all Telfer's doing. He'd seen them playing in the league and reckoned they needed what he called 'a personal message'.

Calder's glorious mantle of first winning Lions captain in fifteen years meant absolutely nothing to the coach. That tour was irrelevant now. He'd seen Calder once, twice, three times for Stewart's Melville and each day he left with the same impression: he's not at his best.

JJ, too. His performances for Kelso had been reasonable but Telfer knew JJ better than JJ knew himself and he was sure that he was holding something back. Telfer was one of the few guys on the planet who could see these things.

'You could hide at a ruck and think you were getting away with it,' said JJ. 'Fifty thousand people in Murrayfield wouldn't notice you taking a breather. But Jim would notice. No matter how clever you thought you were, no matter how well you disguised it, if you didn't do what you were supposed to, he'd spot it. It might be a week or two later, but he'd come up to you in training and say, "I want a word with you about your body position at that ruck, you know the one I mean". You'd be like, "Jesus Christ, is there nothing this man doesn't see!"'

To nearly everyone else Calder and JJ were putting it in big style, hitting rucks, making tackles, carrying ball and winning matches but Telfer wanted to put them under pressure, to remind them that in his eyes nobody was indispensable. He promoted Adam Buchanan-Smith of London Scottish in Calder's spot and Derek Turnbull of Hawick where JJ should have been. And the A team won 45–4.

The newspapers reckoned JJ's place in the Five Nations was in jeopardy after that drubbing. Calder would make it, they were sure of that, but Turnbull had put in a mighty shift in the trial on the blindside of the scrum and had planted himself in the box seat. JJ was trying to be cool but he was concerned. Turnbull was the kind of animal that would take a bit of shifting if he got in the team.

The night of the trial John Reason, the influential rugby corres-pondent of the *Sunday Telegraph*, sat down to file his report. Appalled at the wretched quality of the rugby, he took his big hatchet out and went to work.

'The Blues started by obligingly kicking the ball straight off the field,' he reported. 'The Reds promptly turned the other cheek by putting the ball crooked into the scrum. Again the Blues did their best to be tolerant because they missed the touch with the kick. Again the Reds were equal to the occasion. They gave the ball back.'

Reason was unimpressed with the supposedly elite Blues but he was staggered that the Reds represented the best of the rest in Scotland. It seemed like some kind of joke. He advised the selectors to decamp to England immediately where they could unearth some Anglo-Scots to pad out their squad.

'I would suggest that England's seventh or eighth choices at lock must have some Scottish blood in them somewhere ... or they must have at least one relative who has heard of Edinburgh.'

There was always a feeling about Reason that he was no friend of the Celt. They certainly thought that about him over in Ireland and in pockets of Wales, too. In fact, he wasn't exactly Mr Popular among certain sections of the England squad either. Geoff Cooke threatened to sue him for an inflammatory column he wrote for a magazine once and Mooro, incensed at Reason's constant sniping, vowed that he would stay in the England team longer than the journalist remained at his newspaper.

There was one thing about Reason, though. He very often got it right. And his verdict on the trial was on the money. Geech said: 'I'm not sure what it tells me but I wasn't expecting that scoreline, that's for sure.' What it did tell him was that, unlike England, he had little strength in depth.

England had announced their team to play Ireland while they were still in Lanzarote. They had to do without the injured Deano and they chose to do without Mike Teague, who was on the bench, and Andy Robinson, who didn't even make the bench. And yet even without those three outstanding players they could still pick a dynamic and in-form combination of Skinner, Winterbottom and Dave Egerton of Bath, one of the top performers of the domestic season.

Geech didn't have England's talent, but he had Telfer, his perfect foil. They chatted on the phone and organised the minutiae of the next training session, one of their last before the start of the championship.

'Not long to go now,' said Geech.

'Aye,' said Telfer. 'It's time we cranked things up.'

# CHAPTER 11

# JIM TELFER, I COULD HAVE WHACKED HIM

Jim Murray, the king of American sports writers, might have had Jim Telfer in mind when he said a coach of his acquaintance 'treated his players as if he had bought them at auction with a ring in their noses'.

The boys only ever saw that hardline version of Telfer, but there was another. Away from the training ground he was a different man. If you never knew about his rugby life you would have thought him shy. Sensitive, even. He was easy company. A good storyteller. Smiled a lot, laughed a lot. Had many things he liked to talk about bar rugby, but it was a game he could never escape for long. People always wanted to know what he thought. He was the fount of all knowledge and they liked to hear him speak.

'What do you make of their scrum, Jim?'

'Do you rate their back row?'

'Where's the weak link?'

The furious rugby man was one facet of his personality, sure. But it was largely put on. His players said he was brutal and he was. Some of them called him a bully and he nodded at the accusation. 'But it was an act, you understand? It was my way of getting the best out of them, by putting the fear of death into them. In many ways it was a compliment. I was only really hard on players that were good. I'd only be really cruel with those who could respond. I only did it because I knew it would make them better.'

He never used notes in his speeches but they were all scripted in his head. The rise and fall of his voice was deliberate, the emphasis put on certain words and phrases designed to frighten or inspire, whichever was required. Very little was off the cuff. Even the long silent stares were part of the plan.

On a particular evening in mid-January, Telfer upped the intensity. He got in his car and headed for Edinburgh thinking about the things he wanted to say to them, rehearsing the words as he drove. When his forwards were told they'd be having a meeting with him later their hearts sank. These were the moments they dreaded. Not the sessions. They could handle them. If he wanted a hundred scrums, he got them. If he demanded another hundred on top they jumped to it without a grumble. They understood where he was coming from with that.

'After ten minutes of a Test match, everybody's knackered,' he'd say. 'You're up, you're down, you're making tackles, you're hitting rucks, you're scrummaging, you're out on your feet. Okay. Same for everyone, boys. You think and you move slowly when you're tired. If the body is weak then so is the mind. That's a fact. But not us. No. What we do in training is we sharpen minds as well as bodies. We work and work and work like beasts and get you to a state of mental fitness where you can still make the right decisions even though you're blowing out your arse. Do you get me, boys? "Do I kick, do I pass, do I ruck, do I maul, I'm fucking exhausted but I know what I need to do because up here, I'm razor-fucking-sharp". Yes?'

'Yes!' they'd respond and out they'd go for two and a half hours of torture. But training ground pain wasn't the worst. Aching limbs? They could accept that. It was the assault on their minds rather than their bodies that some of them found hard to take.

*     *     *

Damian Cronin was the first to get it. Del Boy. Had plenty of talent when he could be bothered to produce it, which wasn't nearly often enough as far as Telfer was concerned. Cronin gave the impression that he couldn't care less. Telfer's ambition for 1990 was to break Cronin down and build him back up again, to make him 'putty in my hands'.

'You're a bit of a chancer, Damian,' Telfer started. 'Born in Germany, raised in the West Country, God knows how you ended up here. Not good enough to play for England, is that it? You need to be hit between the eyes with reality. You're a lazy bastard. Look at the fucking size of you. Fat and useless. But something's bringing you up that road from Bath. Eight-hundred-mile round trip. Murder! That's some sacrifice you're making. You've decided to be a Scotsman? Okay. Prove you're worthy.' Cronin kept his head down, pleasantly surprised at having got off lightly.

'Kenny Milne!' Telfer continued.

Milne braced himself.

'You're too loose! Your teammates are working their balls off while you're standing in the midfield waiting for passes. You're the hooker! A coalface man! You're not supposed to be flash! You're looking for the TV cameras when you should be driving hard in the tight where you belong.' Flash! Milne wanted to explode at the injustice of Telfer's words but he stayed quiet and waited for the storm to pass.

Telfer looked to the back row. He saw Calder, JJ and Derek White as the pivotal men in the way he wanted his pack to play. These three were his engine room. If they weren't right, then Scotland wouldn't win one game, not to mind four. If their tackle counts and their ball carries and their impact at the rucks wasn't prodigious then as a team they could forget about it. They needed to lay their bodies on the line. He knew he'd get that from Calder and he was certain JJ would deliver.

Derek White was the one he wasn't sure about.

White was laid back – and Telfer didn't like that. He wanted his No. 8 to be intense, just as he'd been when he was the

Scotland No. 8. White had the talent, no question. He had explosive pace and good hands but he had a tranquillity about him that brought out the worst in Telfer.

This went way back to the summer of 1981 when Telfer rang White and invited him on the tour to New Zealand. White responded with a sigh. Long way to go to sit on the bench, he thought. 'Do you think it would be worth my while?' he asked. More than a quarter of a century later Telfer was still telling that story, shaking his head and laughing incredulously as if it had happened only yesterday. 'Was it worth his while? To tour with his country? In New Zealand? Incredible!'

All the boys knew that Whitey was the main event at these meetings. In terms of Telfer's cruelty, there were many cameos, but he was the marquee act. 'Derek, you were a disaster for the Lions. A disaster! Dropped like a stone after the first Test – and no wonder. The Wallabies came steaming through and where were you? Asleep. Unconscious. An embarrassment. You think you're the kingpin. You've got your head in the clouds. Wake up, man!'

**Derek White:** It was a bloody rant. Shouting and roaring in front of all the other lads. He stormed off and left us looking wearily at each other. At one point he said, 'I'm away to beat my head against a brick wall'. I said, 'Do you want a hand with that?' He never heard me, though. Thank God.

**Damian Cronin:** Jim was going around the room firing questions at us. I was absolutely shitting myself that he'd start on me again. He was grilling Whitey about certain back row moves and he was nose to nose with him. Derek was under so much pressure he could hardly get the words out. I'm sitting there thinking, 'Please Christ, don't come near me' because I didn't know half the moves. Set plays off a scrum? What the fuck would I be doing with them? I had enough in my head as it was.

**Chris Gray:** He was on the edge of pushing it too far. I'd say if one person had hit him then the other seven would have followed up.

**David Sole:** There had been an incident in the changing room in Paris the year before.

**Damian Cronin:** I might have been involved in something.

**Chris Gray:** Jim was having a massive go at Damian just before we went out for the start of the match, calling him a big useless bastard, a lazy fucker. Damian was really chilled most of the time but he had a nasty streak buried deep within him. And when it came out, he was a bit scary.

**David Sole:** Jim was an inch from his face, screaming at him. You wondered how much more he could take. Creamy was pushing him but Damian was giving it back to him.

**Chris Gray:** Did Damian give him a shove? I'm not sure but the collar of Creamy's jacket got stuck on a coat hook.

**David Sole:** I'd just seen the film *Midnight Express*. A prison guard gets impaled on a coat hook through the back of the neck. I'm thinking, 'If Creamy's not careful he's going to end up like that prison guard'.

**Chris Gray:** Jim was in his element. The more furious Damian got the happier he was. He was on the hook shouting, 'That's what we want, boys. Aggression!' We're all going, 'Jesus Christ. Quick, let us out on the pitch to face the French. We'll take our chances against Carminati and Garuet rather than stay here with this madman'. Was Creamy trying to exorcise some ghosts from when he played? I don't know.

**David Sole:** He was one of the scariest men alive. He reduced grown men to wrecks. There were guys you could see physically deflate when they were on the receiving end of it.

**Kenny Milne:** I pushed my heart out in every scrum so for him to tell me I was flash was out of order. He destroyed my confidence when he said things like that. I knew there were more talented hookers than me around the place but none of them wanted it as much as I did, none of them were prepared to put up with the shite that I had to put up with. Jim was playing on my hunger and my insecurities. He knew I didn't have a lot else going on in my life, so this was everything to me. I had a job delivering pies. I was a pieman. There was nothing flash about me at all, but then he knew that. He was only trying to rile me. And he succeeded.

**Derek White:** He was an irritant. What I wanted to do was to play rugby for Scotland and he was one of the things I had to get through. I had to endure him to achieve my dream. He was harsh and he was personal. Not always. But he was that night. On the Richter scale it was an 11 out of 10.

**Chris Gray:** We had a rucking drill and somebody didn't get their body low enough for Jim's liking. We were all piled up on top of each other on the ground and we hear this roar. 'Who's the fucker in the red socks?' And to a man everybody looked down to see what colour they were wearing. You could hear the relieved sighs from seven players and then one groan. Paul Burnell was wearing red. We stood away to the side, puffing and panting, while Jim bollocked Burnell. I was sucking in the air and trying not to laugh at my teammate's misfortune. Jim would be frothing at the mouth, literally.

**Kenny Milne:** He was standing at my shoulder at a line-out and when I got it six inches wrong he fucking screamed at me. 'Kenny! Jesus Christ!' I felt like turning around to him and saying, 'Look, if Sam Torrance was lining up a putt you wouldn't be bawling at him to get the ball in the fucking hole, would you? So piss off!' I never said that, though. I just thought it.

**Chris Gray:** I really wanted to clock him. We were hitting tackle bags. I went into one awkwardly and bounced off it. My neck jolted backwards and I was dazed. He came over.

'Are you conscious?'

'I think so.'

'Well, get up then.'

I could have whacked him. There was no sympathy at all. Deep down, though, I liked it. Maybe I had a sadistic streak.

**Damian Cronin:** We did rucking practice and Whitey had to run off the back of a scrum into a couple of defenders and we had to tread on Whitey as we went over. We weren't allowed not to tread on him. You'd get a bollocking if you didn't.

**Derek White:** I got it more than the rest of them. The forwards got it worse than the backs. Of the forwards, the back row got it worse than the front five. Of the back row, I got it worse than the other two. JJ was the blue-eyed boy.

**John Jeffrey:** Nobody was the blue-eyed boy. He belittled me as well. He gave me some awful doings. But the abuse never hurt me. I got slaughtered for being too loose but I took it because I knew he was only doing it because he thought I was worth it. He made me a player. He did it. Look at our pack. The only one who was out and out world class was Soley. Jim would say to myself, Derek and Fin that he could pick three off the street and make them as good as us and I think he could have done.

He called a back row video session for seven one morning and the three of us were appalled.

*Are we going?*

*Are we fuck!*

*We snub him?*

*Yes!*

I came down the stairs at five to seven and Fin and Derek were already there.

*I thought we were snubbing him . . .*

*Ah, next time, maybe.*

We were there out of respect. And probably fear.

**Kenny Milne:** You got away with nothing. We had a scrum session. I had a knock so I stayed out of it. They took the brake off the scrum machine and drove it downfield at running pace. Jim comes over to me and says, 'When they come past you, I want you to dive in under their feet.'

I said, 'What?'

He said, 'Dive in and let them ruck you out of it.'

This is me, injured. I dive in and the eight of them ran over the top of me. They went easy. Telfer went beserk. We did it again and they kicked me to bits. It was mad but I was almost immune. He had a rucking session in the hotel one morning because it was lashing rain outside. We were in the breakfast room. People were having their full Scottish and Jim is down the far end with the pads. The guests must have been thinking, 'This is a crazy man?' Christ, even we were thinking, 'This is a crazy man'.

**David Sole:** I didn't know Jim. Did I want to make the effort to get to know him? I'm not sure. He wasn't the type to say, 'Hey, let's go for a beer'. I didn't agree with him on a raft of things, but I admired his passion and his pride and his relentless drive to achieve. I respected his rugby brain. We were an average group of players. Sure, we had some great players but we had plenty of journeymen, too. He moulded us. The psychology was cruel, but it was effective.

The reality was that Telfer had great admiration for his forwards, but it just didn't make sense in his mind to tell them that. He thought Derek White was one of the most naturally gifted back rows the country had ever produced but that he needed a kick to get himself going. When friends used to ask him to pick his all-time Scotland XV, he always picked White at No. 8.

Kenny Milne was second only to Colin Deans as Scotland's finest hooker in his view. Chris Gray's straightforward honesty was right up his street. 'He's a public school boy,' he'd say, 'but you'd never know it.' He even had a soft spot for Del Boy, though it was impossible to tell.

He thought about his commitment in making those back-breaking treks up from Bath and warmed to the guy. He thought about David Sole and how different they were and yet how similar.

'David was a deep-thinking man, an intellectual. I could never work him out. I don't think he could work me out either. He was the quietest talking captain I'd ever heard. But he was a committed man and he had the ability to carry out his commitments. We shared nothing except a love of the game. We lived in parallel worlds. He belonged to money and privilege, I was a shepherd's boy. But we had a common goal, him and me.'

Scotland sat out the first weekend of the Five Nations. Instead of playing, they trained. They came together at Gleneagles and Telfer got stuck into White again, pointing out his deficiencies, humiliating him in front of the rest of them once more.

Afterwards, White was talking to JJ. 'I've had enough of this,' he said. 'I'm thirty-two years of age and I don't need this in my life any more. He's just not going to give me a break, is he?'

'Unlikely, Derek,' said JJ. 'Very unlikely.'

# CHAPTER 12

# IT'S NOT NASA, IT'S A
# FOUR-NUMBER CODE

The Scots gathered around the television on Saturday 20 January to watch the action from Twickenham. There was quite a fanfare building up for Will Carling's team. It was pointed out in the morning papers that their run of games – home to Ireland first, then away to France, home to Wales and away to Scotland – was precisely the same as in 1980. And if, by chance, anybody couldn't remember what had happened in 1980, there was a picture of captain Bill Beaumont on the shoulders of his forwards celebrating their Grand Slam on the pitch at Murrayfield.

There was reams of coverage about the resilience of their Lionheart pack and the lethal weapons in their backline. Rory Underwood, 3.7 seconds for the thirty metres, was 'lightning in a bottle' according to Tom McNab. Jerry Guscott, making his championship debut, was singled out by former England greats as the most exciting talent to emerge in the game since Serge Blanco. At scrum-half, Richard Hill, making his first championship start since the end of his Mr Angry period, was looking world class alongside the calm authority of Rob Andrew.

'Christ, they're at it again,' JJ scoffed.

Before England went out to play, Carling told his team that there was no hiding place any more, no excuses. This was a game they were going to dominate, a season they were going to own. Forget the belligerence of the Irish forwards and their dreadnought defence, they were going to go through them, over them and around them. 'In the first five minutes you're gonna look your opposite number in the eye and he's gonna know he's a beaten man,' Carling said.

For seventy minutes Ireland survived on instinct alone. They were losing just 7–0, which was remarkable, for really England should have been out of sight by then. At the Gleneagles Hotel the Scottish boys didn't see much to be afraid of. Not yet.

Seven points was a pitiful advantage against such a limited Ireland side, a group of inadequates that had lost six of their previous seven championship games. But save for the odd flurry, there was no sign of Guscott, Carling or Underwood inflicting serious damage. Instead there was a lot of panicky kicking and chasing from England. 'Fear of failure rugby', as Carling had later called it.

It was Mooro who changed things. England had a penalty near the halfway line and, instead of handing it over to Rob Andrew for a touch-finder, he tapped it to himself and sprinted downfield. It was the kind of inspirational rallying cry the team needed. In the last ten minutes they scorched the ground under Ireland's feet. What the Scots saw now was an entirely different proposition.

Dave Egerton drove over for a try, a reward for England's superior grunt up front. Then the class came out.

Guscott sped away at one point and executed one of the hardest skills in rugby with breathtaking ease: at full pace he floated the most delicious pass off his left side over the heads of two retreating Irish defenders and into Underwood's hands. That one pass showed what wondrous things he was capable of. Underwood had a lot of ground to cover but he sprinted away to score in the corner and history was made in the moment. Underwood's nineteenth try for his country broke a record that had stood for sixty-seven years.

(*Above*) Scotland the brave: the underdogs prepare to go to war on
Grand Slam day, March 17 1990

(*Below*) The Untouchables: England had broken all kinds of scoring records
before they arrived at Murrayfield

(*Left*) John Jeffrey: 'I didn't care who kicked me as long as we won'

(*Below*) David Sole: softly-spoken and born to lead

(*Above*) Jim Telfer: 'I was hard on the boys. Cruel at times'

(*Right*) Geech: teacher and coach and a man under pressure trying to do both

(*Above*) Captain Fantastic:
Will Carling, as complex
as he was brilliant

(*Below*) The Enforcer:
only the brave or the stupid
took on Wade Dooley

(*Above*) Driven man:
Brian Moore had a rage for victory that was scary

(*Facing page*) Scotland says No: poll tax demonstrators hit the streets of Edinburgh (*Inset*) The testing ground: Margaret Thatcher's hectoring *Spitting Image* puppet satirised the Iron Lady's treatment of the Scots

(*Right*) Twickenham terrier: Carling leads the pummelling of the Welsh

(*Left*) Full house: demand for Grand Slam tickets was unprecedented (*Below*) Heart and Sole: Scotland in training the day before the game

(*Above*) The Slow Walk: 'the roar went up and it sent a shiver through me' recalled David Sole

(*Above*) Danger man: Jeremy Guscott, the prince of centres, is targeted for treatment

(*Above*) Try! Referee David Bishop awards the most famous try in Scottish rugby history, but was Tony Stanger's score a legitimate one?

(*Below*) The big men: Wade Dooley gets behind Damian Cronin to win a lineout

(*Above*) The Immortals: Scotland get the party started in their dressing room

(*Right*) Hail the heroes: the front page of *Scotland on Sunday* the day after the Slam was won

This was quality rugby. And before the end of the match, on the back of Carling's initial thrust, Guscott blew through the Irish cover and scored with a grace that brought Twickenham to its feet. England scooped sixteen points in ten breathless minutes and won 23–0, their second biggest winning margin against Ireland since matches began in 1875.

'We were only at 60 per cent today,' said Carling. 'There's a lot of improvement to come yet.' For the cameras he was deadpan. But inside he was buzzing.

In early spring 1990, Will Carling was the most famous rugby player in the world, the game's first media superstar. He was on the cover of magazines, he was on television endlessly, he was to be the leading voice in an official video of England's season called *The Players' Story* and publishers were already offering him book deals.

The perks of being the most wanted man in rugby were considerable. The £80,000 silver Mercedes convertible, on loan from a sponsor, was proof enough of that. He had earners at his fingertips. A golf club offered him £1,500 to speak at a dinner, but he said no. An England rugby fan said he'd hand over £700 if Carling would turn up at a mate's birthday and present a card, but he turned that one down, too. He could have opened pubs and supermarkets, could have done product endorsements by the handful, could have taken a sack of easy money and made life a lot more cushy for himself – but he didn't. He couldn't. Rugby's rules on professionalism forbade it.

As he basked in the attention, the puritans frowned. Before the Ireland match the first stirrings of the Carling backlash were being felt. The blazers at Twickenham were troubled by their captain's profile, looked aghast at his gleaming Merc and practically wept when he appeared on the front of a glossy magazine with his top off.

In the eyes of the RFU establishment he was arrogant, materialistic and posed a danger to the sacred rites of amateur rugby. Carling wanted the game to go open, they were certain of it.

They suspected that the gathering threat of professionalism would be eradicated in one fell swoop if Carling was drummed out of the team, perhaps with Mooro in tow. They felt he was using the profile of the England captaincy to feather his nest and they said as much. Behind his back, of course. But he heard it all.

There was chat about his form, too. He'd been diminished by injury the season before and had missed the Lions tour. His club performances had been inconsistent and some of his detractors said he didn't seem bothered about playing for Harlequins any more, that it was only the Test match arena he was interested in. He was presented as something of a prima donna. Paul Ackford, a fellow Harlequin and close ally, would wind him up about it. 'Will, forget what they're saying. They're only jealous. You're a very busy man. If you only turn up for training once a fortnight then fair enough.' There was petty sniping. When Harlequins won an easy victory in the league in early January the best that one of the dailies could say about his performance was: 'Such was the paucity of the opposition, even Carling looked quick.'

Carling's defences were robust but occasionally things would crowd in on him and Geoff Cooke would feel the need to intervene. In the months before the Ireland game he saw his captain's insecurities close up. Carling went to Cooke and suggested that the fine Bath centre Simon Halliday partner him in the midfield against Fiji in November. Cooke could see Carling's thinking: Hallers was his pal, so he wanted him in the team. Guscott was a rival and so he feared him. Guscott had scored a hat-trick in his one England Test to date, then he'd gone to Australia and been one of the stars of the Lions tour.

'Here was Will's lack of self-confidence emerging again,' said Cooke. 'He saw Jerry as a threat. He thought he might lose his place, thought we might give the captaincy to somebody else.

He needed the reassurance. People forgot that he was a young man. I said that publicly. I said he has moments of doubt and uncertainty, the same as the rest of us, that he was only twenty-four, that he wasn't the finished product yet.'

The problem was that he didn't exactly have an understanding audience in the media. There was no love lost there on either side. Halliday was being talked up a lot in advance of the Ireland game partly because his play for Bath warranted it, but also because it helped apply a bit of pressure on the captain. And, to some, that was no bad thing.

The press coverage when Carling was made captain wasn't negative, it was just disbelieving. 'It was, "Will who?" They were shocked that I'd got the job, but they couldn't have a go at me right away because we had beaten Australia. Then we drew 12–12 with Scotland in the '89 Five Nations and that's when it started. About a week later I was sitting in a press conference with about fifteen journalists and it was quiet. They said, "Will, are you down about something?" I said, "Since you ask, some of your criticism after Scotland was out of order". I had a little go for a minute or two and there was silence in the room.

'As I was leaving one of them came up to me and said, "What are you doing? You can't have a go at us". I said, "Hang on, your articles are read by millions and I privately say to you that you're wrong and that upsets you?" He said, "Yeah, you'll get our backs up". I thought, "Okay, fuck off then".

'That was my attitude. This had been my dream since I was six years old and they were picking away at me. There was never much affinity there. It was my fault. It was only later on that I started to see it from their side. They had a job to do but all I could see at twenty-two, twenty-three and twenty-four was fellas picking holes.'

Carling needed a big performance against Ireland to counter this negative press and felt much happier about himself when he delivered it.

\*    \*    \*

A week before Scotland entered the fray, word went around the squad that all was not well with Geech. Something about the flu. Something else about sinuses. He was struggling. Hadn't been out of his bed all week apparently. He was rated as 50–50 to make the trip to Dublin. Make that 60–40 against. No, now he wasn't going.

The players would like it recorded that their first thought was for their shivering coach, coughing and spluttering in Leeds, but that wasn't the case at all. Faster than a McGeechan sneeze they were over his plight and on to Telfer and the sudden sense of foreboding that hung over the trip to Ireland.

'Marvellous,' remarked Derek White. 'Three days of uninterrupted Creamy. Just what I need.'

At least White had JJ and Finlay Calder for company again, the pair of them having found their focus and regained their pre-eminence among Scottish flankers following the miserable experience with the also-rans at the trial.

White was still talking about jacking it in after the Ireland game. It was a Telfer thing but it was also a time thing. He was living in London and his life was mad. He played for London Scottish on a Saturday afternoon, came up to Scotland on a Saturday night, got shouted at by Telfer on a Sunday, went back down on Sunday night, back up Tuesday, re-entered Telfer's world of pain from Wednesday evening, game on Saturday and back down to London the morning after. He wasn't sure if this was what he wanted to do any more.

The flight to Dublin was a hellish experience. The 737 was in the air for just ten minutes when the pilot announced that they were returning to Edinburgh on account of 'pressurisation problems'.

'Pressurisation problems?' repeated Damian Cronin.

'It means you shouldn't lean too hard on that emergency door, Del Boy,' said JJ.

The ride back to Edinburgh was turbulent and unpleasant. Having a door hanging off its hinges at 25,000 feet wasn't exactly the ideal way to start the weekend. And Telfer hadn't even begun to lay into them yet.

Telfer's quickfire quiz took place when they sat down at their team base in Dun Laoghaire, by the sea.

'Kenny Milne! We're in our 22, the ball is going to JJ, what's the line-out call?'

'Er, 6–4–5–8.'

'JJ, we're between the 22 and the halfway line and it's going to Finlay, what's the call?'

'That would be 4–7–5–6, Jim.'

'Derek, we're in the England 22 and it's going to Chris Gray, what's the call?'

'Mmmm . . .'

'Come on!'

'I know it . . .'

'It's not NASA, it's a four-number code. You think you're going to have time out there tomorrow? It's Donal Lenihan and Willie Anderson you're dealing with. What's the call?'

'7–6–5–4.'

'At last!'

'Right boys,' said Telfer. 'Last season you put thirty-seven points on this lot. You scored five tries. You conceded three, mind. But we've spoken about that, haven't we, JJ? They have home advantage but we are fitter and faster. Our scrum is good, our line-out is good, nobody rucks more aggressively than us, nobody works harder. Let's make all that work worthwhile.'

With thirteen minutes left to play, Ireland were ahead 10–9 and Telfer was brooding. The clock was ticking and with each second that passed came the certainty that whoever scored the next try would win. When the heat was on, one player stood out above all others: Derek White. If it hadn't been for Whitey, Ireland would have already been home-free, for it had been his try just after half-time that pegged back a 7–0 deficit, a score that arrested Scotland's apparently imminent demise.

Now Whitey was thinking of glory again. Scotland had a

scrum about twenty metres from the Irish line. In his younger days he wouldn't have had the confidence to make the play but all those Telfer bollockings had put him in a bolshie mood. 'Telfer might not like it,' he thought, 'but when this ball comes to me I'm going for that try line.' He did. And he made it. His pace off the base of the scrum was too much for Ireland. He was up and away and over for the score, a load of green jerseys hanging off him as he thumped the ball down. This was the seminal moment of a dreadful match. The team came back in and none of them said a word. For ten of the Scottish team this was their first away win in the championship; for the other five, the Hastings brothers, JJ, Calder and White, it was only the second. But there was no happiness on their faces, no hint at all that they'd won the game.

Maybe that's what threw Jimmy McNeil. Wherever the president of the Scottish Rugby Union had been – and given the hospitality on offer at Lansdowne Road they could all make an educated guess – he hadn't been paying attention to the match. 'Bad luck men,' he said. 'You'll get them next time.' At least the president's eccentricity lightened the mood in the dressing room. JJ sidled over to Whitey and congratulated him on his heroics.

'Are you still thinking of quitting?' JJ asked.

'Ah, I'll give it another game or two,' he replied.

Somebody asked Telfer what he thought of Derek now.

'I've always said he was a good player,' he grinned.

They all decided that before a drop of booze passed their lips that night they were going to have a think-tank about what went wrong. Telfer liked the sound of that. The need for the debrief became all the more essential when news started filtering through to them from Paris. England, by the sound of it, had done something remarkable over there, something truly historic.

# CHAPTER 13

# SOMETIMES THINGS GO DIZZY FOR A WHILE

With its bells and bugles and its dozen brass bands playing all at once, Parc des Princes was like no place on earth. The crowd was noisier, the game was faster, the collisions were harder. There were cockerels. Even the ball, with its distinctive black tips, was different. There was a 50,000 capacity but many more got shoe-horned in. They sat in the aisles and on each other's laps. On the best days, when Les Bleus were playing like gods, they made the noise of 100,000 people.

Some of the French players were semi-pro, everybody knew it. Cash under the table. *Ssssssh, merci bien.* They came from curious places: from Poitiers in Poitou-Charentes, Arcachon in the Gironde, Eymet in Aquitaine. They had exotic nicknames: The Bayonne Express, The Dax Bull, Les Trois Mousquetaires, Le Professeur.

It was the only stadium in the Five Nations where the teams met in the tunnel beforehand and walked out together. The French pack would line up caked in sweat and Vaseline and sometimes blood. They'd headbutt the wall or each other and then glare at their opponents as if they were going to eat them whole the first chance they got. Those stand-offs in the tunnel were fearsome.

There'd always be legends in the stands, throwbacks to more malevolent eras, reminders of the dark side of French forward play, when men were maniacs: Gérard Cholley, the nineteen-stone prop who once knocked four Scots senseless in a single match; Alain Estève, the Beast of Béziers, as cruel as they came; Michel Palmié, as frightening an enforcer as ever set foot on the Parc.

Mooro loved everything to do with a Test match in Paris. The sights and smells but especially the sense of menace. This was rugby's steamiest cauldron.

He knew that on days like this so much hinged on what the front row did. Of course, there were individual battles all over the park, hugely important ones, but the tone would be set up front and there were three wars in particular he knew England had to win.

*Pascal Ondarts, thirty-three, tempestuous Basque, veteran head-banger, prodigiously strong loosehead, versus Jeff Probyn, thirty-three, quietly spoken East Ender, formidable tighthead, cowed by no man.*

*Jean-Pierre Garuet, thirty-six, potato merchant from Lourdes, first Frenchman to be sent off (for gouging), cornerstone at tight-head since 1983, versus Paul Rendall, thirty-five, streetwise north Londoner, world-class prankster, steady operator.*

*Louis Armary, twenty-six, prop playing hooker, immensely powerful clubmate of Garuet's in the holy city, versus Brian Moore, twenty-eight, four inches smaller and over a stone lighter than Armary.*

England brought Mike Teague into the team for Paris, put his considerable weight at No. 8 and reckoned they had the boys to get the job done. The French begged to differ. The great Jean-Pierre Rives met talk of England's possible glory with heavy sarcasm. 'Yes,' he said. 'It's a great mystery, this pattern of English success at Parc des Princes.'

If Rives was sold on French invincibility at the Parc then it was hardly surprising. He listed the names in the team. The forwards: Ondarts, Armary, Garuet, Devergie, Erbani, Champ, Rodriguez, Roumat. 'I respect the England pack but this French eight is massive,' said Rives. 'These are huge men.' And behind them: Blanco, Andrieu, Sella, Charvet, Lagisquet, Mesnel, Berbizier. 'One of the great French backlines.'

Paris was the fortress to beat all fortresses. France hadn't lost at home in the Five Nations since 1982. In that fifteen-match winning streak, they had scored forty-two tries and conceded just seven.

Between them, Blanco, Sella, Charvet and Lagisquet had seventy-five Test tries and many of those were the type of epic scores that the Parc specialised in. When the English boys closed their eyes they could almost hear the commentary.

*Blanco, behind his own posts, steps away from the tackle and there's the acceleration. Across the 25, Garuet in support, to Erbani. Feeds Champ. Halfway line. Berbizier inside to Rodriguez. The power comes on. Mesnel has it. Wide to Lagisquet. Ghosts through a gap. Fantastic rugby. Charvet now. Sella on his shoulder. Only the full-back to beat. Sidestep. Sella to the line. Try! What innovative brilliance from France! What adventure!*

England couldn't let the French get momentum or they were dead men.

Typically, though, the French were in wildly unpredictable form. A fortnight earlier in Cardiff they had played more than half the match with a one-man advantage – Welsh lock Kevin Moseley having been sent off for stamping – but had struggled when trying to close out the game, the brilliance only coming with seven minutes left to play when Wales were out on their feet.

That autumn they had been annihilated by the Australians in the first Test before producing some wondrous stuff for victory in the second Test. Nobody ever knew what they were going to get from the French. Their autocratic coach Jacques Fouroux, Le Petit Caporal, was as much in the dark as everybody else.

The majesty of their play was being compromised by the coaching of Fouroux. He wanted a colossal forward unit and wasn't afraid of sacrificing brain for brawn. He thought beautiful rugby would only get France so far, but it wouldn't beat the All Blacks. The Kiwis haunted his dreams. Everything Fouroux did now was part of a grand plan to fell the New Zealanders by brute force at the next World Cup. So Armary was in at hooker not because he knew how to hook but because of his daunting physical strength. After nine years in the back row and at the age of thirty-three Dominique Erbani was picked at lock. Having established himself as one of the world's best No. 8s, Laurent Rodriguez was selected at openside.

The England boys had a hunch that some of the French forwards weren't happy playing in their new positions, that some of them weren't as fit as they ought to have been and that Blanco, thirty-one, was beginning to show his age. At their base at the Trianon Palace in Versailles, the English came up with a gameplan: hit like howitzers and hound Blanco as if he was a hare at a course.

At half past midday on Saturday 3 February, a police motorcycle cavalcade led the England coach out of the hotel and on to the motorway. They switched on the sirens and sped away to rue du Commandant Guilbaud in the city's 16th *arrondissement*. Parc des Princes was already alive with activity.

A gale had blown into Paris overnight and the wind was swirling in the Parc. An hour before kick-off Mooro walked on to the pitch. There were only five or ten thousand people there and yet the noise was ridiculous. The bands were striking up, trumpets were going off, the atmosphere was electric. For all the noise he couldn't hear what Winters was saying to him – and Winters was standing right next to him.

Mooro went back in the changing room. And that was something else that was different here. The French team were housed in palatial comfort; the visitors were stuck in a broom cupboard.

As Ondarts did his stretches on the floor of the home team's special warm-up room, Probyn cleared a square foot of space and jogged on the spot. Rendall said he was going to do the same – in the bath. Eventually they went into the corridor and bashed themselves about. Down the hall they could hear the guttural roars of the French pack. 'It was like there was a rhino running loose,' said The Judge.

'Time ticks by,' said Mooro, 'and your focus gets narrower and narrower as the hour gets closer. You're not thinking about winning or losing, you're thinking about surviving. You're thinking about the first scrum and getting as low to the ground as you can because this is Paris, this is the Parc and in this place of all places if you don't go low you'll get fucked.

'There's excitement but there's also fear. You're thinking about the shock of the first engagement, the two packs coming together, that terrible thud and the way your body judders on impact. There might be a punch or a butt or their tighthead might force his head into your jaw trying to unsettle you, trying to put you in a bad position where you might bend double, where your ribs might pop or your neck might snap.

'You know that's what can happen if you get it wrong. There's eight of them driving through on you and you're concertinaed. It's scary. You can hyperventilate down there with all those bodies on top of you. Sometimes things go dizzy for a while – if you get it wrong. The first scrum is everything. If they shove you around first time, it's a long, long day.'

The plan was that Carling would lead the team into the tunnel with Dooley, Ackford, Skinner and Teague right behind. Mooro wasn't having any of it. 'I'm pack leader, I go second,' he said.

'But Mooro, we want our big men to line up beside theirs and stare them out.'

'I'll fucking stare them out.'

That was the end of that. Mooro went second.

England were in the tunnel when they heard the French coming. Laurent Rodriguez went first. When it came to intimidation he

was the real deal. Big and wide and with sweat and blood trick-
ling from his nose down on to his moustache, the only thing
more menacing than Rodriguez's scowl was his smile. He came
rumbling down the corridor shouting something that sounded
like 'Death to the English!' and looked across to Dooley, who
looked straight back. 'He was one ugly man,' said Dooley. 'But
Christ, was he tough.'

Will Carling didn't know what was going on up front but one
thing he was sure of: whatever Mooro, Probyn and The Judge
were doing, it was working. The scrum was steady. There wasn't
a bit of movement in it. Garuet had thrown a haymaker at one
point but all he'd caught was fresh air and some of Mooro's
derision. Ondarts had attempted a headbutt as he engaged for
a scrum but Probyn had seen it coming.
   'You learn to smell trouble in Paris,' said Probyn. 'It's a psychological game they're playing as much as a physical one. When
they rough you up, they're testing you. They want to see what
you do. If you start throwing punches back at them or start
hunting them down, then you're not concentrating on your job.
You're distracted. They've got to you. If you just soak it up, they're
thinking, "Hang on, he's one of us", and they'll leave you alone.
You don't hit back immediately. You wait. You'll always get a
chance to land one. Ref not looking? Bang! They respect you
for it.'
   The French pack were blowing after half an hour. Winters was
the first to every loose ball. The power of Skinner and Teague
was too much for even Rodriguez to cope with. At the line-out,
Dooley and Ackford dominated Devergie and Erbani, who
suddenly looked every day of his thirty-three years.
   *What's up, Dominique? You a bit old for this, my son?*
   The French backs didn't exist. Blanco may or may not have
been past it but no one could tell because he'd hardly touched
the ball. The television cameras picked up an exchange between
Charvet and Sella; no words, just a simultaneous shrug of the

shoulders. 'You could see in their eyes a sense of bemusement,' said Carling. 'They'd no possession to play with. They didn't know what was happening.'

The twisting breeze was blowing the advertising boards across the field but Simon Hodgkinson barely noticed. He put England 6–0 ahead with two fluent kicks at goal. There was a sinister look to the French pack now. Dooley stole a line-out and Rodriguez smacked him in the mouth. Dooley tried to break free but Rodriguez took hold of his jersey and hit him again. As the England forwards galloped away to follow the ball they could hear their besieged teammate shouting: 'I've taken one, boys. And another one. Fuck me, and another . . .'

Ackford felt like laughing at his partner's plight but he was too busy watching Rory Underwood screaming over in the corner for a try, his twentieth in thirty-six Tests. In the final minute of the first half, Ondarts tried to decapitate The Judge and gave away a penalty, which Hodgkinson duly kicked. At the break it was 13–0 to England. Not since 1925 had the French trailed by so many points at half-time on home soil.

**Laurent Rodriguez:** I felt like I had forgotten how to play rugby.

**Pascal Ondarts:** I felt in shock.

**Jean-Pierre Garuet:** I felt like all the energy in my body was gone. England had taken away my spirit.

**Brian Moore:** I felt twelve foot tall.

**Will Carling:** Four minutes into the second half Denis Charvet gets the ball and we all close in on him. He's nowhere to go. This wizard of a rugby player is trapped. He tries to kick it away but I block it. They're scrambling backwards now. Blanco goes to pick it up but Jerry is all over him. Jerry puts his boot to it and races after it. Blanco's on the floor, helpless. Jerry runs on to score at the posts and Hodgy lands the extras; 19–0. Jesus, what a scoreline. I look over at Blanco and Charvet and Sella and Lagisquet and their heads are down and I'm thinking, 'Does life get any better than this?'

Soon he would have his answer.

With a minute to go and England leading 22–7, Teague surged off the back of a scrum and France were in trouble again. It took three men to bring Iron Mike to the ground. Two more to stop Dooley. Another couple to halt the immense Richard Hill. This was humiliation for France. A scrum-half breaking the tackles of their biggest men.

Carling got the ball and saw Blanco in his path. The captain fixed his man with a jink inside and then left him for dead with an outside break that Blanco never read. Try; 26–7 final score. France's biggest hiding at the Parc in sixty years. Out of camera shot but audible on the tape is a Frenchman, coming back up the tunnel at the end of the game. As the England players walk past he is saying one word over and over: 'For-mi-dable. For-mi-dable. For-mi-dable.'

The England dressing room was impressively calm. Partly down to exhaustion; Carling liked to think that it was a sign of maturity, too. 'We're growing up as a team,' he said. 'We're on a journey and we're only halfway there.'

At home, though, the press weren't so circumspect.

**Robert Armstrong, Guardian:** *England rolled inexorably through the Parc des Princes towards the 1990 Grand Slam that would be the only appropriate reward for their magnificent triumph in France.*

**John Mason, Daily Telegraph:** *So complete in every respect was England's victory over France that confident talk of championship titles and Grand Slams is not out of place this season – or next. Even New Zealand, the world champions, need to take heed.*

**Stephen Jones, Sunday Times:** *Lou Reed's 'Perfect Day' was on all the trendiest turntables in the 1970s. It is a song about a blissful day's loving and courting in New York. Lou Reed probably never heard of Will Carling, but a few hummed bars of his old classic would have been so richly appropriate as England's travelling thousands moved through a mild Parisian Saturday evening.*

\*   \*   \*

Some were moving a lot slower than others. Winters and Mick Skinner drank for Harlequins that night, strolling from bar to bar and getting hailed in every one. They got to their beds at, well, they'd no idea. They woke at, ah, that was a mystery, too.

All Winters knew was that by the time he opened his eyes on Sunday the rest of the England party were halfway to Heathrow. 'There is sleeping it out – and then there is *really* sleeping it out.'

He wondered if any of the other boys were left behind. Best bet: Skins. He dialled his room and lay back in the bed. It rang and rang. Thirty seconds, a minute, two minutes. And then: 'Uggghhhh?'

'Skins?'

'Where are we?'

'France, mate. We've missed the plane.'

'Fuck! We'd better have a drink, then. Downstairs in twenty.'

The legends of the Parc drank all day, everything going on the slate, which John Burgess, the president of the RFU, happily paid for. 'Not having my boys forking out for their pints on a weekend like this!' Eventually, Winters and Skins made their way to the airport. It was coming up for 11.30 at night and all they had was standby tickets on the last flight out of town. They got in the queue and then a funny thing happened. Everybody moved aside.

*Go ahead, boys. Famous day yesterday.*

*Take my place, fellas. You've earned it.*

*Right up the front, chaps. Least we can do.*

It was a humbling gesture, an indication of what the victory meant to people. They thought about that as they took their seats and closed their eyes and remembered their perfect day.

CHAPTER 14

# IGNORE HIM. HE IS NOT THERE

When JJ heard the news from Paris, its significance was immediately apparent to him. France were coming to Murrayfield next and he knew now that they'd be arriving with their eyes on stalks after the fortnight-long slagging they were going to get from Jacques Fouroux and the entire population of France.

'Wait and see, boys,' said JJ. 'Ten changes minimum. These guys will be out for blood.'

When the French team was announced there were exactly ten changes – five fewer than the enraged Ferrasse wanted but still one of the great French purges of the age. Jean-Pierre Garuet, Dominique Erbani, Eric Champ, Denis Charvet and the captain Pierre Berbizier were all dropped. Garuet and Erbani never played for their country again.

Fouroux's intent was not lost on JJ. First of all, he'd made the bogeyman, Laurent Rodriguez, his captain. Shifting from little Berbizier, his previous skipper, to The Dax Bull made a fairly unambiguous statement. Next, he brought in Marc Pujolle at loosehead. Pujolle, of Nice, was a converted lock forward, a man well known in the game despite having just two caps to his name. They called him the new Gérard Cholley. He was a piece of work. Everybody knew it.

But on top of Rodriguez's promotion and Pujolle's arrival there was a third selection that told of the French mindset. It was the return of Béziers' Alain Carminati on the openside flank.

Carminati was a big man: six foot five inches tall and almost seventeen stone. He was quick and he was skilful. He was only twenty-three but with fourteen caps he already seemed a veteran. He'd been a Test player since not long after his twentieth birthday and a part of the French back row that had bullied JJ, Finlay Calder and Derek White so completely at the Parc the previous year. He played the game on the edge – sometimes way over the edge. In the French championship he was respected as a hard man – and respect did not come easy in that league. But the Scots knew that better than most.

They'd encountered him four years before on a summer tour to France. 'He was a total shocker,' said Derek White. 'The worst I ever saw. He was very young at the time; maybe nineteen. When we knew he'd been picked for Murrayfield I said to JJ, "You watch, he's going to do somebody, he's dangerous".'

Scotland hadn't lost to the French at Murrayfield since 1978 but Jim Telfer wasn't one for stats and records. Stats and records wouldn't help the boys win the first scrum, the first ruck and the first line-out, so he wasn't interested. He didn't care what had happened before, he just dealt with the now.

They all thought long and hard about what had gone wrong in Dublin. Geech, fit and well again, pored over the tape on his new VCR, rewinding and pausing and making notes for the gameplan.

*Target Blanco with garryowens, he looks vulnerable now.*

*Watch for Rodriguez at the back of the line-out, put a blocker there.*

*Speed up line-out, must be quicker.*

Telfer was on the end of the phone with his own theories and solutions and there was input, too, from Derrick Grant and Dougie Morgan, both of them valued advisers.

When the squad met up, Telfer got to work on the deficiencies in the line-out, which meant he got to work on Kenny Milne. Kenny Milne became the new Derek White.

'Okay, boys, line-outs,' said Telfer. 'On you go, Kenny.'

*Do you have to stand so close, Jim? Can't you just move back a bit, so I don't feel the spray on my face when you bollock me?*

'Well taken, Damian Cronin. But we want it faster. Come on.'

*I can do fast. I can do fast all night. Here's a fast one. Zzzzip. Oh fuck!*

'Terrible, Kenny. Over the back. Carminati is away with that and it's your fault. Do it again!'

*Ignore him. He's not there. Focus. This is going to Chris Gray. Zzzip. Yesss!*

'Excellent catch, Chris.'

*Excellent catch? He couldn't not catch it. Excellent throw. Come on Creamy, say it. Excellent throw . . .*

'Hurry up, Kenny.'

*Zzzip to JJ. Beauty!*

'That's more like it JJ.'

*Zzzip to Fin Calder. Nailed it.*

'Better, Finlay.'

*Zzzip to Whitey. On the button.*

'Well done, Derek.'

*Well done, Derek? Well done, Derek! Who's he all of a sudden, teacher's pet? Zzzip to Del Boy. Oops, bit wild that one.*

'Hopeless, Kenny. Bloody hopeless. You do that against the French and they'll eat us alive, you understand me? This is useless. Come on, get your finger out! We nearly got beaten in Dublin because of the line-out. Let's go!'

*Look at you. Hands on hips. Staring at me. Trying to psyche me out. Testing my nerve. Pushing me and pushing me.*

Fearless Fred Howard of Lancashire was the man in the middle. Howard was nobody's fool. He had sent off Kevin Moseley in the Wales vs. France game a month earlier, more proof, if it was needed, that he wasn't a referee you could take liberties with. Just in case the message hadn't got through, he stressed it beforehand. 'Any dirty stuff, boys, and I'm telling you now, you'll be off. You don't believe me? Ask the fella Moseley.'

Scotland wore white, France wore blue and 'Flower of Scotland' was played for the first time before a championship game. The vibe in Murrayfield was transformed. No half-hearted singing from the players now, as there had been with 'God Save The Queen'. No booing from the stands either. It was loud and raucous and uplifting. Even the French, used to ear-splitting noise at home, were impressed. Some of their team applauded. Nationalistic fervour was something they could all identify with.

And within a minute of Fearless Fred blowing his whistle to start the match there was another moment that resonated with the French: havoc at the first ruck. A blue jersey dived in to protect the ball and Telfer's heavy brigade gave him such a shoeing that he got off the floor with his hands in the air in surrender mode.

Alain Carminati looked across at the Scotland players and winked.

*Très bon, JJ. Un zéro pour l'Ecosse.*

Fred Howard was not happy. 'Okay, Scotland, we are now one minute into this match and you're testing my patience already. Don't push your luck.'

The gales of Paris had turned up in Edinburgh and the wind blew hard on Scottish backs in the first half. JJ reckoned it was worth ten points, maybe twelve. When Scotland managed only three, to France's nil, in the entire forty minutes he was disgusted. They'd missed kicks at goal, they'd messed up chances of tries, they'd left a dozen points behind them and now they were in serious trouble. 'We're fucked,' JJ said. 'We've made a balls of this. These bastards have got us now.'

After five defeats on the trot at Murrayfield the French felt their time had come at last. Laurent Rodriguez gathered his players together and urged them to listen to the silence of the crowd. 'The wind is our friend,' he said. 'Kick it down their end and corner them like animals.'

So France kicked it down Scotland's end and Gavin Hastings kicked it back again – sixty metres. Everybody stopped dead. Either Hastings had a bazooka for a right boot or something weird had happened. Carminati bent down and picked up some grass and threw it in the air. The grass blew straight into his face. In the space of a few minutes during the break a meteorological freak had occurred – the wind had changed direction. Scotland had it in the first half and they were getting it in the second half, too.

The body language of the French players altered in an instant. They were cranky now, convinced that the world was against them. With eight minutes gone in the new half, JJ found himself on the floor on the side of a ruck. He saw a Frenchman's leg and instinctively grabbed hold of it. It was JJ's misfortune that the leg belonged to Alain Carminati. When JJ looked up he knew he was done for. Carminati slammed his right boot down on to the Scot's chin, opening up a cut, then slammed the studs down again and caught JJ on the side of the face, lacerating his ear. JJ's head was jolted back under the force of the blow, thumping off the ground with such a thud he was lucky he stayed conscious. Carminati walked on serenely, as if strolling on the Royal Mile.

Fred Howard had the Frenchman under surveillance – and he knew what he had to do. 'I'm not having that,' he said. 'You're off. Off! Get off the field!' Carminati didn't move for a moment. He said it was out of disbelief. Where he came from, shaking a guy loose with some heavy shoe was commonplace. In his world, what he had done was routine. He crossed himself as he left the field. A few days later he was banned for seven months. It would be another five years before Carminati played for his country again.

JJ got to his feet, put some tape on his cuts and carried on. The French threw their arms in the air and cursed their luck. And Scotland cruised to victory. At the end, it was 21–0. Telfer knew what the cynics were going to say. The newspapermen from the south would focus on how the wind change dug Scotland out of a giant hole and how Carminati's stupidity handed them the win on a plate. And he was right.

*Mark Reason,* **Sunday Times:** *With their two hardest games to come, Scotland do not look like a Grand Slam team.*

*Bryan Stiles,* **The Times:** *Scotland swept to victory thanks mainly to France's ability to throw themselves under the guillotine.*

*David Irvine,* **Guardian:** *Once Carminati departed, France seemed to lose all hope. Forwards and backs ran around like head-less chickens, uncertain where to go or what to do. Quite simply: France badly selected, badly prepared and totally lacking in self-discipline were a rabble.*

Telfer was pleased; he liked the look of his pack, liked Sole's quiet authority and Milne's raw hunger, liked the way his second rows followed orders to the letter and the way his back row pushed the laws to the limit. This was a unit he could go to war with. So he threw them some crumbs. Kenny Milne reckoned his ears were deceiving him but he was sure he heard half a compliment about his line-out throwing. Damian Cronin was startled when he caught praise for his performance. Chris Gray, the same. He said, 'Not being funny, Jim, but you know what you said about me having a good game? You wouldn't mind writing that down and signing it for me, would you?'

'Aye, Chris, no problem.'

The boys made the most of Telfer's munificence. For as sure as night followed day they knew it wouldn't last.

CHAPTER 15

# IT WAS CRUEL WHAT WE DID TO THEM

After England had stormed Paris, Mooro was chatting to a mate who'd been in the stand at the Parc.

'Even before the teams came out it was magic,' said his pal.

'How'd you mean?'

'The guy on the PA system was announcing the England team, right? He gets to Carling and there's booing and whistling and all sorts. Then he gets to you. *Numéro deux: Breeean Moore.* The place went fucking mental. It lasted about a minute. You got it way worse than Carling.'

Getting barracked by the French crowd was like an Oscar to Mooro. He couldn't think of a greater compliment in the game than the thought of the Parc booing his name. It gave him another lift. He was floating now. And he wasn't alone. The blazers who bitched about Carling changed their tune after Paris. There wasn't a word of criticism about his leadership. Quite the opposite. Now there was self-congratulation on a grand scale. For their wisdom in appointing him, the old guard took a bow.

Carling bit his tongue. He had to do that a lot. The day before England played their third match of the championship, against Wales at Twickenham, he held a press conference at Feltham Community School near Heathrow. The papers had been praising him to the hilt but the relationship hadn't warmed up much. He spoke because he had to, not because he wanted to. And the line of questioning that morning wasn't going to improve matters much.

'Will, what about this psychological hold the Welsh have over England?'

'I don't believe in it,' said Carling. 'If they want to believe in it, then fine.'

'But England have lost the last four games against Wales. You've only won four times in a quarter of a century. It's not a coincidence, surely?'

'It's not something I worry about.'

Carling wanted to say more, but he held fire. He wanted to point out that part of the reason why England had lost the previous year was because the Welsh forwards, cynically and brutally, took Mike Teague out of the game on the first whistle. (Teague had been concussed by a flying punch at the kick-off. As he was carried away by the medics he remembers Mooro shouting at him, 'You lasted three seconds, you useless Gloucester bastard!') The captain also wanted to say that if the Welsh forwards tried a stunt like that for a second time, they'd live to regret it.

He didn't think much of the Welsh team, but he kept it diplomatic. He could have said that Wales looked weak up front without Dai Young, who'd gone to rugby league, and Bob Norster, who was injured. There was also word doing the rounds that their chief scrummager, Mike Griffiths, was hobbling about on one leg.

The more the press boys banged on about the curse of the Welsh the more he wanted to tell them, 'Look, fellas, we're going to murder these guys', but he left it to Geoff Cooke to sum up the mood of the squad. 'I honestly believe that they cannot beat us.'

Mooro was more Geoff Cooke than Will Carling. He didn't do diplomacy. He said that Wales were going to get crushed and he, personally, was going to take great pleasure in their demise. He had a long memory, see. Welsh supremacy: he'd been on the receiving end once too often. He remembered the atmosphere of the Arms Park and how he felt when he lost there, remembered what Clive Rowlands, the Welsh manager, had said after his team were knocked out of the 1987 World Cup by New Zealand: 'Ah well, we'll just have to go back to beating England every year.'

Mooro was fond of Rowlands but that kind of attitude bothered him. 'I never forgot it. Little things like that I remembered my whole life. I really liked Clive, but when he said it I remember thinking, "If I ever have a chance of reversing that kind of shit then I'm gonna take it". And this was the chance.'

**Jeff Probyn:** The Welsh were always interesting. In some ways they were on a par with the French. Some of them used to gouge. They did anything they liked. Our backs hadn't a clue. People like Will Carling had it easy. He was scoring tries and then swanning about in his free Merc. Me, The Judge and Mooro, no free motor for us. But we were the ones making it happen.

**Paul Rendall:** I was up against Laurance Delaney, a Llanelli boy. Knew nothing about him apart from that the Welsh seemed to fancy him a bit. Himself and the hooker were supposed to be immovable objects. That's what the Welsh press was saying anyway. 'Rendall won't get any change out of Laurance Delaney.' I thought, 'That right?' I'd heard it all before.

**Jeff Probyn:** I had Griffiths. He had been a Lion in Australia the summer before. A good player. But there was this talk about him being crocked. He'd done his ankle in the first game of the championship and hadn't recovered fully. I paid no attention. It's all gossip. You find out if he's injured or not at the first scrum. You know everything you need to after that. And what I knew after the first scrum was Griffiths wasn't ready for the kind of test I was gonna give him.

**Brian Moore:** The game was over after the first scrum. Maybe ten minutes gone, but it was finished. We destroyed them. It was cruel what we did to them. You get shoved back like that and it affects your mentality. It's a macho thing. You're not supposed to go backwards. It was total physical domination and it was embarrassing.

**Jeff Probyn:** There's nothing like that feeling. You get a nudge on and then the nudge becomes a shove and then a shove becomes a drive and there isn't a thing they can do about it. They're helpless. They're going back and the only thing they can do is collapse it – and that's more humiliation.

**Brian Moore:** I looked at them and they'd gone. They had a glazed look.

**Jeff Probyn:** It was the best scrum I'd ever been involved in. You could hear them wheezing.

**Brian Moore:** We'd heard about what they'd done to us down the years, but nothing we'd experienced was anything like as bad as what we did to them. Every facet of their game, annihilated. A total demolition. Fucked from first to last.

Mooro didn't just go for the win, he went for the jugular. His head dripping blood, he was in his element. He galloped fifty metres along the touchline at one point, leaving a string of Welshmen in his wake. He popped up on the wing and in the midfield, giving and taking passes and waving his arms at the crowd, demanding their noise. When Andy Allen, the Welsh second row, tried to sink his knee into Will Carling's midriff, Mooro was the first to react, standing over the prone Welshman and growling at him. Later, the boys asked him what he'd said to Allen. 'Can't remember,' he smiled. 'But it wasn't Proust.'

England were playing a different game from the Welsh: faster, more skilful, more powerful. The captain scored again and there were two more for Rory Underwood and one for Richard Hill. Wales got off lightly with a 34–6 defeat. The records tumbled, just as they had done in Paris. England had never scored so many points against the Welsh before and in over a century of the championship Wales had never been beaten by such a margin. It had been sixty-six years since England had scored as many tries in one game against Wales. No wonder there was delirium in the ranks.

A BBC reporter took Roger Uttley to one side and asked him to rate the performance. 'That was the most outstanding display any of us have witnessed from any England side from any era,' he said.

Geoff Cooke was next. 'The combined running of our backs and forwards was breathtaking,' he remarked. 'We haven't seen this in English rugby before.'

Cooke said there was a 'stamp of greatness' about Carling and his team, a theme the English papers adopted with relish.

**Stephen Jones**, **Sunday Times:** *It strains credibility when you see a once-in-a-lifetime performance reproduced in a fortnight, but there were aspects of England's seething, glorious victory which rendered the demolition of France two weeks ago almost a failure.*

**Robert Armstrong**, **Guardian:** *The majority of Five Nations matches are tight, meanly fought affairs, yet in this competition England have been ripping their opponents apart with the kind of ruthless abandon usually reserved for the likes of Romania. Wales, France and Ireland have in effect been reduced to the status of banana republics.*

**John Mason**, **Daily Telegraph:** *England, brisk confidence illuminating every purposeful stride, were magnificent. Comparisons with New Zealand's All Blacks, the world champions, are inevitable. Nor are they out of place.*

Will Carling knew he was captain of something special now. Still one win away from a Grand Slam, the papers were already weighing up their place in the annals. Comparisons were made with the 1980 Grand Slam team. How did Ackford and Dooley rate alongside Bill Beaumont and Maurice Colclough, the locks from ten years before? How good were Carling and Guscott compared to Clive Woodward and Paul Dodge? Was Peter Winterbottom a better openside than Tony Neary? Was Mooro as good as Peter Wheeler at hooker?

Carling tried to ignore the hype. Instead of thinking about 1980 he focused on 17 March 1990 and the team he was taking to Edinburgh to play Scotland. A disparate bunch: some mates and some who were virtual strangers.

*Hodgy at full-back. I got him wrong at the start. I didn't want him in the team but he's proven himself. Good kicker, great tactician, dry sense of humour, top boy.*

*Hallers on one wing: a highly educated nutter. Strong and brave. If the shit hits the fan he won't shirk it. Rory on the other wing: I have no words to describe how fucking good he is.*

*Jerry: him and me, we're complicated. He talks about the Varsity Brigade. The university boys. He forgot his dicky bow for a function once and his missus asks me if Jerry can have one of my spares. You must have another on you, she says. What's that about? I carry them around for fun, do I? That's what Jerry thinks of me: black-tie posh.*

*I don't know Jerry as a person and he doesn't know me. We're shoulder to shoulder on the pitch but we don't have a clue about each other's lives. And that's fine. He sees himself as the laid-back working-class rebel and I'm the middle-class Establishment. Whatever. I worry about him if it gets nasty out there. But he's special. He's got more class than any other rugby player on earth. He's capable of genius. Nobody can do the things he does.*

*Rob Andrew and Richard Hill: Everybody thinks Rob is a sweet guy. Let me tell you, he's a tough bastard. Intense. Hilly's calmed down. Used to be a lunatic. Now he's up there with the best scrum-halves in the world.*

*Front row: The Judge. Good bloke, old school, I like him. No badness in him, which is probably a fault. I tell him I want more from him than scrummaging and he looks at me strangely. What the fuck would I know about a prop's life. It's like a speech bubble coming out of his mouth. Probes: awkward bastard. Whatever you say, he'll say the opposite. He's got a problem with me, I know he has. Doesn't like me much. I'll get over it. They tell me he's a world class prop. Fair enough. Mooro? Don't get me started.*

*PC Plod: Wade and Ackers in the row. Cops. Brilliant, the pair of them. Their line-out work has been key to what we've been doing. Nobody can live with them. They're too damn good.*

*Skins: saved me from a kicking once and spent years telling me about it. 'Next time Skins, just leave me there, right!' A character. Good to have around. Hard as nails.*

*Winters and Teaguey: I love 'em. Wints was my schoolboy hero. Still having a hard time being his captain. What do I say to the man who has done it all? Teaguey's the bravest of the brave. He'd lay his body down for you without blinking. I'd do the same for him but I doubt it would have the same effect. He's a colossus.*

England had a month off before heading to Scotland. Far from ideal, but at least it gave them time to take stock of the mayhem they had caused.

The post-mortem in Wales lasted a fortnight. Many of the legends were involved; Gareth Edwards, Phil Bennett, Barry John, Ray Gravell, Brian Price – all of them held their head in their hands at what England had done to them. Just as the French greats had done a few weeks before.

John Ryan, the Welsh coach, resigned the day after the loss. The embarrassment was just too much for him. Ron Waldron took over. A proud son of Neath, he left the Principality in little doubt about the depth of his passion. 'The only sin I will not commit for Wales is murder,' he said.

On Saturday 3 March, the England players sat down together at the Petersham Hotel and watched the preamble to Wales vs. Scotland at the Arms Park. Carling knew that his team were going to be playing for the Grand Slam at Murrayfield on the 17th. What he wanted to know was whether the Scots would be doing the same.

# CHAPTER 16

# IF THEY ASK, ENGLAND ARE AWESOME

Mick Skinner lay back in his chair, simulated a yawn and made a pronouncement on the action from the Arms Park in Cardiff. 'Not exactly champagne rugby,' he said. He had a point.

Del Boy had scored an early try for Scotland and, save for a ten-minute spell just before half-time, the visitors had complete control of the match. They were doing damage in the scrums, just as England had done, and they were bossing the line-outs with ease. All the physical confrontations were being won by Scotland yet their own crass errors stopped them from shaking the Welsh loose. It was 13–9 after an hour and some of the England players were losing the will to live watching it on television. Bill McLaren summed it up in commentary: 'Ian McGeechan won't be burning the midnight oil watching this one on video, I can tell you.'

Rumour had it that the RFU had sent twenty men to Cardiff to analyse every facet of Scotland's performance, from the scrummaging technique of David Sole, to the line-out work of Chris Gray and Damian Cronin, to the infernal law-breaking of JJ and Fin Calder. It was the biggest surveillance mission in the history of the game – and Skinner reckoned it might also have been the biggest waste of money in the history of the game.

Skinner wasn't sure Scotland needed much inspection. They had no flair, no ambition, that much was obvious.

'How many tries have the Jocks scored in their three games?' Skinner asked the room.

'Five,' came the reply.

'And how many have we got?'

'Eleven.'

'Exactly,' said Skinner. 'They've got five and two of 'em came when the French were down to fourteen men. And only one of 'em came from the backline. We've got eleven and nine of 'em came from our backline. Rory's got four to himself, for fuck sake.'

The way Skinner saw it – and his wasn't a lone voice – Scotland played to a conservative gameplan and stuck rigidly to it. They kicked it in the air and they rifled it into touch. They could defend but they couldn't create. They were one-dimensional. Didn't need twenty blokes to figure that one out.

They were streetwise, though. There was no denying that. At the Petersham, the England boys didn't have a lot to get excited about, but when they got animated it was invariably a response to some devilment from the Scots that hadn't been spotted by referee René Hourquet.

'Watch Sole in this scrum,' Jeff Probyn was saying. 'He's taking the piss there. You're not allowed do that.'

'Look at Lineen!' shouted Richard Hill. 'Five yards offside and he's getting away with it.'

'Have a butcher's at JJ at this ruck,' said Mike Teague. 'Here he comes, keep your eyes on him. And . . . bang! Textbook cheating, that. Outstanding. Ref can't see it. The perfect crime. Scotland steal the ball and they're away. From defending to attacking in one fell swoop. Thank you and goodnight.'

When it came to chicanery, JJ was king. He was everywhere. When there was a line-out to be won, he won it. When there was a tackle to be made or a turnover to be secured, it was his big blond head in at the heart of it. And when there was a bit of momentum in attack it was invariably The White Shark who provided it. The England players marvelled at his ability to play the referee. Ultimately, that was his genius, they said. Persuading the ref he was onside when he was actually a mile offside was a trick he had mastered better than any other player in the world. Even when the Welsh complained, he avoided censure. How he did it, nobody quite knew.

'How long to go?' asked Skinner.

'Three minutes,' said Wade Dooley.

'Terrible bloody match, this. What is it, 13–9 to the Jocks? We had over thirty points in the bag against the Taffs at this stage . . . How long to go now?'

'Two minutes,' said Will Carling.

'Any danger of Scotland throwing it wide? Look at poor Iwan Tukalo on the wing, he hasn't had a pass. And Tony Stanger on the other wing. Tony Stranger more like. Stranger to the ball! He wouldn't recognise it if he saw it. Has Bill McLaren even mentioned him yet? How long left now?'

'A minute, Skins. Shut up, will ya?'

'They know what they're doing up front, I'll give 'em that much. JJ, Calder, Derek White; they know what they're about, them three. Time's nearly up. Gonna be us against them, then, eh? There's the whistle. That's it then. Fuck me: Scotland vs. England for the Grand Slam.'

There were things the Scots didn't want the English to know. Secrets and lies.

David Sole got a bang on the head against Wales. He couldn't remember getting it and couldn't remember much about the match either. He was all over the place. Concussed. Felt sick. Couldn't do the press conference afterwards. A little deception was called for. The management made up some excuse about Sole's absence and everybody bought it.

'By rights,' said Sole. 'I probably should have been ruled out of the Grand Slam game.' But losing their captain wasn't an option at this stage.

Before the night was out in Cardiff, a plan was being hatched. JJ predicted that Grand Slam fever was going to hit Scotland in the next twenty-four hours and they needed a plan to deal with it, something that would take the pressure off the younger lads.

'From now on,' said JJ, 'the only players who speak to the press are myself, Soley, Finlay and Gavin. And here's what we say. If they ask us about England we say that England are awesome, probably the best side the championship has ever seen. We talk about all the tries they've got, all the records they've broken, the brilliance of Underwood and Guscott and Carling, the power of Teaguey, Dooley and Skinner – and Mooro's will to win.

'If they ask about us we say, "Ah, we're just muddlin' along". Nobody outside Scotland thinks we can win. The bookies will give us no chance. Let's hype that up. We're singing England's praises, okay? We're playing that card for two weeks, non-stop. We're talking them up.'

Jim Telfer reminded them of the enormity of what was to come. 'Us against them, boys. First time in history Scotland have played England for the Grand Slam. It's ours for the taking: the Calcutta Cup, the championship, the Triple Crown and the Slam.'

'Nae worries, Jim,' said Kenny Milne. 'We're bound to win one of them, eh?'

For his wisecrack, he felt the gentle slap of Telfer's notebook across the back of the head. It was the closest Telfer got to being playful.

Geech got on the road to Leeds the morning after and was glad of the solitude. Four hours in the car on his own was a godsend; four hours to think and to plot, to figure out why all the possession at the Arms Park the day before had not turned into points, why they hadn't exerted the kind of control on the game that they should have. He needed videos and he needed hours in front of the television. He hadn't even thought about England up to now. He knew they were good, but no team was *that* good. Every team has a chink and he had to find it. Down in the Borders, he knew that's what Telfer was doing, too. Derrick Grant and Dougie Morgan were doing likewise. All trying to find the weakness in this team of all the talents.

Geech went to school on the Monday. He got home at 6 p.m. and was on the phone for the next five hours. Every time he finished with one call he'd barely moved from his seat when it rang again. And again. And again. If it wasn't Telfer, it was Derrick Grant, if it wasn't Derrick Grant it was Dougie Morgan, if it wasn't Dougie Morgan it was Norman Mair of the *Scotsman* or Bill McMurtrie of the *Glasgow Herald* or one of the English journalists or somebody from the Union or somebody looking for tickets. At one point Judy even screamed in frustration. There was two more weeks of this to come.

# CHAPTER 17

# SHE'S FROM ANOTHER PLANET

The dividing line between rugby and politics began to blur in the week after Cardiff. All the bitterness that surrounded Margaret Thatcher's premiership and her early introduction of the poll tax into Scotland had seen a surge in nationalist sentiment that only ratcheted up when the Auld Enemy were pitched together for the Grand Slam decider. Scotland's relationship with England, sporting and otherwise, was a talking point on a daily basis now. And there was a growing edge to the debate.

On Monday 5 March the *Glasgow Herald* ran an editorial titled 'The whingeing English'. It was a caustic attack on the double standards of their neighbours to the south over the vexed business of the poll tax.

The levy was three weeks away from coming into force in England – and the country was in turmoil. In one evening, five hundred protestors pelted police in Bristol with missiles; in Weston-super-Mare, a crowd one-thousand strong clashed with officers outside the local council building; a mob of three hundred attacked the council office in Reading, and there were violent scenes in Birmingham, Bradford and Maidenhead.

In the days that followed, pockets of disruption opened up all across the country. In Hackney, four thousand people fought running battles with police on the streets.

The poll tax had sparked the kind of civil unrest in England not seen since the worst days of Toxteth and Brixton. The lunatic Militant fringe were inflaming things behind the scenes but the anger of ordinary people towards this new tax was stark.

There was acres of coverage in the media. Huge debate on the iniquities of the tax and the seismic impact it would have on normal folk in England. 'The whingeing English' spoke to this mindset. It was one of many such commentaries in the Scottish press. When the poll tax had been imposed on Scotland eleven months earlier by a Tory party it never voted for, the fear and loathing of the Scots had been dismissed down south as just another manifestation of the whingeing Jock.

The Scottish papers brought a stream of stories about the frozen bank accounts of the poll tax refuseniks, the intimidation of the non-payers, sheriff officers turning up at the doors of the poor and seizing their radios and their toasters as payment for unpaid bills, aggressive demands dropping through the letter-boxes of grieving families looking for money for the portion of a month a late relative was alive. Did this outrage of eleven months even register in Middle England? Had they not read the *Daily Record* columns of a Labour firebrand called Gordon Brown in which he forensically proved, with his economist's eye, that doctors and dustbin men in Scotland were paying the same amount? Were they aware that middle-class Scots found the tax almost as much of an abomination as the put-upon working class?

'Can it be true?' asked the *Glasgow Herald*. 'Those who remember the impatience of English MPs with Scots' protests against the Poll Tax will find ironic amusement in the squeals now emanating from the fat heartlands of the Tory vote ... There is very little love in Scotland for a government that has for so long, and with such seeming arrogance, told us all where we have been going wrong – indeed that we are a miserable bunch bludging off the state in the dependency culture ... It is obvious that, like the comrades in *Animal Farm*, some whingers [in Thatcher's Britain] are more equal than others.'

Things were tense – and relations between the nations weren't helped when Margaret Thatcher paid a visit to Scotland ten days before the Grand Slam showdown. A poll in the *Scotsman* showed that 77 per cent of Scots were dissatisfied with her leadership, the worst rating she'd received in eleven years.

Nothing touched the raw nerve of Scotland's capacity for anti-Englishness quite like a Thatcher charm offensive. Anti-poll tax protestors vowed to hound her from the moment she arrived, claiming they knew every detail of her schedule. 'There is nowhere for Thatcher to hide,' said Andy Clachers, an activist in the fight against the tax. 'She's about as popular here as Ceauşescu was in Romania.' When she landed, Thatcher was cosseted by more police security than any PM before her.

The demonstrators barely got within shouting distance. They were shadowed by police and stuck behind barriers. When they chanted at her to get back to England and take her poll tax with her, they were so far away she could hardly hear a word. When they threw eggs they splattered on the ground pitifully short of their target.

The agitators had the comfort, though, of the grapevine. Out of Whitehall came rumours of a Tory plot against the prime minister, talk of disaffected cabinet members deciding that Thatcher had not only lost her touch but that she had become vaguely delusional. Her unwavering support of the poll tax was proof of it. Her insistence on going to Scotland to woo the locals was another. In Scotland, she got on with business as if she was among her own kind, opening a shopping centre in Glasgow and meeting whisky barons in Edinburgh, talking to school kids in Linlithgow and cuddling a Russian cashmere goat called Gorby on a farm in Aberfoyle. She said, and sounded like, she believed that a great Tory resurgence in Scotland was imminent and that the poll tax was a success.

'It's almost as if she's from another planet,' said the Scottish Labour MP George Foulkes. 'She doesn't seem to have the normal instincts of humility, fear or embarrassment.'

On Friday 9 March Thatcher went to the BBC studios on Queen Margaret Drive in Glasgow for a thirty-minute interview with the indefatigable Kirsty Wark. The PM's people didn't want Wark in the interrogator's chair, knowing that Thatcher didn't always respond well to women as equally feisty as her.

She had form there. She had virtually blackballed the BBC's Sue Lawley after an 1983 interview during which the presenter had famously allowed Diana Gould, a geography teacher from Cirencester, to upbraid the prime minister for the sinking of the *Belgrano* in the Falklands War. Thatcher thought there was more than a hint of Lawley and Gould about Wark – and she was right. The interview went ahead and Wark's questioning was relentless. In many senses it captured the national mood and it produced responses from Thatcher that made Scotland's skin crawl.

The prime minister's tactic was to try and ingratiate herself with the Scots, a naive plan that merely confirmed how wildly out of touch she was. She declared it a great honour to be 'prime minister of Scotland', conveniently forgetting that Scotland had shunned her in record numbers at the last election.

Throughout the interview she referred to 'us in Scotland' and 'we in Scotland', as if she was a native instead of the alien George Foulkes had talked about. Backstage, two of her key lieutenants, Michael Forsyth and Malcolm Rifkind, held their heads in their hands, knowing only too well how her attempted charm offensive was going to be received the next day.

Margaret Thatcher's flying visit reminded Scotland of the reasons why they hated her so completely. She was, as the journalist Allan Little, said: 'So grandly, aggressively, self-confidently, irritatingly and irredeemably southern.'

No sooner had she departed than the English rugby team

were on their way north. The Iron Lady had cleared the stage, but her hectoring personality and her incendiary policies had left a nation in ferment and ensured that the Grand Slam on 17 March had, for some, gone beyond a game.

# CHAPTER 18

# ONCE MORE UNTO THE BREACH, DEAR FRIENDS, ONCE MORE

A week before the Grand Slam, Jim Telfer's dream came true: Melrose beat Jed-Forest and won the Scottish championship, a momentous event in his rugby life. As player and coach, Telfer had spent thirty-three years at the Greenyards. And Saturday 10 March, was the most joyful of them all.

His team and his old teammates say they had never seen him happier, not even on that exultant afternoon in 1984 when he had coached Scotland to their first Grand Slam in fifty-nine years. That's how much Melrose meant to him. Through all his days as the club's No. 8 and captain he never imagined that they would ever topple the dynasties of Hawick and Gala.

'It was something you always hoped for, but never expected to see,' he said.

The Greenyards celebrated, but Telfer didn't stick around. Nobody was surprised. He had somewhere else he needed to be, another team that required his intensity. While the revelry was going on at Melrose, Telfer was on the road to Edinburgh, his mind already turning to the Grand Slam.

At the Braid Hills Hotel, they gathered: the players and the management, the underdogs called Scotland. Geech and Telfer,

Derrick Grant and Dougie Morgan talked of gameplans over dinner, dissecting England's season, probing for a weak link, not leaving the table until they were sure they'd found something.

At six the following morning, Iwan Tukalo, the earliest bird in the team, went downstairs and was heading out of the door of the hotel for a walk when he heard voices in the team room. Through the gap in the door he saw Telfer, nose pressed to the TV screen, watching, pausing and rewinding over and over a single England line-out in their game against France.

How long he'd been there Tukalo had no idea. How long Telfer was intending to stay, he didn't know that either. He stood for a minute, awed by the determination. Twenty years on, Tukalo still remembers the sound of the tape whirring and the vision of Telfer in the half-light, notebook in hand, illuminated only by the pictures on the screen in front of him.

Jim Telfer watched the hysteria develop. Grand Slam on the front pages and Grand Slam on the back. People everywhere. Newspaper people, radio people, television people, sponsors, union men, merchandisers, publicists.

*Hello, this is the BBC*, we'd like to arrange interviews for next week. Please get in touch . . .

*Hi there, Terry Wogan's office here. We'd love to have one of the boys on the show on Monday. Do call . . .*

*Good afternoon, this is Downing Street, the prime minister wishes to extend an invitation to Number 10 to David Sole. Phone for details . . .*

To be ignored, the lot of it. But it was hard. The newspapers brought stories of people making ties, T-shirts, hats and scarves and badges, making and selling things in tartan, a tenner a time.

And the loaves and fishes queues for tickets: four hundred people outside Mackenzie's sports shop on Nicholson Street from midnight, eight hundred at the door of Intersport on Hanover Street, hundreds more outside Sports Conscious on Castle Street. Tickets like gold dust. And the touts patrolling the tailbacks with accents you wouldn't mistake for sons of Melrose or Hawick. *Awright, guv. Prime seats. Princess Anne's lap, as God is my judge. Eight hundred a throw, sixteen hundred the pair, and I'm giving 'em away.*

**Norman Mair, Scotsman:** *There are desperate men abroad who might sell their daughters into bondage for a couple of tickets – and if they were Centre Stand, furnish a dowry into the bargain.*

**John Reason, Sunday Telegraph:** *The whole of the UK is searching for tickets with the determination of eels making for the Sargasso Sea. The demand is unprecedented in my view ... The wallet-emptier is nationalism, naked and unadorned. Us versus Them.*

It wasn't like this in 1984. But France were the opposition that time. This is England. And it's a circus. None of it matters, says Telfer. Nothing matters, only this ...

*England's line-out is their key, boys. Their key. Great players, Carling, Guscott and Underwood, magic finishers, world beaters on the evidence. Andrew and Hill, outstanding. Brian Moore? Superb.*

*But they'd be nothing without Ackford and Dooley.*

*Ackford and Dooley, boys.*

*To fix a problem, you go to the source. And they are the source. They are the foundation, the rock on which everything sits. It's Ackford and Dooley we have to destroy.*

Geech is talking now. Not showing his hand, not fully. He's keeping quiet about a lot of stuff. Issues about his teaching job, concerns about money – all a secret. That's just for him and Judy, the wife he's hardly seen in two months, the mother of his kids who he's spotted only in passing since the championship began months ago.

He's speaking about comfort zones. England are in one, he says. They've won their games without being asked a question, without ever being behind.

Eleven tries for and only two against. Eighty-three points

scored and only thirteen conceded. Nobody has put them under pressure, nobody has given them cause to doubt. Every team doubts itself sometime. England are no different.

*What happens when Ackford and Dooley can't find any space at the line-out, can't win ball as they please, can't build a platform for the rest? They look at each other and say, 'This ain't right. We're not used to this'. What happens when Mike Teague takes the ball up and gets smashed in the tackle? He gets up and wonders, 'What's going on here, then?' cos he's not used to it, not this season. He's used to breaking tackles and offloading and causing mayhem. What happens when Will Carling and Jerry Guscott and Rory Underwood have no room to run? They have to come up with a Plan B. They've had no need for a Plan B because Plan A has been killing teams. Let's see what happens when Plan A refuses to work. Let's see if they can find their way out of trouble.*

Geech wasn't sure Carling would stand up in a crisis. He was only twenty-four! Nobody knows it all at twenty-four.

JJ had something on his mind. A secret dread. Out there somewhere, in a folder in a library in a newspaper office in rural England, there was a photograph of him in an England shirt. Him playing for the England university team against Scotland while he was a student in Newcastle. Him scoring a try for England Universities against Scotland – and looking delighted.

That photograph in the wrong hands was dynamite. Imagine if Mooro saw it. Imagine the slagging.

*Here he is, John Bull Jeffrey.*

*Ah, come on, Mooro, it was only a Universities international.*

*Pictures don't lie, JJ. That's you in an England top.*

*It was a long time ago. I was only a boy.*

*Doesn't matter. You turned your back on Scotland. You're one of us now.*

'I was checking the newspapers, petrified. Jesus, the thought of it.'

\*    \*    \*

David Sole was talking to the boys; Finlay, JJ, Gavin, all listening to his grand plan for Saturday.

'I want us to send a message to the English as we come on to the field,' he said.

'Sounds good,' said JJ.

'I like it,' said Hastings.

'We're gonna walk,' said Sole.

'Walk?'

'Walk. All teams run on to the field. England will have sprinted on before us. The crowd will be expecting us to do the same. But we're gonna walk. Nice and slow. Single file. Like an army going to war. "This is our country, these are our people and we're here to fight". The crowd are gonna see us and they're gonna love it, the English are gonna see us and they're gonna think, "Christ, I don't like the look of this". The noise will be deafening. We're walking, boys.'

'Fantastic,' said Hastings. 'And we'll have kilts on.'

'Aye, Gav,' said Calder. 'But what about the claymores?'

'Don't be stupid, Fin,' said Hastings.

'Well, you started it. Kilts!'

Calder wasn't sure. A slow walk. Sounded good in theory but it wasn't original. He'd done it himself as Lions captain in Australia the previous summer. First Test at the Sydney Football Stadium and he walked the Lions on to the field.

The Lions got annihilated.

Soley said it'll be different this time. Home stadium for a start. Think of the noise; sweet music to the Scottish team, a bloody cacophony to the English team. Calder thought it through and relented.

Come Saturday, they were walking.

Wednesday night at training. Jim Telfer's final beasting. Del Boy on the receiving end. You're lazy, you're fat, you're useless, you're going to get emptied on Saturday. Why are you here? Why?

He had his reasons. Rugby was never much of a big deal to Del Boy. He could take it or leave it. After school, he left it for three years and never missed it. Never pined for a scrum the whole time. People like Telfer? The game was their life. It was never that way with Del Boy. Still wasn't.

It was his mother who brought him back. Called him up one day and asked if he'd think about playing again – for his father, a rugby lover who missed those Saturday afternoons supporting his son. 'The driving force was my dad. It meant the world to him. I did it for him.'

They all had their own motivation for being there, their own rationale for putting up with Telfer's rage.

*Scrums, boys. Let's be having you.*

*Rucks now, no fucking about.*

*Line-outs, we're in for a hiding if we don't get this right.*

Derek White on the floor getting shoed. Kenny Milne on the touchline getting barked at. Del Boy in a scrum getting smacked on the back. *Get your arse lower, Damian!*

Telfer looking on with a scowl, giving nothing away. But he's smiling inside. 'The papers were saying we were going to get mullered in the scrum. That's when the confidence started to grow. If they believe that, then that's good for us.' This is as good a session as Telfer can remember; focused and furious. He can't ask for more. They've no more to give in any case.

He talks to them later, breaks them down and builds them up again. All the work, all the pain, he wouldn't have pushed them if he didn't think they were worth it. That night, he sits down with Geech. Tells him the boys are as technically accomplished as he's ever seen them. He thinks they're ready.

The forwards, worn out, need the comfort of a pint.

'Come on, JJ,' said Calder. 'We're going down the Golf Tavern.'

'But it's the Buxton we go to.'

'Not tonight.'

They sat down in the snug of the bar, chatted awhile about England, about the slow walk, about what the day might mean to their lives if it went right and what it might mean if it went wrong. Halfway through the first pint, the door swung open.

A woman stared daggers at Calder.

'I need a word,' she said.

'Sit down,' said Fin. 'Have a drink.'

'I don't want a drink. I'm pregnant. What are we going to do, Fin?'

Calder got up and left. They didn't see him for the rest of the night.

JJ and Soley and the rest were frozen to the spot, their pint glasses stationary at their open mouths. 'Oh, Jesus Christ!' said JJ. 'Oh, fucking hell! How could he do this? Finlay, you arse-hole. You stupid bastard! Poor Liz and the kids! Oh, Christ almighty!'

This couldn't get out. 'This does not leave this pub,' JJ demanded. 'Not a word to the rest of them, right? We keep this to ourselves. Nothing has happened here. Nothing has happened.'

They returned to the hotel and Craig Chalmers was lurking.

'What's up with Fin?'

'Nothing,' snapped JJ. 'What do you mean? There's nothing up with him. Why?'

'Well, he's just come storming through here and he's blanked me.'

'It'll be nerves. Long day. He's tired. Get to bed, Chick.'

Next morning, JJ was up first. As he always did, he went to the hotel reception and got the telegrams and the cards that had come in for the boys – and then he read them all. It was customary. He didn't do privacy, JJ. Everybody knew it.

There was nothing for Fin. At least, nothing that mentioned the trouble he was in. But at breakfast, the talk was of the commotion in Calder's room in the night-time. The phone ringing and the sound of an irate woman on the other end. The phone ringing again and Calder's anger as he pulled the cord out of the wall.

Then a forwards meeting later in the day. They were dealing with line-outs and the effect the wind would have on Kenny Milne's throwing.

'What if it's really blowing and the call is a long ball to the back?' asked Milne. 'It's risky. What do we do?'

'Uhm, we abort!' said Whitey, suppressing a snigger.

If JJ had been close enough he'd have kicked him in the arse. 'Shut up, Derek!'

On the bus back from training, Sean Lineen reached into his pocket and pulled out a letter. You missed this one this morning, he told JJ. Must have slipped down the back. 'It's actually addressed to you,' said the centre.

Lineen stood up on the bus and read the note to a rapt audience.

*Dear JJ. About the pregnancy* . . .

'Oh, for fuck sake,' said JJ.

*Revenge is sweet. You've been had! Lots of love, The Lads.*

The squad erupted in laughter and cheers. The wind-up to beat all wind-ups, the champion prankster beaten at his own game. *Hook, line and sinker, big man!*

'Bastards!' shouted JJ.

Up the front of the bus, Geech and Telfer chuckled quietly. Sounded like the boys were nice and relaxed back there. Just as they wanted them.


After training on Thursday, Will Carling spoke to the press at Twickenham. He was unflappable, singularly unwilling to crank up the tension with some loose talk of Scotland's shortcomings, despite the best efforts of the reporters.

Well, he didn't need to, did he? They were capable of doing that all by themselves. The man from the *Daily Mirror* reckoned that the big question to be answered at Murrayfield on Saturday wasn't so much who was going to win the Grand Slam – that was England's already – it was could England get the twenty points they required to become the highest scoring team in Five Nations history. *Daily Mirror*'s view: *We'll get thirty!*

And there were plenty of veterans knocking around with similar opinions. Bill Beaumont was in the vanguard. 'England should have too much artillery for the Scots,' the former captain told the *Daily Record*. 'I cannot think of too many Scottish players I'd put in this English side,' he said. 'We'll wreck your dream,' he concluded.

Low-key, that was Carling's way. Humility. Respect. He'd have gambled his life on an England win, but he wasn't going to say it publicly. No way was he going to stoke the fires of the Scots. He hadn't been around very long, but this much he knew: in Scotland they'd be looking for signs of English arrogance in the build-up and they'd be papering the walls of the dressing rooms with every newspaper homage to England's greatness.

Unassuming was the only way to go. 'It's an important game, but it's still only a game,' he told reporters. 'We're very impressed with Scotland. I really don't understand how the bookmakers can say we're overwhelming favourites. Don't they know what happens to a Scot when he pulls on the jersey to play England? It's going to be tight up there, very tight.'

From a side room, Mooro appeared. Without saying a word, he went to his captain, handed him a book folded over on a page, and walked off again. The book was *Henry V.* The page was Act III, Scene I – *Once more unto the breach, dear friends, once more.*

Carling looked at it for a moment.

> *But when the blast of war blows in our ears,*
> *Then imitate the action of the tiger;*
> *Stiffen the sinews, summon up the blood,*
> *Disguise fair nature with hard-favour'd rage*

Thanks a bunch, Mooro.

*For there is none of you so mean and base,*
*That hath not noble lustre in your eyes.*
*I see you stand like greyhounds in the slips,*
*Straining upon the start. The game's afoot:*
*Follow your spirit, and upon this charge*
*Cry 'God for Harry, England, and Saint George!'*

Carling held the book in his hands as if it was a ticking bomb.
Low-key was officially out of the window.

England arrived in Edinburgh in the late afternoon on Thursday
and were bussed to the tranquillity of their base in the Borders
– the nineteenth-century Peebles Hydro set in the hills over-
looking the Tweed Valley.

Will Carling took a look around. Good facilities, friendly staff,
gorgeous scenery – this place looked the part. He pushed open
a door and walked into an empty conference suite – and immediately felt a chill. A giant mural swept around the room, covering
three walls and depicting battle scenes from Bannockburn.

Maniacal Scots in chainmail, wielding spears and axes over
the bodies of the slaughtered English. The Lion Rampant waving
in the breeze.

'Don't think we'll be having our team meetings in here,' said
the captain.

He closed the door behind him but couldn't shut out the images
of war. Bannockburn was everywhere.

On Saturday, the Scottish team would be singing an extra
verse of 'Flower of Scotland'. The words were in all the papers.
*Sing it out loud and sing it proud, readers.* A local reporter asked
Carling what he thought about that. Carling said it made no
odds to him. The reporter didn't believe him. Carling didn't care
what the reporter believed or didn't believe.

'All I knew was that the guy was looking at me like he detested
everything about me. "You hate me, do you? Well, I'll hate you
back".'

'Flower of Scotland': inspiration or embarrassment, a symbol of Scottish identity or an anti-English dirge? Mooro had some thoughts on that. Kept them to himself for a while but they came out soon enough.

*You think about it. You want to be an independent country which, by the way, I think you should be because then you might stop moaning all the time. Is this anthem really the summit of your ambition, the song you define yourselves by? A thing about a seven-hundred-year battle with England which, may I remind you, was only the first leg, the second leg of which you got fucking butchered in. The day you go and be a nation again is the day you stop talking obsessively about us. 'Flower of Scotland'? Is that it? Is that all you've got?*

The England players were watching television, a Grand Slam special on the BBC. David Sole was talking about his life in rugby, telling the nation about the honour of wearing the jersey, the pride he was going to feel when leading the team out on Saturday.

David Sole, Scotland's hero. Some of the England players thought that funny. Jeff Probyn, Paul Rendall, Simon Halliday, Richard Hill: they all remembered Soley from before, from his days in England when he propped for Bath and was talked about as the next big thing in English rugby.

**Jeff Probyn:** He's not Scottish. He's from Suffolk or Oxford-shire.

**Paul Rendall:** Berkshire, I reckon. He's an Englishman.

**Richard Hill:** He was born in Buckinghamshire, moved to Hertfordshire and stayed there until he was eight. David was a teammate of mine at Bath for years. He was a good lad. Not a Scot, but a good lad. His grandfather was Scottish. Colonel somebody or other.

**Simon Halliday:** I was already at Bath when he arrived from Exeter University in 1983. He was polite, cultured, intel-ligent. Not a trace of Scottishness, though. Not that I could see anyway. I mean, he was playing for England Students. And he was outstanding. Hard and mobile. Wonderful athlete. Would have been a revelation for England. We took the piss out of him when he was capped for Scotland. All of a sudden he started talking like a native. I'd say, 'David, I've played beside you for years, mate. Stop bullshitting me with this Scottish accent'.

**Richard Hill:** He had a nice, soft West Country voice and then, all of a sudden, he didn't. He was a West Country boy one week and Rob Roy McGregor the next.

**Jeff Probyn:** Ian McGeechan was born in England as well.

**Paul Rendall:** And Del Boy.

**Richard Hill:** Lineen's from Auckland.

**Paul Rendall:** Iwan Tukalo's from Siberia.

**Jeff Probyn:** Is he?

**Paul Rendall:** Nah. Edinburgh.

**Jeff Probyn:** Same difference, Judge.

**Paul Rendall:** Hehehe. You're not wrong, Jeffrey. You are not wrong, son.

On Friday morning, both teams trained at 10.30, England in Peebles, Scotland at Meggetland, home of Boroughmuir. Bill McLaren, BBC commentator and favourite son of Hawick, had a decision to make as to where he was going to go. He opted for Peebles and stood on the sideline as Will Carling and his men ran on to the field.

Despite a tacky pitch and a stiffening breeze, McLaren saw forty minutes of perfection. Not one pass was dropped, not one line-out went astray, everything was done at pace and with telepathic understanding.

Geoff Cooke and Roger Uttley didn't interfere. They had no need. Things came to a stop only once, and only briefly, when a Jaguar fighter plane roared into view above them and started doing tricks in their honour. Rory Underwood, an RAF pilot, played dumb. 'Nothing to do with me, lads. Honest.' In fact, he knew all about it. That was his mate Pete up there. He'd been expecting him.

When the session ended, Mooro and McLaren got talking.

'What did you think of that, Bill?'

'Oh, aye, very impressive, Brian. Very impressive. We'll have a job to beat you tomorrow.'

'You'll be commentating, I presume?' asked Mooro.

'I am, aye.'

'So can you keep dispassionate or not?'

'Och, I've been through it all before, son.'

'You've not done one like this though, have you?'

'No, no.'

'That's what I mean.'

'Aye, this is unique.'

Will Carling went to his room and got to work on his speech. He needed to be confident and in control, he needed to put up the mask as he always did and be the composed leader they all expected him to be.

His speech to the team that night was short and sharp, full of passion and laced with history. 'We can go down as the greatest English side ever tomorrow,' he said. 'We know we're good enough. We've shown it. Let's show it again one more time.'

Thirty miles away in Edinburgh, Geech and Telfer were having coffee, content that they could do no more, saying that it was up to the players now to do what they'd been told to do.

*Control the line-out: make it chaotic, cut off their space, shove them, barge them, hassle them, give them nothing.*

*Control the tempo: make it fast and make it furious, don't let them settle, don't miss a tackle, hit them hard and hit them often.*

*Control the referee: don't question him, don't react to him, be nice to him, we need him.*

'I think we're going to win this match,' Geech said.

Telfer said nothing.

'I think they have it in 'em to do it.'

Telfer stayed quiet.

'What do you think?' asked Geech.

'If they win,' said Telfer, 'I think their lives are never going to be the same again. If they win, tomorrow never ends. It lasts forever.'

# CHAPTER 19

# HATRED IS NOT THE WRONG WORD

In the early hours of Saturday morning the players began to stir. In his bed in Peebles, The Judge was woken by the sound of the television and by the chuckles of his room-mate and soul brother, Jeff Probyn.

'Jeffrey, what time is it?' he asked.

'Dunno, Judge. Best go back to sleep.'

'I can't, can I? You've got the bleedin' telly on again.'

'Sorry, mate. You know how it is. I'll turn it down.'

'What's on anyway?'

'*Fraggle Rock.*'

'Fuck sake.'

At the Carlton Highland Hotel in Edinburgh city centre, JJ's eyes were opening. By his estimation, that would make it around about six thirty, the same time he woke nearly every morning. Any minute now he was going to get up and go downstairs and check the papers for the photograph. He reckoned he was in the clear. He thought if they had it, they'd have used it against him by now.

'Hey, Chick, you alive?' he asked his room-mate, Craig Chalmers.

'No.'

'Make us a cup of tea anyway, will ya?'

Being the junior partner, Chalmers got up and made the tea, handed it over and went to the bathroom. He began the biggest day of his young life by splashing water on his face. Then he looked in the mirror – and shrieked.

'Oh, my God!'

Chalmers was a superstitious sort. During the championship, his hair was getting too long for his own liking, but he had refused to get it cut. Friends advised him to, but he was having none of it. And now, on Grand Slam Saturday, he paid the price – a hideous, Thatcheresque bouffant had appeared on his head.

'I came out of the bathroom and JJ was going, "Chick, what's up with your barnet?" In the history of hair, this was the lowest point. I was disgusted.'

But for Chalmers things were soon going to get a whole lot worse.

At breakfast, Geech looked out of the window and saw the flags fluttering in the breeze and was glad he'd pre-arranged a session at Murrayfield: all hush-hush and just for the kickers, to give them an idea of how the wind was going to affect the ball in the air.

Chalmers was launching garryowens, Armstrong was dinking box kicks, Hastings was hitting touch-finders, long and true. Chalmers heard a cry in the distance, something from Hastings' country. He looked up and got smacked on the nose by the falling ball.

Chalmers put his hand to the wound and ran to the dressing room, his nose pumping blood through his fingers, down his arm and on to his shirt. He stuffed some toilet roll in his nostrils to stem the flow and caught sight of himself in the mirror; face a mess and hair a disgrace. 'Great fucking start to the day, this,' he said.

JJ rifled through the morning papers for the photograph. Not a sign of it anywhere. But a headline caught his eye.

*Grand Slam decider just a stepping stone to World Cup prize.*

A stepping stone! He laughed, imagining what would happen if he went to Jim Telfer and said, 'Creamy, it doesn't matter if our body positions at the rucks aren't perfect or if we're too high in the scrum or if we leave Ackford and Dooley plenty of space in the line-out. Today is only a stepping stone. Look, it says so in the *Telegraph*'.

He kept flicking through. Lots of Bannockburn. Lots of everything. Pages and pages of stuff. The words to 'Flower of Scotland' printed yet again. A column from Ally MacLeod, the former Scotland football manager, saying: 'Scotland is a downtrodden nation and this is a chance to avenge a lot of things. It's Bannockburn all over again.'

There was a news piece about a guy in Surrey walking into the bookies with forty grand in cash and having it on England at odds of 1–4. It wasn't so much the forty grand that caught the eye, it was the 1–4. Did England really deserve to be such red-hot favourites?

The first of the team meetings was scheduled for 11 a.m. but Jim Telfer was there half an hour early, pulling the chairs into a semi-circle around him, dragging some tables across the room and spreading fifteen jerseys on top, fronts up, so that the players could see the thistle.

In his head he had rehearsed his speech, the words, the tone, the timing. When the team arrived, he was ready. Told them to sit down. Paused for a moment and then began.

*Look boys, you're going to get hammered today, you're going to get crucified, there's no way you lot can live with this juggernaut England eight that I keep reading about.*

**Michael Calvin, match preview, *Daily Telegraph*:** In the first scrum at Murrayfield today, Scotland will find the spirit of D'Artagnan, alive and well and living in the England pack.

*If I believe what I read in the English papers we've got no*

*fucking chance at all. We may as well pack up and go home to*
*our families. Are we wasting our time? Are the English media right*
*about you? Journeymen! Not in England's class! Lucky to get this*
*far! That's what they're saying. Are they right? Only you can answer*
*that question*

*But here's what I think. You're better than they are. You're fitter,*
*stronger, hungrier and cuter. You've worked harder than they*
*have. You want it more than they do. Days like this don't come*
*around very often, boys. Take it from me, I know. I can only*
*imagine what it must be like to be in your shoes today. To play for*
*a Grand Slam in front of your own people! What an opportunity.*
*What a privilege.*

*Your jersey is there, boys. Don't put a hand on it until you're*
*ready to accept the responsibility that comes with it. Pick one up,*
*turn it round and see whose number it is. Hand it to the man it*
*belongs to, wish him luck, make a commitment.*

David Sole and Iwan Tukalo returned to their room in silence,
Telfer's war cry still ringing in their ears. Tukalo switched on
the television just in time for the opening credits of *Grandstand*,
only it wasn't the usual beginning, it was a special Grand Slam
package of great sporting battles between the Scots and the
English.

There was Jim Baxter and Bobby Moore, Jim Clark and
Stirling Moss, Sandy Lyle and Nick Faldo and Ken Buchanan
beating the head off somebody, presumably an Englishman. And
a picture of Eric Liddell. All the history was there. 'Myself and
Soley stopped in our tracks and just stared at it,' said Tukalo.
'When it was over, we looked at each other and went, "Fuck!"
We were almost in denial about the hugeness of the occasion
up until then. Not now.'

The plan was to get everyone on the bus at 12.40 p.m. That left
Geech a window of about five or ten minutes to talk to the
whole squad. And that was all he needed. He knew what he
wanted to say. Somebody had given him cards and faxes from

fans, folk wishing the team well, and a lot of them were from Scots abroad.

It triggered a thought. 'It got me thinking about my father, a man who had spent a great deal of his life outside Scotland, but who was Scottish to the core of his being. These people's lives had taken them away from their birthplace, but their hearts were still here, just like my dad's was until the day he died. I told the boys that on top of the five million Scots at home, these people would be with them today, these proud people watching from all corners of the world. I knew that because I did it myself as a kid. I knew what it was like to be on the outside looking in.'

**Derek White:** We were close together in a darkened room and you could cut the atmosphere with a knife.

**David Sole:** It was emotionally charged, that's all I'll say.

**John Jeffrey:** Tears were shed, aye.

**Scott Hastings:** Geech's speech? Sorry, it's gone.

**Gavin Hastings:** Scott was wired to the moon. He wasn't taking anything in.

**Scott Hastings:** Aye, true. I was crying on the bus – on Friday! I was very emotional.

**Sean Lineen:** What Geech said was very powerful. Look, I qualified to play for Scotland because of a grandfather who lived in a small croft in a place called High Borve, the tiniest dot on the landscape in Stornoway on the Isle of Lewis in the Outer Hebrides. He was my mother's father. Jock Macdonald was his name. But I didn't come to Scotland to discover my roots. I didn't even know I had Scottish roots until I got here.

The truth is I came because I accepted I was never going to be good enough to play for the All Blacks. I arrived off the plane in Edinburgh in a T-shirt and flip-flops. What I'm saying, I suppose, is that Geech's words were so powerful that they resonated even with somebody whose Scottish ancestry was two generations old. I wasn't born here, but I bought into what he was saying, big time.

**Iwan Tukalo:** Geech really got to me. It was like he knew my story. On the bus to the ground, I started thinking about my mother and father. My mother is Italian, my father Ukrainian. When World War II began, my mother was sent from her hometown, near Monte Cassino, to friends in Edinburgh. She worked in a café on the Corstorphine Road. When the war ended and Dad was released from his POW camp in Dalkeith he got work in a paper mill in Balerno. On his way home he'd pop into the café and buy his smokes. And that's how they met.

Neither of them had anything but they worked hard to give me something. Dad told me that the papers at home were writing about the match. *Son of Ukrainian takes on England.* He got a big kick out of that. Geech was saying that Scots around the world were watching us. Well, I like to think there were some Ukrainians watching, too.

Dick Best had been on the phone all week, talking to his boys, wishing them luck, warning them, if they'd only listen, that nothing is guaranteed in this world.

Best was coach of Harlequins, London Division and England B. As such, he knew most of the players intimately, knew where they were strong and where they were weak.

He told them that himself and the wife were going to the match, that his missus had been bridesmaid for Kenny Milne's sister and they were all staying in the Milne family home. 'That's going to be an uncomfortable place to be if we lose this fucking game,' he said.

The boys told him not to worry, but Best was sensing arrogance. 'I kept saying, "Look, there's a trap lying in wait up there, it's not your God-given right to win this Slam", but I wasn't sure they were listening to me.'

**Paul Ackford:** We weren't overconfident, I'll say it to my dying day.

**Mick Skinner:** I was sure we would win.

**Simon Hodgkinson:** I didn't think they had a great deal to hurt us with, to be honest.

**Richard Hill:** I really couldn't see us getting beat.

**Paul Ackford:** I'll rephrase that, then. Some of us weren't overconfident. This was a serious Scottish pack we were up against. We knew what they were about. Good players with a great coach like Telfer in charge of them. They say Chris Gray was underrated as a second row. Well, not by me he wasn't.

**Brian Moore:** Their pack, right. David Sole: great ball carrier, not a great scrummager, was going to be targeted in the scrum. Kenny Milne: different story. Strong, good technician; I knew I was gonna have a battle there. Paul Burnell: journeyman, made the most of what he had, which wasn't a lot. Chris Gray: tremendous competitor, but not the biggest. Damian Cronin: great bloke, but not the fittest. JJ: a fucking nuisance. Finlay Calder: a mate and an icon, but actually a very limited openside, not the greatest of hands, not that quick, but for fearlessness and sheer bloody-mindedness, there's nobody like him. And Derek White: ball-player.

It was a good pack, but we were better.

**Paul Burnell:** We all thought the England side was fairly arrogant. I didn't really rate Brian Moore that much. Having played against him before, I thought he was overhyped. Him against Kenny Milne? Not a contest in my view.

**Kenny Milne:** Some of the boys didn't like Mooro. I thought he was okay. A bit gobby, but fine. It was all an act with him. Some of the team were very nationalistic and saw the game as different somehow. I wasn't like that. 'We need to raise it now' they were saying. Well, I raised it all the fucking time: I couldn't raise it any higher!

**John Jeffrey:** Me and Mooro, we're a bit similar. If you're going to be the bad guy you may as well be the real villain, there's a certain honour in that. Brian took it as a compliment, and so did I. What would you call him? An aggravating little bastard. First boy you'd want in your team, though.

**Will Carling:** I think we gave them respect. I know I did. I went out of my way to be respectful, all the good it did me.

**Gavin Hastings:** Will was a superstar, in all the papers, on telly, on the front of magazines. Fair to say that there was a bit of resentment there. Will was this and Will was that. I had no problem with him but if we needed any extra motivation, there it was.

**Jim Telfer:** England were waking up to the fact that everybody was against them. There's no doubt that fellas like Carling and Guscott can be cocky devils and they're not afraid to give opinions. Richard Hill and Skinner and Brian Moore, they could all be anti-Scottish. Fine players, but they'd rub you up the wrong way, some of them.

I'm not one to go along with this English arrogance stereotype. Considering where I'm from, I have more in common with people from the north of England than I do with people from the north of Scotland. But there's a certain type of Englishness that provokes this reaction in the Celts, a particular type of southern Englishness. I use the word supercilious. If it's snowing in London, it's a disaster. If it's snowing anywhere else, it doesn't matter. That type of thing.

They're a bit like the Americans in that they are so wrapped up in their own importance, nobody else is any good at all. They have no interest in us. They treat you like some kind of foreigner. They don't think Scotland is relevant. Ten years before, they came up with a very good side. They won by five tries, slaughtered us and took the Grand Slam. I think they thought they were going to do that again.

Bannockburn, Bannockburn, Bannockburn. Jeff Probyn was wondering when the Scots would give it a rest, when they'd tire of the endless stream of bullshit about Robert the Bruce and his relevance to a game of rugby seven hundred years after he died of leprosy or syphilis or whatever the hell it was that killed him in the end. Maybe it was boredom he died of. Maybe he keeled over from the sheer tediousness of listening to Scots going on and on about how bloody great Bannockburn was.

The way the Scots were talking, they thought they had the monopoly on bitterness. Or so it seemed.

**Jeff Probyn:** Well, they didn't. I couldn't put me coat on some days I was so bitter and twisted. I was thirty-one when I won my first cap and I felt cheated. Didn't go to the right school, did I? When I was a lad I played in the England U-15 trials, played three out of the four games, destroyed my opposite number in the scrums and scored a try. They went for a kid from a posh school instead. The prop selector said later that he hadn't even been watching me. How the fuck could he miss me? I was the one doing all the damage. Snobbery and corruption. Rugby was full of it. So don't give me all that bollocks about Scotland wanting it more than us. I'm not having it.

**Paul Rendall:** Jeffrey was badly treated. I wasn't exactly given a red carpet myself.

**Brian Moore:** We left our hotel in Peebles on Saturday morning. Everyone was really nice to us down there. It was, 'Hello, Mr Moore. Play well at Murrayfield, sir'. And we were going, 'Oh, thanks very much, very kind of you'. When we got to Edinburgh, it was edgy on the streets. Every fucker hated us all of a sudden. It didn't take me long to figure it out. There was something different about the atmosphere right away.

**Jim Telfer:** It was Bannockburn and Culloden rolled into one. The press hyped it up. You had Margaret Thatcher and the poll tax thrown in. There was no escaping it. Was it different to a normal Calcutta Cup? Oh, aye.

**Kenny Milne:** I remember walking past some youngsters and they were singing, 'If you hate the fucking English clap your hands'. Then they spotted me. 'All right, Kenny, how's it going, pal!' I just walked past. They were no pals of mine.

**Peter Winterbottom:** There's not a lot of distance between Peebles and Edinburgh but it was like we'd stepped into a different world. As we made our way to the ground it was all V signs and 'English bastards'. This was my fifth time playing there and there was a harshness about it that was new. It was a bit of a gauntlet. It bothered some, but not me. I was thinking, 'Okay, that's fine, we'll soak this up and use it against you'.

**Wade Dooley:** I was a bit like Winters. Soak up the abuse and let it inspire you. Look, it was bad, but I'd been through some hairy situations in the force by then, so something like this wasn't going to bother me. A while before, while I was off duty, some fucker pulled a gun on me. A house was being burgled and I disturbed them, they jumped in a car and couldn't get it started and I was trying to open the door. The guy reached under his seat and pulled a shooter out and pushed it up against the window. I thought, 'Okay, I'll back off now'.

So when they told me to fuck off back to England, I didn't bat an eyelid. I just said, 'We'll see how smart you are later on'.

**Dick Best:** It started off as good natured piss-taking, which we can all cope with, but the longer it went on the more like William Wallace it became. My wife got me out of three scrapes just before I decked somebody.

**Brian Moore:** Half of England hated Thatcher but most of Scotland despised her. I understood why we were hated. I got it. There's always an anti-Englishness in Scotland but this was of a more virulent strain. Thatcher was desperately unpopular for a variety of reasons, not least because of the poll tax. She used the Scots like they were experimental rats. That's how it looked anyway. That's how it felt to the people and they hated her for it and we were English and so came along with that. And you could feel all of that in the atmosphere. You could. They saw us as Thatcher's team. We drove straight into something powerful.

**John Jeffrey:** I'll always maintain that the ditching of the football fixture had something to do with it. People needed an outlet – and they found it in that game. All of Scotland was

behind us, even west coast people in Glasgow. Normally these
people would see us as kinda English. We were rugby players,
therefore we were snobs. Public school aristocracy play rugby
and the working class play football. That's nonsense, yet some
of them would see it that way. But even those boys were behind
us. I really, really did feel it; 1990 was a fix for the anti-English
brigade. There was anti-Thatcherism in the air for sure.

**Will Carling:** Up until then we were really only getting a
taste of the anti-English feeling through the media. Now it was
in our faces. If you'd told me a week before that I'd have
Margaret Thatcher, the poll tax, Butcher Cumberland and
Bannockburn thrown at me, I'd have told you that you were
on drugs. Butcher Cumberland? I'm not sure I'd even heard of
him. They said I was Thatcher's captain. The Scottish media
stuck that label on me and everybody bought it. People just
assumed things about me that were wrong. Most of my teammates didn't really know what was going on in my head so I
don't know how the Scots thought they did. Thatcher's blue-
eyed boy. Bloody stupid.

**Brian Moore:** If you're faced with the barrage of abuse we
got, what are you going to do? You're going to bridle, aren't you?
What sort of person is going to say, 'I'm an English bastard, am
I? Oh right, thanks for that'. No, you say, 'Well, fuck you, pal'.
That sort of atmosphere wasn't in Ireland or France and it wasn't
even in Wales – and it was hardly pleasant down there. Because
of all the things going on at the time in Scotland, the atmosphere was nasty. It was nasty and hard. Fair play, if I was a Scot
in that climate I'd have been the same. Hatred is not the wrong
word. Not on that day. It wouldn't have gone into physical
violence, but it was total enmity.

David Bishop had been in Scotland for two weeks, acclimatising
after his long trip from Te Anau on the South Island of New
Zealand, taking in some games and attending functions at clubs
around the capital in preparation for the big one.

Bishop, a forty-one-year-old sports shop manager, went walking near Murrayfield a couple of hours before kick-off. He stopped at a stall and looked at the merchandise.

'Scotland or England, sir?' asked the huckster.

'Neither, actually,' Bishop replied.

'Neither? There's no such thing as "neither" today!'

'There is if you're the referee, mate.'

**David Bishop:** The build-up was extraordinary. I had never seen anything like it. The amount of chat in the newspapers was just neverending. There must have been about ten articles on me alone. The English papers were saying, 'Watch the Scots, especially JJ, coming up offside', and the Scottish papers were saying, 'Maybe you should look at England at the breakdown'. I knew what I needed to look for. I didn't need any telling.

The second stall I stopped at seemed to be an England-only venture. There were T-shirts and flags and hats and they all had 'England: Grand Slam champions 1990' written on them. I said, 'You're confident!' And he said, 'Nothing surer, mate'.

**John Jeffrey:** I got off the bus and all I wanted to do was get started. I hated that hour before a match, hated stretching and warm-ups and team talks. I just wanted to get on with it. 'Start it early. Come on, I'm ready.' I threw my kitbag in the changing room and went out on to the pitch to try and walk off some of my nerves and doubts. But England were already there. If the other team is out there first, you wait until they come in before going out. We were waiting and waiting.

**Ian McGeechan:** The wives and girlfriends were on the pitch taking pictures. Those are the bits that irritate you. They felt they only had to turn up and it was theirs.

**Iwan Tukalo:** They were getting filmed or whatever. I was thinking, 'You've got this one wrong, England'. All these little things fuelled the fire.

**John Jeffrey:** 'Is there nobody gonna tell 'em to get off the field? Nobody? Right, fuck it, we're going on.' I'd had enough. I looked at them taking pictures of each other. Jesus. There was a voice in my head telling me what they were saying. *And this is where I'm going to score the winning try. And . . . click!* I thought, 'You're not quite switched on here, are you boys? You're not totally focused on this game. Do you believe what you've been reading in the papers?'

**Iwan Tukalo:** In the changing room half an hour before, it starts to get very serious. Some needed to knock nine bells out of the wall, others needed to be calm. Me? I withdrew into my own world. Each to his own. Not everyone is wired the same way. Everyone needs their own space.

**Tony Stanger:** I was just glad to be there. The week before I was playing for Hawick against Stewart's Melville and Alex Brewster fell on me and my collarbone shot out. Until the Wednesday that week it didn't look as if I was going to be able to play. The sorest movement was when I put my hands above my head. Creamy put me through a tackling and rucking session with the forwards and it was unbelievably hard, I survived, but I was thinking, 'Am I being stupid here? Will I let everybody down?'

I reckoned I'd be fine as long as I didn't have to lift my arms directly above my head. And what were the chances of that?

**Iwan Tukalo:** I had a small crucifix with me. My grandmother gave it to me at my christening. Pasqualina Pettesse was her name. I went and found a quiet corner, blessed myself and kissed the cross. I did that every game. You sometimes look for that divine intervention, that little bit of support. None of the guys knew about it. It was my twenty-second cap and nobody had ever seen me do it. I'd just find a spot, in the showers or wherever, and if I couldn't find that spot I'd get agitated. It was part of my preparation.

**Brian Moore:** The bigger the occasion, the more specific your preparation should be. The closer the hour the narrower the focus, so you stop thinking about destiny and history and you start thinking about the first scrum – where your feet are going to be, where your hands are going to be, because that gives you a focal point and stops your mind wandering. There was too much big-picture stuff going on with us and not enough of what I'm sure the Scots were doing. We were going on about 'Our time' and 'Our moment', which means fuck all, really.

**Roger Uttley:** The boys were good. Mooro was going around from player to player, like he always did. Will was calm. Or appeared calm. Mick Skinner was on his feet, looking like he was going to kill somebody, Mike Teague alongside him. Winters was sitting there quietly, like it was just another game. It was no different to Paris. Will said his piece and it was strong. England expects and all that. We wanted to cut them open with our power and our pace and we thought we could do it. Everything looked normal.

**Kenny Milne:** Soley came across as a bit strange sometimes. I was never that close to him. We got on fine, but he didn't open himself up, didn't invite a lot of warmth. Quite a guarded person. Finlay filled the gregarious role. Finlay and JJ and Gavin. Soley was more distant. But if you were looking for a man to lead by example, you didn't need to look an inch beyond David Sole.

**David Sole:** Creamy had spoken and so had Geech and now, as the time was closing in, it was my turn. I couldn't match Geech's emotion from the hotel, but I said we were about to experience something out there on the field that would never happen again. *Boys, no matter what happens in the next eighty minutes, life will still go on, but this afternoon we have a chance to make history. Let's go out and grab it. Let's enjoy it, but let's go and win this game.*

**Jim Telfer:** I could hardly hear him. I felt like saying, 'David, speak up!' But it wasn't my place. The time comes when you just have to retreat, when you have to accept that there is nothing more you can do. This was the time. The players were on their own. It was up to them now.

When England took the field, they did so at speed, 'like an SAS hit squad', wrote Ian Wooldridge in the *Daily Mail*. Carling jogged them down the ramp and then broke into a sprint as he crossed the running track.

Scotland planned to walk out in numerical order, David Sole first, Kenny Milne second, Paul Burnell third and right on down to Gavin Hastings, who was meant to bring up the rear.

But that was never going to work. Iwan Tukalo's superstitions put a spanner in the works right away; nobody was going out after him even if he had to sit in the dressing room for an hour.

And then there was Scott Hastings.

**Chris Gray:** Scott jumped the queue and went in third. I was saying, 'Scott, get back'. He ignored me. 'Scott, you're thirteenth in line'. No response. I looked at him – and he was gone. He was in another world. We were lining up in the corridor, ready to walk, but there was a delay. Don't know what it was, but there was a hold-up. I was thinking, 'If Scott doesn't get on the move soon he's going to blow a gasket'. He was like a horse down at the starting stalls. He had to be let loose.

**Scott Hastings:** I was in a trance. I relied on passion. I cried all the way to the ground, I cried in the dressing room beforehand, cried on the way out to the pitch.

**David Sole:** There's a gradual slope at the entrance to the pitch, so if you start jogging at the top you'll nearly be sprinting by the time you get to the bottom. You wanted to sprint. Everything in your body and the noise of the crowd was telling you to sprint. But we couldn't. We were walking.

**John Jeffrey:** *Walk! Walk!*

**Tony Stanger:** I didn't even know about it until we were standing there, waiting to go.

**John Jeffrey:** *Walk!*

**Tony Stanger:** I didn't know why, but fair enough. I was only twenty-one-years old. I wasn't going to turn around to JJ and say, 'Why are we doing this?'

**Derek White:** The weight of expectation put fear into me because normally the expectation was not that high. Now it was sky-high. The Scottish people were watching in their millions, throughout the world, just as Geech had said, and they were expecting something from us. Losing in front of our own people, it would have been a disaster. I was feeling the pressure.

**David Sole:** We emerged and a big roar went up and then a weird thing happened. It just subsided for a second or two. It was almost as if you could hear the thought process of more than 50,000 people. 'Hey, they're walking.' Then the roar came back and it sent a shiver through me.

*Ian Wooldridge, **Daily Mail**: Scotland came out in measured single file, ominously self-possessed, an invisible Piper Laidlaw VC at their head. Whoever dreamed up the theory of body language was vindicated. The tension was numbing and not a ball had been kicked yet. Readers not privileged to be present may think it absurd to write thus of a mere football match. But this was not a mere football match. I am nonplussed to define precisely what it was but it certainly embraced ancient history, modern politics and the constant personas of Anglos and Celts.*

**John Jeffrey:** England saw us walking out. Fantastic!

**Chris Gray:** I looked over at the English and they were going, 'Bloody Nora!'

**Brian Moore:** No we weren't. People said we were quaking in our boots. Urban myth.

**Rory Underwood:** We saw nothing. We were in a huddle. The first I heard about a slow walk was when I picked up the newspaper the next day.

**Jerry Guscott:** I didn't care if they walked out, ran out, came out in a taxi or on motorbikes.

**Will Carling:** I was talking to the guys, so we didn't see their famous walk. I heard the reaction to it, though. Jesus, did I hear it.

**Ian McGeechan:** Myself and Jim missed it. As David led them out we were walking under the grandstand en route to our seats – and the whole edifice shook. It was like a train passing overhead.

**Mick Skinner:** You know how the first row of the stand down by the pitch is normally kept for kids? Well, before the anthems, I looked at some youngsters and they were screaming and roaring and they had saltires painted on their faces and See You Jimmy wigs on their heads. Little nutters, everywhere.

**Tony Stanger:** The crowd were feeding off something. Something powerful was unleashed.

**Simon Halliday:** The hostility from the Scottish players was major. Scott Hastings was verbally and physically very aggressive. He was very vocal, trying to piss us off.

**Jerry Guscott:** Scott Hastings was like a zombie. He wasn't there. He was away at the races, gone from the emotion and the history of it all. After they came out I was looking for the players that I'd toured with eight months earlier with the Lions – and there was no recognition from any of them.

**Chris Gray:** Before the anthems started one of the bandsmen's music sheet blew away as he was marching past me. I picked it up and gave it him. 'Thanks very much,' he said. 'Now get stuck into the bastards!'

**Simon Halliday:** The real panic was when 'Flower of Scotland' was played and their guys knew the words. That's when I knew we were in trouble. Previous years they didn't sing anything. I had a little look across at them and they were absolutely screaming it out. I thought, 'This all looks a bit different to other years'.

**Jim Telfer:** I stood up for 'Flower of Scotland'. When I went to weddings and things around Scotland, they'd sing it and I'd be saying, 'You've no right to be singing that. That's our team song'. But it was everybody's song.

**David Bishop:** When the pipers started on 'Flower of Scotland' the hairs on the back of my neck stood up. My God, it was powerful. Haunting and moving. The two touch judges were Derek Bevan and Les Peard and I remember at the end getting a dig in the ribs from Peard, a big Welsh copper. 'Hey, boyo, if you didn't know you had a game on your hands, you fucking got one now'. I said, 'Thanks, mate, but I had kinda figured that out for myself'.

CHAPTER 20

# SKULDUGGERY AND THE SLAM

A daunting feeling came over David Bishop. He knew the Grand Slam was a major deal, he knew that the locals would be hostile and the players obsessive, but the reality was even harsher than he'd imagined. In the seconds before he blew his first whistle he took a look around the field and saw trouble.

*This is ominous. JJ, Calder, Mooro, Dooley, Skinner – things could get out of control pretty quick. You gotta be strong here, gotta be strong.*

**David Bishop:** As a referee, you're looking for an early opportunity to stamp your authority on a game, a bit of foul play that you can act on, something that will remind the players 'I'm not a man you want to annoy, fellas'. I was looking for that. Hoping for it. After forty-five seconds it landed in my lap.

**Mick Skinner:** He gave Scotland a penalty for offside and I didn't exactly applaud the decision.

**David Bishop:** Skinner opened his trap. I thought, 'Thank you very much. That's right up my alley. We'll be having an extra ten metres, gentlemen'. I hauled Carling over. 'Any more talk like that from one of your players and we're gonna have a problem today. Sort it out!' An opportunity like that? Sent straight from God.

**Will Carling:** I told Skins to put a sock in it.

**Mick Skinner:** I couldn't hear him. I had 50,000 people telling me what a prick I was at the time.

**Wade Dooley:** It was a frantic beginning. No time to settle down, no chance to find your feet. It was full-on mayhem. We got a line-out early on. 'Okay, great, let's win this and get these guys where we want them.' We had controlled the line-outs all season. Not being cocky, but me and Ackers gave the rest of the team a hell of a platform in the other games.

**Paul Ackford:** Wade was a big lump. It was impossible to shift him.

**Wade Dooley:** I was six foot eight and knocking on for eighteen stones. All the Dooleys are big. My great aunt Amy was six foot five. She was a sergeant in Wigan. A bit of a legend. Like I say, we're tall people.

**Paul Ackford:** Our line-out was all about creating space, getting guys like Probyn and Rendall moving about and then myself or Wade would jump into the hole and Mooro would find us with the throw. It was a very slick operation. Four people working together. The first time we tried it at Murrayfield there wasn't any space because Gray and the Jocks closed it off. That would have been Telfer's doing.

**John Jeffrey:** Finlay went into No. 2 in the line-out. Paul Ackford was going, 'What are you doing here, Fin? You should be out the back?' That was the plan. Mix it up, confuse them, make it claustrophobic, give them nothing.

**Paul Ackford:** I tried to step into the gap and all I hit was bodies, which was very unusual. The space we'd created all season, and we're only talking half a metre, wasn't there all of a sudden.

**Brian Moore:** We lost the first line-out. Okay, it happens. But after three or four minutes we had the first scrum. Now was the time to start making some statements.

**Jeff Probyn:** We wanted to send them a message. 'You think your scrum can survive, Scotland? Have a bit of this, then – bang!'

**Kenny Milne:** I got in under Mooro. Popped him right out of there. Penalty for us.

**Jeff Probyn:** So much for sending them a message.

**Jim Telfer:** Fin Calder tapped the penalty and drove at England's heart. I've been around the game a long time, but I never heard a roar like it. He smashed into Teague and Skinner and was held and then our forwards came in behind him and mauled England fifteen metres downfield.

**John Jeffrey:** Teague and Skinner stopped Fin dead in his tracks. To be fair, it was a fucking great hit. But then David Sole and the rest of us came blasting in and England were swept backwards. Physically and mentally, it was a colossal moment.

**Jim Telfer:** Low driving, great body positions. Exactly what I wanted them to do, exactly what I would love to have done myself. We got a penalty out of it and Craig Chalmers kicked it over. The crowd went crazy. The prickles were up on the back of my neck.

**Chris Gray:** It was the first time England had been behind all season.

**Ian McGeechan:** England didn't touch the ball for the first fifteen minutes. They were frustrated and were giving penalties away. Suddenly you could see them looking around, a bit stunned.

**Will Carling:** They were doing these quick line-outs and we didn't react. We were going, 'What's all this about?' They were putting pace on the game and we didn't expect that. That was a reflection of my captaincy.

**Rory Underwood:** My confidence was never higher. In the four games before Murrayfield, I'd scored five tries against Fiji, one against Ireland, one against France and two against Wales. The boys were creating so much space for me. The first ball I got at Murrayfield was a garryowen – and a millisecond after I caught it I was hit in the tackle by four Scots, Calder and JJ being two of them. They threw me into touch like they were putting out the rubbish.

**Paul Ackford:** I gave away a penalty and it was because I was offside at the breakdown and I remember thinking as I gave it away, 'This should not be happening'. It was a stupid penalty, but they were forcing me into that position. I hadn't experienced this before.

**Will Carling:** Our forwards underestimated what happens to a Scottish player when he puts on the jersey, especially when it's against England, especially when it's at Murrayfield. People were going on about Cronin beforehand. 'He's crap'. Well, he was playing pretty fucking well from where I was standing.

**Brian Moore:** We'd had good discipline all season. Gave away precious little. But then Probyn trod on Sole at a scrum and suddenly we were 6–0 down.

**John Jeffrey:** When Jeff Probyn stamped on Soley, Derek spotted it and came charging in and threw a punch, which kinda caught me more than it did Probyn. Derek says, 'Oops, wrong Jeffrey'. I thought, 'That's very good, Whitey'.

**Will Carling:** They were faster and sharper. Their tackling was precise, their speed to the breakdowns was electric, their speed of thought a lot quicker than ours. We were off the pace mentally. I wasn't worried, exactly. But I was thinking it would be nice to get some ball at some point, because we hadn't had any.

Jerry Guscott was cocky. But he had every right to be. Between England and the Lions, Guscott had played seven straight games at international level before Murrayfield, winning all seven and scoring seven tries.

In the fifteenth minute, England put-in a monstrous scrum on halfway, shoving the Scottish pack backwards. Mike Teague picked and went off the base and made some hard yards. At the breakdown, Scotland panicked. And Guscott began to see an opportunity.

**John Jeffrey:** I fucked up. I should have seen the trouble coming to my right but I stepped off to the left and Whitey came with me. Richard Hill and Will Carling spotted it.

**Scott Hastings:** No, it was my fault. I made the mistake. Hill threw out a pass and I came up too quickly. Got sucked in and Carling went outside me. He's done me, completely. A total nightmare. He was away. I couldn't do anything about it.

**Tony Stanger:** Oh shit! I had Carling to my left and Guscott to my right. I went for Carling and he gave it to Guscott.

**Jerry Guscott:** Gavin Hastings in front of me. A little dummy to Rory Underwood on my outside and I'm over for the try. I glided in. There was no way anybody was going to stop me. There were no boundaries for me. No fear.

**Will Carling:** Clinical. I thought, 'Yes, that's more like it'.

**Mick Skinner:** Sweet as a nut.

**Richard Hill:** Game on.

**Simon Halliday:** Hodgy missed the conversion, but we were up and running now.

**Scott Hastings:** Jerry Guscott was one of the most talented rugby players in the world. He was horrendous to play against. Incredibly quick, great hands, instinctive. I didn't have a clue where he was going to run. He was a class act, but he was full of himself. It was important to keep him in your pocket, so I was devastated when he scored. I got on with him, but there was always a rivalry between us.

**Jerry Guscott:** Scott's mouth was bigger than his body. Geoff Cooke always used to say, 'Engage mind before mouth', but with Scott there was no engagement of anything really. Whether you wanted to hear him or not, you heard him. He wasn't as bad as Timmy Mallett, but he was close.

**Mike Teague:** I picked and went off another scrum just after Jerry's try and I ran about twenty metres. I'm thinking, 'This is looking much better all of a sudden'.

**Mick Skinner:** We were losing 6–4 but we were in control. They were struggling with our power. It was just a matter of time before we broke them.

***Bill McLaren, in commentary*:** There's Michael Skinner.

Sometimes looks like a moving thatched cottage with his hair-style, but he's a very handy citizen to have.

**David Sole:** Skinner: The Big I Am. I wasn't a fan.

**Jeff Probyn:** In international rugby if you're a prop and you're under pressure it's the most desperate feeling you can have. You're on your own. Nobody can help you. And just before half-time David Sole was on his own. I had respect for Sole. He was a great ball carrier but my job was to knacker him in the scrum so he didn't have the energy to carry ball. I didn't have any great animosity towards him.

**David Sole:** I didn't particularly like him. He was all yap, yap, yap.

**Paul Burnell:** We're five metres from our own line. England had a penalty. They could have opted for the kick at goal. But they took the scrum instead. The psychology was huge. England were looking for the pushover try. They wanted to humiliate us in front of our own people.

**David Sole:** We had to get in close to them at the scrums because we didn't want them to get a big hit on us. If they come crashing in on engagement, they're going to do damage because their pack is bigger and heavier than ours. So you're looking for ways to survive. You're disrupting all the time. You're going as low as you can in the scrum so it's difficult for them to push you back.

**Paul Rendall:** There was a lot of skulduggery going on at the other side. Me and Burnell, we were steady. The action was with Sole and Probyn.

**David Sole:** As a loosehead you want to get your head under the tighthead because you can manipulate him then. It's all about two guys wanting to get their body in the right position. You get in that right position first and the other guy has nowhere to go.

**Jeff Probyn:** All my schoolboy rugby was at loosehead. Even when I joined Richmond in 1980 I joined them as a loosehead. I came up against some right bastards, I can tell you. You see, at that level, you was coming up against blokes who were happy to scrummage. They were big and hard and they had no interest in getting about the field scoring tries. They lived for the scrum and they knew every trick. That's where I learned my trade, from blokes nobody ever heard of at Charlton Park and Ilford Wanderers and Old Albanians and Streatham & Croydon. So when Sole tried it on, I knew what he was at.

**Wade Dooley:** Great player, David. Bloody outstanding. But he was very wary of the destructiveness of Probyn. A lot of people didn't like the way Probyn scrummaged. I don't know how Jeff did it. Probes would be doubled up in a scrum and he'd be talking to me through his legs, holding it rock solid. He could just work his opposite number into a frenzy. A lot of them had no answer to him. So, so strong. Such narrow shoulders and yet amazingly strong.

**Kenny Milne:** I was reasonably big and technically I was very good. Burnell was a good scrummager as well. We compensated for Soley. It's not that he was bad in the scrum, it's just that he was better in the loose. Soley and Probyn didn't get on and it was all kicking off.

**Jeff Probyn:** After the first scrum goes down, Bishop says to Sole, 'I know you took it down, if you do it again, it's a penalty try'.

**David Bishop:** I'm not sure I ever said that.

**Jeff Probyn:** So it goes down again. And Bishop talks to Sole again. 'I know it was you, once more and it's a penalty try'. Mooro says, 'What's happening?' I say, 'Once more and they're fucked'.

***Bill McLaren, in commentary*:** All kinds of panic stations for the Scots here.

**Derek White:** I did my knee ligaments a few minutes earlier. Calder tackled Skinner and then one of them bashed into me and my leg went numb. You think it'll be okay, but then you start running and it starts wobbling and then you know you need to get off, sharpish. I knew after the first scrum that I was a passenger. I was making frantic signals to the touchline. I'm on one leg. I'm a total liability. I switched to the flank and let JJ push from No. 8. I was hoping like crazy that England wouldn't come down my side. If they had, I would have been helpless.

**Jeff Probyn:** It goes down again. Sole can't hold it up. Any prop would do what he done. You go down rather than back. You take a chance.

**David Sole:** I'm telling the ref I'm losing my footing and I'm hoping he'll buy it. It's a bit of a con job but you hope. It's knackering.

**Paul Burnell:** We were just hanging on for grim life but Telfer had us scrummaging and scrummaging in training for situations like this because we knew they saw our scrum as a potential weakness and if they got close to the line they were going for it. For us, it was mind over matter. We were not going to be pushed over.

**Chris Gray:** They were sure the ref was going to give a penalty try. They kept asking him and asking him and the ref was annoyed because he didn't like being shouted at. We didn't say a word. England had the best kicker in Britain playing full-back. Simon Hodgkinson was my teammate at Nottingham. A brilliant kicker. But England didn't want to kick it over, they wanted to push us over, wanted to humiliate us. Mooro wanted it more than anybody. He forgot that there were eight guys on the other side who didn't want to be humiliated. Well, seven and a half guys. Whitey wasn't all there.

**Simon Hodgkinson:** I wasn't consulted. You'd like to think you'd have slotted the kick if you were asked. But it was a wind where nothing was guaranteed.

**Damian Cronin:** Mooro seemed to be calling the shots, not Carling. They had a bit of a conflab after three or four scrums went down and then Mooro decided to go for the tap penalty. He calls up Hilly and Hilly gives it to The Judge. He trundles it up and we eat him. I was going, 'We can defend this all day long, boys'.

**David Bishop:** 'Offside, Scotland! Penalty, England!'

**Damian Cronin:** The Judge has another trundle.

**Robin Marlar**, **Sunday Times**: *Did England really think if they threw themselves at the Scots from a tapped penalty they would carry all before them? Thus, in their wisdom, did English generals murder a generation in World War I.*

**Derek White:** I'm still on the field, still on one leg, still helpless.

**David Bishop:** 'Penalty, England!'

**Brian Moore:** 'Scrum!'

**Jeff Probyn:** Sole droppin' it was a problem, but so was Kenny Milne. Kenny was strong and he was hard, hard work. He was holding it together for the lot of them.

**John Jeffrey:** 'Come on, boys!'

**Kenny Milne:** It feels like we've been there an hour, trapped in our corner, hanging on for our lives. Probably should have been a penalty try. I didn't understand why Soley was collapsing because I didn't feel Paul or myself were under any pressure. I said to Soley, 'Just keep it up', and Soley did and the ball comes flying out the tunnel and Craig Chalmers hoofs it away. There was this immense roar from the crowd. Just the most incredible noise swept around the stadium.

**Will Carling:** People talk about not going for goal being the turning point. The abuse I got for that. Fucking hell. Not being funny, but bollocks. We should have had a penalty try but, okay, we never got it. My view is, it's far out on the right hand side, it's a hard kick, so keep ploughing on in the scrum.

That was a lesson for me because I asked the wrong guys. I asked Mooro, who loses all rational thought from about Thursday. 'Can we shove them back, Mooro?' 'Course I fucking can, course I fucking can'. And Richard Hill, a similar sort of guy. 'Take the scrum! Bastards!' I should have asked Winters or Ackers. They were calmer. Winters might have said, 'Mate, have a go for the posts, what harm would it do?' That was a lesson. I didn't know my players well enough. There was no point in asking some of those guys for sensible advice in those circumstances. With Mooro, maybe it was an ego thing.

**Wade Dooley:** People say we were cheated. No. You do what you have to do. If Sole collapses the scrum two yards out on six occasions and gets away with it, all credit to Sole. It's up to me and Probyn to keep him up. Sole survived. That's what you do. You try and survive, by any means necessary.

**David Sole:** Correct.

Derek White was taken out of his misery and removed from the field, the Hawick policeman Derek Turnbull replacing him. Turnbull was only the sixteenth player Scotland had used in the entire championship.

Nobody had any doubts about his ability to get the job done, Telfer least of all. At the beasting session during the week, Telfer used Turnbull's uncompromising spirit to make a point to his pack. 'Would you kick your granny to get the ball off England?' he asked. But before the boys had a chance to answer, Telfer pointed to Turnbull and shouted: 'He would. And he's only a sub!'

A Craig Chalmers penalty shortly before half-time made it 9–4 at the break, a complete triumph for a Scotland team that had conceded the only try and had spent long periods on their line defending a series of scrums with only seven fit forwards.

**Chris Gray:** Everything we did right was roared to the rafters by the crowd.

**Iwan Tukalo:** Didn't matter if it was an inch or twenty metres. It was my eleventh time playing at Murrayfield and the noise was never like this before. Or after.

**John Jeffrey:** There was a hostility there, definitely. It wasn't the normal atmosphere.

**Brian Moore:** You can pick out individual faces and hear what's being said. Oh yeah, absolutely. I collect the ball for a line-out and you look into the crowd and you can see it clear enough.

**Simon Hodgkinson:** My parents were up – and they hated it. They'd been watching rugby for twenty-odd years and they said it was the most aggressive atmosphere they'd ever seen. The national pride and patriotism, which you'd expect, spilled over into something more. It was vitriolic. They said they'd never go back again.

**Jerry Guscott:** I'd never played a Test match in Edinburgh before. I'd heard everybody saying what a wonderful place it was, but I didn't see that. As an Englishman you weren't welcome there. As far as I was concerned I was just a young guy playing the game I loved. But in Scotland I figured out that the Calcutta Cup was more than rugby. I didn't mind banter. I enjoyed it. But hate and jealousy, they're evils really.

**Geoff Cooke:** We should have been in control of the game by half-time, instead of being 9–4 behind. But I was confident the points would come. Scotland had got lucky, that was my view. And they couldn't get lucky the whole game.

**Gavin Hastings:** I kicked off the second half, gave it too much welly and the ball went out on the full. First time I'd done it since my debut four years earlier.

**Geoff Cooke:** So we had a scrum back on the halfway line and I'm rubbing my hands. Excellent. We've rehearsed this a hundred times. It goes right, Hodgy comes up from full-back and kicks it down in the corner and we're back on the Scottish line.

**Kenny Milne:** It was their put-in, but we got a wee movement in the scrum, about six inches. And six inches in a scrum is a lot.

**Mike Teague:** The ball came through the scrum at a hundred miles an hour. I tried to pick it up and dropped the thing.

**Geoff Cooke:** Why Mike Teague went to pick it up, I don't know.

**Mick Skinner:** You could ask Teaguey, but I bet he wouldn't know himself.

**Mike Teague:** Bollocks, I knew what I was doing. I didn't hear them complaining when I picked it up at the back of the scrum and made the surge for our try. I didn't hear them giving out when I tried it again a few minutes later and ran about a mile and a half downfield. I did it because it had worked the two times I'd tried it before.

**John Jeffrey:** It was our scrum now. What happened with Teaguey made me all the more conscious that I had to get the pick-up spot-on. We called a set move: Fiji. We'd tried it in the first half and it went wrong.

**Gary Armstrong:** That was my fault. Gavin gave me a bollocking.

**John Jeffrey:** We needed fast ball and we got it. I was up and away, drew in the wing-forward, and gave it to Gary.

**Gary Armstrong:** The first time we did it, I gave the pass to Gav too early. I wasn't making that mistake again. I held it and held it, waited for Rob Andrew and Mike Teague to get to me and then let it go.

**Gavin Hastings:** I was looking for a gap to run into, but there wasn't one. Rory Underwood was coming across to me. I'd no choice. I had to kick it. Just kick it infield a bit and hope that someone was around to chase it.

**Tony Stanger:** The Scottish way, from when I was starting off in the game, was to minimise the mistakes. 'No errors, lads, that's the most important thing'. That's what I was told since I was a young fella. Across all of Scottish rugby it was drilled into you, mistakes are not acceptable, which is fair enough, but you're not going to try anything, are you? It's easy to fall into the trap of saying, 'I must not make any mistakes today', and you put that down as a success if you achieve it. But it's not really.

I never got much ball, not in the big games. Against the Fijis and the Romanias I got plenty, but when push came to shove we played it through the forwards all the time. It made sense, I knew that. But my biggest challenge sometimes was to stay focused and be ready for any chance that came my way. And here it was.

**John Jeffrey:** The ball was in the air. It was Stanger versus Underwood. Our fastest guy against their fastest guy.

**Mick Skinner:** I'm running behind the two boys, knowing that the bounce is crucial. It bounces straight or a bit to the left, then Stanger scores. It bounces a bit to the right and Underwood saves us. The Jocks got the right bounce.

**Tony Stanger:** This will sound strange, but I don't really remember it. I look at the video now and it's like somebody else scored that try. Twenty years on, I can't quite believe that it's me. I don't remember seeing the ball in the air in front of me. I think instinct had taken over. Like driving a car. You go from A to C and sometimes you can't remember going through B, but you did. Chasing the kick, reaching up for the ball, I did it automatically, without even thinking. It was only later that I thought about my collarbone – and then suddenly I was in pain again.

**Mike Teague:** A bloke comes into my bar in Gloucester and says, 'You're Mike Teague, you fucked up at that scrum in Murrayfield'. This was in 2008! Twenty years I've been listening to that.

**John Jeffrey:** I'm not sure Tony got the ball down, you know.

**Mike Teague:** What?

**Jim Telfer:** I maintain it wasn't a try. He didn't touch it down.

**Mike Teague:** Now you tell me.

**Jim Telfer:** Every time I've seen it I think, 'Look at that, the most famous try in the history of Scottish rugby and he didn't get it down'.

**Tony Stanger:** It was a definite try.

**Jim Telfer:** It's always been dubious to me.

**Brian Moore:** Bishop gave it. End of story.

**Roger Uttley:** We're 13–4 behind. It's a travesty, really. But there's a long way to go. We had cut them open once, we can do it again.

**Wade Dooley:** We regained control of the game. We're deep in their half and I hit a ruck and whatever I collided with, my neck was jolted backwards and I got this indescribable pain across my shoulders and pins and needles down my arms and fingers and a terrifying numbness. I just rolled over, convinced

I'd broken my neck. I was lying there, absolutely certain that something fucking terrible had happened to me. Some of the Scottish boys came over. Fair play to them. Soley and Finlay had a word. After three or five minutes I started to feel okay again so I carried on. The wife nearly killed me for not going off.

**John Jeffrey:** I gave away a penalty after about fifteen minutes of the second half: 13–7 now.

**Scott Hastings:** Just after that, I made a comment and I deeply regret it.

**Jerry Guscott:** I didn't hear it.

**Scott Hastings:** Jerry was down getting treatment and my head was buzzing and I just blurted it out: 'Get off the pitch, you black English bastard'. As soon as I said it, it felt like Murrayfield suddenly went quiet. There was all this noise and then I said it – and then silence. Jesus, I was embarrassed. I cringe even now. It wasn't meant to be racist. It was just something stupid I said in the heat of battle.

**Jerry Guscott:** If I didn't hear it, then it didn't bother me. These things happen in that kind of environment. People do strange things.

**Rory Underwood:** The longer the match went on, the hungrier I got for the ball. 'Just gimme it, boys. I'll find space, we'll get through, we'll definitely get through'. We were banging on the door but the door bloody well wouldn't open. Scotland were scrambling like lunatics. There was no shape to it, no system. They were all over the place but they kept making their tackles.

**Will Carling:** The crowd is raucous the whole game. In our ears non-stop. Anytime I go near the touchline I get a mouthful of abuse. Some of it is nasty. You think, 'Right, we're going to get this try and we're going to win this game and you lot are gonna be sickened'.

**David Sole:** There was an anti-English feeling that went beyond a healthy sporting rivalry. I didn't like that side of it.

**Paul Ackford:** Will and Mooro were the real targets. Mooro had a chip on his shoulder about the Scots. He thinks he's right about everything. He just crusades through life. You don't have an argument with Mooro. He doesn't entertain any other opinion. He's good at internalising anything that can give him an edge. Anything he thinks is unfair or if something is said against him he'll use it as a motivation. And there was plenty said against him at Murrayfield.

**Rory Underwood:** Finally, I spot a gap. Between Scott Hastings and Iwan Tukalo there is a lovely big space for me to attack. Carling sees it, too. Out comes the ball and through I go. Yessss!

**Will Carling:** No!

**Rory Underwood:** I'm down. How the hell am I down? I should be roaring over the try line now. I should be turning to take the congratulations of my teammates. It should be 13–11 with Hodgy's conversion to come. But I'm down!

**Scott Hastings:** I got him at the knees, slid down to his boots and managed to hang on.

**Gavin Hastings:** Scott always says he made a try-saving tackle. Underwood still had me to beat which, clearly, he would have struggled to do.

**Scott Hastings:** It would have been a try. Gavin was useless tackling on his inside.

**Jim Telfer:** When Scott tackled Underwood I began to think that maybe this was going to be our day. Our defence was superb. The commitment was outstanding. I couldn't fault it. I just didn't see how England could break us down.

**David Bishop:** Towards the end, England were totally bereft of ideas and started with the tap penalties again. Up came The Judge. I was thinking, 'This failed dismally in the first half, so I don't see how it's gonna work now'.

**Will Carling:** Nah, it didn't work. Nothing did. With three minutes of normal time to play I decided to have a cut. I went past Lineen and Armstrong and gave it to Rob Andrew. Scotland were all over the shop. Mark Bailey had come on for Jerry and he took Gavin Hastings on the inside. But there was always one last defender. No matter how many tackles we broke, there was always one too many.

**Iwan Tukalo:** We were camped on our own line and all the action was over in Tony's corner. All I wanted to do was get over and help, but you have your beat to control. I was like a dog on a leash.

**Jeff Probyn:** The Scots weren't dirty but they were cynical. JJ was offside that often I thought he was playing for us. He spent more time in our backline than Guscott. The longer it went on, the more I thought of Deano. Out injured all season. Hadn't missed him – until now. He was policing a football match and listening on the radio, apparently. Christ, we could have done with him. Deano would have done something to dig us out of the hole. He'd have worked it out.

**Geoff Cooke:** I thought we were going to win the game until about five seconds from the end of the match. I always felt we had a bit of magic left in our locker and it was only a matter of time before it came out.

**Mike Teague:** We were in injury time. We couldn't win the Slam now, all we could do was stop them winning it, which was a great prize in itself, to be fair. We had an attacking scrum. Me and Winters work something at the back of it and Hilly's away. JJ's trying to get to him but he runs into Bishop and falls on his arse. Go on, Hilly!

**Mick Skinner:** Hilly gives it to me and Scotland concede a penalty. It's a scrum, eight metres from their line. Sole collapses again. We tap the next penalty. We're three metres away from denying them the Slam!

**Jeff Probyn:** All sorts went on at the ruck. Calder's pulling fast ones. The ball goes out the line to Carling.

**Will Carling:** JJ nails me in the tackle. It's just desperation on our part, just blind panic. Time's nearly up. You can sense it. The crowd can sense it. They're screaming their heads off. We ain't never gonna get through this lot. It just ain't gonna happen.

There's 54,000 people in the stadium, but you feel pretty fucking lonely. I look at Bishop and he's looking at his watch. Any second now. Any second . . .

**David Bishop:** *That's it, boys. It's all over.*

**John Jeffrey:** I ran. I just bolted. Oh, my God, the elation!

**Damian Cronin:** The crowd came sprinting on to the field. It was like the charge of the light brigade. All that was missing was the trumpet blast. I was outta there.

**Kenny Milne:** Half our team ran. They wanted to get in before the crowd swallowed them up. But I said, 'No, I'm going to enjoy every minute of this'. I let the fans wash over me. Calling my name, slapping me on the back, telling me what a hero I was. I went slowly through the throng and I soaked up every second of it.

**Brian Moore:** When the final whistle went, I crouched down on the field. It was just despair, really. Absolute devastation. I know Finlay came over to sympathise with me. And it was a lovely thing to do. But to be honest, I was so fucked off it wouldn't have mattered who came up to me.

**Hugh McIlvanney, Observer:** *It is hard to exaggerate the exquisite, unforgettable pleasure the Scots took from leaving the ancient enemy dazed among the rubble of their delusions. A couple of the English players clutched their brows at the end of the match as the shock and lasting pain of what had happened to them began to penetrate. Plenty of Scots will be holding their heads this morning but the causes will be more temporary and less regrettable.*

**Jeff Probyn:** Our dressing room? Hard to describe how grim it was.

**Paul Rendall:** There was fellas crying, for sure.

**Will Carling:** I used it for years afterwards. 'Remember how we felt at Murrayfield'. Bloody horrible.

**Roger Uttley:** I walked in there and it was like a morgue. There wasn't a word spoken, just the sound of boots being discarded and heavy sighing. I'd been in a lot of disappointed dressing rooms before, but this was unlike anything I'd experienced. The silence was murderous. And all the time you could hear the roars of the Scottish crowd outside and then the sound of 'Flower of Scotland' being sung in the opposition dressing room.

**Jerry Guscott:** I didn't feel the emotion the others were feeling. I'm not all that emotional a person, to be honest. If you haven't got it in you, you haven't got it in you. It doesn't mean you're not passionate. I thought the game was a bit of a 'mare, but that was about it. There'd be other days. Grown men were crying next to me, showing everything on the outside. I was gutted, but I wasn't crying.

**Mick Skinner:** I went out of the dressing room to talk to somebody for five minutes, went back in and my jersey was gone and in its place was a can of McEwan's Export. Marvellous. They denied us a Grand Slam and now they were robbin' us as well.

**Paul Ackford:** We went back to the Carlton Highland Hotel. There was a Scottish bloke waiting for us at the door. He was well pissed, but harmless.

'You enjoy yourself, big man?' he says.

'I've had better afternoons.'

'How'd you fancy buying a Grand Slam tie?' he asks.

'You want the honest answer?'

**Brian Moore:** We were dignified in defeat. I know we were. They all said it. But it was hard.

**Dick Best:** It was a complete and utter fucking nightmare. I had been invited for drinks back to the Heriot's club after the game and I said to my wife, 'I don't really fancy this'. She said, 'No, we're going'. Of course, the Scots were ecstatic. And who was the only Englishman in the Heriot's clubhouse? Yours truly.

**Mick Skinner:** I thought I was the dog's bollocks before that game. I was Jack the Lad, the best No. 6 around. It was all a load of shite. I'm in my hotel room thinking, 'What the fuck! I've got to go downstairs now, into a dinner with the Scottish team, all giving it large on the whisky. Nightmare!' There were punters shouting, 'Do you know how much you cost me!' Sorry, boys. I put a good show on that night, in fairness. Tried me best. Learned a bit of humility. Became a better person, I feel. I gained from it. I immediately stopped believing in my own press. I questioned myself from that day on.

**Will Carling:** I was twenty-four years old and deep down I knew I would have other days. But I wasn't thinking like that. I was thinking, 'This is the end of the world'. For me, it stopped right there, round about half past four on Saturday 17 March 1990.

**David Sole:** We had a royal delegation come in to see us. Peter Phillips, son of the Princess Royal and first grandchild of the Queen, turned up in a Scotland cap and a tartan scarf. I gave him my jersey.

**Derek White:** Was Telfer complimentary? He was pleased, but he didn't go overboard with his praise.

**Damian Cronin:** He was probably watching the video somewhere, probably saw me going into a ruck about a millimetre too high at some stage and was getting the evidence together to berate me.

**Kenny Milne:** No, he'd have been looking at the line-outs again. 'Kenny, one of your throws was an eighth of an inch offline. You're a disgrace, man!'

**John Jeffrey:** He'd have been thinking about the penalty I gave away to make it 13–7. 'JJ, about your fuck-up . . .'

**Chris Gray:** We were knackered. Totally spent. I sat down and didn't get up for ages. I looked over at Creamy and he was happy, but his emotions were in check, as ever. I looked at him and thought to myself: 'I owe that man my career'. But you wouldn't tell him. Oh, Christ, no. But it's true.

**John Jeffrey:** All Jim ever wanted was for us to win. That's all that mattered to him. Victory, not popularity. All the pack would have had their moments with him, their nights when they thought he was the biggest sadist that ever walked the face of the earth. But when it came down to it, the respect we had for him was immense.

**Kenny Milne:** Yes.

**Damian Cronin:** No doubt about it.

**David Sole:** Absolutely.

**Derek White:** Aye.

**Jim Telfer:** I can't remember saying much after the game, but I was elated. We'd beaten England and that kind of thing didn't happen very often. We'd beaten them to the Grand Slam and that was a first. If I was quiet in the dressing room it was probably just me letting the players get on with it. Because it was their victory, their day. They were a fantastic group. Especially the forwards. Hard as nails. Honest. Hungry. All the things you look for. I was proud of them, every last one of them. Oh aye. Proud.

# CHAPTER 21

# ENGLAND'S RETREAT – AND THE AFTERLIFE

Will Carling was magnanimous in defeat. He had no gripes with the result, no moans about the penalty try that never was. He went into the Scottish dressing room and paid tribute to the victors. Everybody said he handled the disappointment with a lot of class.

But Carling was a man under fire. The press were on his case about his captaincy and the fact that it looked like Mooro was the one calling the shots out there.

*Did you bottle it, Will?*

*Did you go AWOL?*

He soaked it up, but just wanted to get away from Murrayfield as fast as he could. On the way back to the hotel, he looked out of the window of the team bus and saw the masses heading for town. When the Scottish supporters saw the England team coming through the traffic, they shouted and waved their flags, one of them a giant saltire with *Bannockburn 1314* printed in the middle and *Murrayfield 13–7* added just below.

The captain retired to the hotel bar and drowned his sorrows. Later – much, much later – two friendly porters at the Carlton Highland helped him to his room, while a third, less sympathetic, colleague brought up the rear, landing frequent boots to

Carling's backside as they swayed down the corridor. Carling was in no state to respond. All he wanted was his bed.

He was the first of the England team to leave town the next morning. For reasons that are a mystery to him now, he had to get to London early on Sunday, so he threw his stuff in a bag and headed for Edinburgh airport. The place was awash with dishevelled rugby folk, up-all-nighters still giving it a rattle. Some were English, some were Scots, but all of them were on Carling's back from the moment they saw him. 'One Scottish guy came over to me, spat in my face, and walked off. I mean, bollocks to that. The whole thing had moved over from a keen rivalry to something personal, something spiteful. It was a political cesspit. A nasty environment. I thought, Right, okay, if this is the way it has to be, then fair enough. I don't like it, but I'll deal with it. And I'll never lose to you bastards again'.

He got pelted with flak post-Murrayfield. The papers forgot about his tumultuous performances in the first three games and rounded on him for his lack of authority in the Edinburgh maelstrom. 'Is it all so shallow that one match makes all the difference?' he asked. But he knew the answer to that already. Only rarely did the mask slip and the insecurities show. In a brief glimpse of the hidden Carling he said: 'I can't always fool myself that I enjoy it'.

In the summer of 1990, England toured Argentina and lost their opening game against a club side from Buenos Aires. The captain went nuts. 'I absolutely fucking ripped into them. Hilly was saying, "Will, woah, woah, calm down", and I thought, "Hang on, if Hilly is telling me to calm down then how bad have I got?" I had a huge amount of pent-up frustration after the loss of the Grand Slam. How long did it last? Years.'

Carling made good on his promise. He played the Scots eight times after 1990 – and won all eight games. In 1991 he made his return to Murrayfield and beat JJ and the boys 9–6 in a fractious World Cup semi-final. He led England to the long-awaited

Grand Slam the same season. The following year, they recorded their biggest victory in Edinburgh since 1921 – and Carling claimed a second Slam.

He went on to use the aggression of the Scots as a motivational tool throughout the 1990s. Somebody told him of an Edinburgh bar that had pictures of Margaret Thatcher, Saddam Hussein and himself placed in their urinals. He spoke to the manager. 'Well, Saddam gets the least amount of business', he said. 'Our customers seemingly forgive mass genocide and prefer urinating on Maggie and yourself. I've seen them bursting for a pee but hanging on until either you or her come free. Then they let you have it.'

'That doesn't surprise me,' said Carling.

'It's actually not even that close between the two of you,' said the manager.

'No?'

'No. I'd say it's about seventy per cent you.'

'I feel honoured,' said Carling.

'Aye, you're a very popular man.'

Five years after Murrayfield, England and Scotland met again in a Grand Slam showdown, this time at Twickenham. Carling's pre-match speech was Hillyesque, a thunderous denunciation of all things Scottish. He was banging on about settling old scores and 'doing to them what they did to us' when he noticed a certain unease in the ranks.

'Er, Will, what are you talking about?' asked the full-back Mike Catt.

'Nineteen bloody ninety!' Carling snapped.

'But we weren't there in 1990,' said Kyran Bracken, the scrum-half.

Carling looked around the room and counted the survivors: Mooro, Guscott, Rob Andrew and himself. Only four of them left. Time was moving on.

England won that Grand Slam, too. His success didn't go down well in Scotland, even among those who had only a passing interest in rugby. On the morning of the 1996 game he went for a walk through the streets of Edinburgh and happened upon a group of kids standing outside a shop, none of them more than nine years old.

'There's that Will Carling,' said the leader. And then his mates chirped in the background. Carling was a dick, he was an arse-hole, he was going to get his head kicked in at Murrayfield, he was going to be taken home to his mammy crying. The wiseguys fell about the place laughing. Carling didn't say a word, but he saw an opportunity.

He went into the shop and headed for the pick 'n' mix. He got the largest bag he could find, a veritable sack, and started shovelling sweets inside. Kola Kubes and Cola Bottles, Pear Drops and Lemon Sherbets, Dolly Mixtures and Liquorice Allsorts and Chocolate Mice. He filled it up to overflowing, handed over his money and stepped outside.

'Hey, guys,' he said to the kids. 'Got sweets here. Anybody want some sweets?'

The group went quiet.

'Mmmm,' said Carling, unwrapping a Fruit Bonbon and drop-ping it in his mouth. 'Fantastic.'

The boys were looking at each other now. 'What do we do? He's got sweets!'

The leader stepped forward. 'The bag is all yours,' said the England captain, 'but you gotta say something to me first. You gotta say, "Will Carling is a good guy!" You think you can do it, big fella?'

The kid looked inside the bag, looked up at Carling and looked to his pals, who looked away. He was on his own now. 'Okay,' he mumbled. 'Will Carling is a good guy.'

The booty was handed over and the boy backed away, then turned on his heels and ran, his mates sprinting in his slipstream. They got fifty yards down the road when suddenly they stopped and roared as one, 'No, you're not, you're a bastard!' Carling could hear them laughing. He laughed, too. As for the last laugh, though, he had it to himself. England won the game 18–9. Then in 1997, in his sixty-ninth cap of an eventual seventy-two, he scored a try in a 41–13 pummelling of the Scots at Twickenham, a record England win in his final appearance against the Auld Enemy.

As the decade moved on, Carling started to make headlines less for his rugby and more for the turbulence in his private life. When, in 1995, the *News of the World* revealed details of his friendship with Princess Diana, it removed the final string that was holding together his unhappy marriage to Julia Smith. The couple separated and divorced soon after. Mooro's definition of tragedy comes to mind again. 'Tragedy is not tree falls on man but tree falls on man because man has a habitual tendency to walk under trees, when he shouldn't do.'

In 1998, Carling ended his relationship with Ali Cockayne, his bride-to-be and the mother of his eleven-month-old son. He left the family home for a new life with Lisa Cooke, the wife of a former teammate at Harlequins. A few days after their split, Cockayne was photographed by a paparazzo. She was in tears with baby Henry in her arms. The *Sun* put it on the front page. Overnight, Carling was Britain's biggest cad. His business interests collapsed under the tidal wave of hostility. Plans for a testimonial game and dinner were abandoned, ITV dropped him from a sports series and a nationwide theatre tour, *An Evening with Will Carling*, was ditched. His new autobiography tanked. The *Daily Record* discovered that sales of his life story in Scotland amounted to two copies – and then appealed to the purchasers to come forward and admit their guilt.

The man who had had it all suddenly had nothing. He considered driving a taxi to make a living. He withdrew from public life and hoped that the storm would pass by one day. And it did. Carling married Lisa Cooke in 1999 and they have two children together, as well as two from her previous marriage and young Henry, who comes to visit. 'Lisa is very extrovert,' says Carling. 'She's very sociable, she's part Italian and gets her energy from being around people. She's changed me for the better. Every-body says it. All the guys with England and Harlequins say that I'm a different person now. I'm still shy and I'm still insecure about things, but I'm not as serious as I used to be. I'm more relaxed. I can take the piss out of myself.'

He is still heavily involved in the game, both as an occasional media pundit and as owner of a successful sports corporate hospitality company, Will Carling Management. He says that 1990 doesn't get thrown at him that often any more. 'About a dozen times a day, tops.'

Mooro woke with a heavy sigh the morning after. There was something he had to do that Sunday, something he'd committed to, something he was dreading but couldn't back away from now. He had to go to a Grand Slam bash at Myreside, the home ground of the Watsonians club in Edinburgh, the heartland of Hastings country.

A week earlier, Mooro had told Chris Gray he'd go to the Sunday bash. Gray had told Gavin, Gavin had told Scott and word had got round after that. 'See, I thought I was going to walk in there as a Grand Slam winner,' said Mooro. 'I thought I was going to have a marvellous time. That's why I said yes in the first place. If I'd known we were going to lose, I'd have told them to bugger off.'

Myreside was packed from early morning. People were merry on tequila and champagne from breakfast time onwards. A brass band turned up and started playing jive music on a makeshift stage. There was singing and dancing and record amounts of drinking. By the time Mooro walked in, the place was like the maddest disco on earth.

'If I'd pulled out, it would have looked cheap, so I went through with it. From the second I walked in the door it was a searing experience. They rubbed it in, in a very public way. There was gloating on a grand scale. Some of it went over the line, little snippets. Most of it was good-humoured, which made it worse, actually. People were laughing at me. I'd rather they just abused me. Then I could be violent.'

They called on him to make a speech. 'I made myself do it. I didn't want to, but there were catcalls and all sorts and I said, "No, this is something I have to do". I was pretty handy on my feet and had a few put-downs ready. I just congratulated them on their victory, said it was well deserved, said they seemed to want it more than we did. I wished them luck. I was affable. Or as affable as I could be in the circumstances. But I was hurting. The whole thing really did cut me. It was hard.'

**Iwan Tukalo:** I always stick up for Mooro. I talk to Scots and they all say what an absolute arsehole he is: 'He's just a biased, arrogant little man'. So I say, 'You don't understand the guy'. Would I have had as much dignity as him if the roles had been reversed and I was down in England having just lost a Grand Slam? I'm not sure I'd have been as gracious as he was. That's the side of him people never saw.

**Scott Hastings:** Brian spoke to a silent crowd. And he spoke brilliantly. You had to say fair play to the guy. That took some amount of balls.

**Paul Burnell:** I didn't particularly like him, but I was at Myreside that day as well and I thought, 'Maybe I'm going to have to reassess you, Mooro'. Because it was a classy thing to do.

**Chris Gray:** I was really embarrassed at the way some of the Watsonians guys were shooting their mouths off. They'd had too much to drink and were coming out with a load of anti-English rubbish. People thought, 'Ah, this won't bother Mooro, he's a tough old boy'. But it did bother him. Christ, it did.

Mooro left town that night with the funereal beat of 'Flower of Scotland' playing in his head. For the rest of his career he took immense pleasure in inflicting defeat upon the Scots, particularly the 1991 World Cup semi-final at Murrayfield. In a gesture that illustrated how sour things had become between the teams, some of the Scottish players turned up at the final at Twickenham wearing the colours of England's opponents –

Australia. He stored away the image of the Scots bedecked in Wallaby gold for future reference.

At Murrayfield in 1994, England won a tight match thanks to a Jon Callard penalty late in the game. Mooro was standing near the touchline as Callard prepared to kick. 'I took on board the advice from the crowd, some of it physically impossible even if I had been a contortionist,' he said. 'When the ball sailed between the posts, I gestured to the Scottish fans with both hands in a Churchillian manner to acknowledge the win. I was lucky I wasn't lynched.'

Over the years, a lot of Scots have got in touch with Mooro. 'I got hate mail,' he says. 'Sheds-full. I got one letter and he was still swearing on the ninth page. Remarkable. People kept writing to me, saying "The day of devolution is coming, Moore, and you'll have played a great part in it". I said, "Good. If you think I'm that influential, marvellous! Fuck off on your own, then. If you're on your own you can't blame us for anything, can you?"'

Mooro won the last of his sixty-four England caps at the 1995 World Cup, but his battles with the Scots have continued periodically in the years since. The year after he retired he went to Edinburgh for the Calcutta Cup and the first three taxis at the airport refused to take him. 'I was at a dinner in Scotland with Fin Calder and I was getting a bit of stick. Fin said to the punters, "Look, can you get off his back, he's a good friend of mine, please show him a bit of respect". Then everybody stood up and sang "Swing Low Sweet Chariot". I told them, "I'm genuinely astonished by that. Thank you very much. But what you don't know is I fucking hate that song. Mind you, it's not any worse than that dirge of an anthem you've got". And there was this great "Booooo!"'

'It's true, though. "Flower of Scotland" is cheap and juvenile. It's a crutch. It's like the bogeyman. It's an excuse to hate us. After I said my piece, loads of people came up to me. "Dinnae tell anyone I told you this, Mooro, but I agree with you". Hehehe. Brilliant. Nowadays, I ham it up with the Scots. It's just me being mischievous. I haven't watched that game again, though. Never have, never will. I've no need to watch it. I have it all in my head. I can tell you everything that happened that day. I'll not forget it. Ever.'

Mooro's professional life has gone off in all sorts of directions since 1990. He is a qualified solicitor and a trained manicurist but earns his living nowadays as a sports columnist for the *Daily Telegraph* – he was shortlisted for a prize at the British Press Awards in 2009 – and a rugby analyst for the BBC, where his uncompromising take on things regularly causes ructions among old friends north of the border.

Jerry Guscott grew to dislike Calcutta Cup games in Scotland. He played at Murrayfield on four more occasions and, though he won all four, he doesn't look back on those with any affection.

Hyped as the Prince of Centres from his earliest days at Bath, he had no trouble living up to that billing. In a storied international career, he won sixty-five caps and played on three Lions tours – memorably sealing the 1997 series in South Africa with one of the most famous drop goals in rugby history.

His partnership with Will Carling in the England midfield stayed largely intact for seven years. They started forty-four Tests together, as well as one for the 1993 Lions, but there was always an edge between them. Guscott was the rebel, Carling the Establishment figure. Guscott was the working class boy, the hod carrier in his previous life. Carling came from money and the army. Both of them had a desperate desire to be the match winner every time they played, so their egos collided.

After 1990, England decided that a more pragmatic and less flamboyant style of rugby was required if they were going to win a Grand Slam. Carling endorsed the shift in emphasis. Guscott opposed it, but had no choice but to go along with it. When they secured their Grand Slam in 1991 they did it by playing forward-dominated rugby. They scored just five tries, compared to their twelve in 1990. 'When we lost the Grand Slam in Scotland, it had a profound impact on the way we played the game for the next two or three years,' said Guscott. 'We took less risks, we played down-to-earth rugby through the forwards. I can't say it was always fulfilling on a personal level because I wanted us to throw the ball around and express ourselves. But we won three Grand Slams. And you can't argue with that.'

After ten years at the very top of the game, and with thirty England tries in his sixty-five Tests, Guscott retired in 1999. He is still a regular on the circuit as a rugby analyst for the BBC.

Geoff Cooke is credited with restoring pride to the England side after their years in the doldrums. As team manager, he inherited an ill-disciplined, demotivated rabble and brought order and, eventually, success. He oversaw two Grand Slam victories and was manager of the 1993 Lions tour before resigning from the RFU in 1994. He says he had done what he had set out to do by then, but some of his players believe that he went, at least in part, because he was fed up of dealing with the politics of the Union. For the past few years he has been involved in consultancy work for the RFU but intends to retire in the summer of 2010. 'Time to go out to pasture,' he says.

Roger Uttley's relationship with some of the Scottish forwards on the Lions tour in 1989 was testy at best, so getting beaten by them at Murrayfield was a bitter blow. And it was made worse by the fact that his flight home on the Sunday after the game wasn't until late in the evening. 'I had to mooch around Edinburgh with everybody going ballistic,' he says. 'It was a long, long day.'

After 1990, Uttley's rapport with Will Carling took a nose-dive. Carling, on the advice of some of his senior forwards, encouraged the involvement of his Harlequins coach, Dick Best, in the England set-up. Uttley took it as a challenge to his position. 'It was all part of the fallout from the Murrayfield match. I was a bit wary of Will from that point onwards, but it was a long time ago now. He said a few years ago that he regretted that we never sat down and spoke about things. And I regret that, too, to be honest.'

Uttley departed as England coach after the 1991 World Cup, returned as team manager in 1997 before exiting the sharp end of professional rugby two years later. For more than twenty years, he was Director of Physical Education at Harrow School in Middlesex. He retired in 2009.

To the undoubted relief of his parents, Simon Hodgkinson never played at Murrayfield again, winning the last of his fourteen caps at the World Cup in 1991. He is now co-owner of the burgeoning rugby clothing equipment company Samurai International Sportswear.

Rory Underwood had gone to Murrayfield in the form of his life, scoring nine tries in the four Tests before the Grand Slam. Denied his one sniff of a score by Scott Hastings, he resumed his prolific strike rate in his very next game, claiming a hat-trick against the Pumas in the autumn. He stayed at the top level for twelve years, calling it a day in 1996 having scored a record forty-nine tries in his eighty-five Tests. Only Jason Leonard has won more England caps than Underwood.

In his eighteen years as an RAF pilot, Underwood rose to the rank of flight lieutenant. He left the RAF in 2001 and became a business performance consultant. In 2009, he set up a new company, Wingman, from his home in the East Midlands. He maintains a connection with his old club, Leicester, where he is a non-executive director.

Simon Halliday played for England until 1992, when a persistent ankle injury ended his playing days. 'The RFU told me they'd look after me if I ever needed an operation on the ankle,' says Halliday. 'Then, when I told them I had to get the op, they sent me a letter saying they couldn't be seen funding the medical bills of former players. That was disgusting, to be honest. But it was the way it was back then. It left a nasty taste in the mouth.'

Halliday stayed involved in rugby in an administrative capacity, spending nine years as a member of the council of the RFU and another two as a non-executive director at his old club, Bath. He left that position in the summer of 2009. He earns his living in the City of London, where he is a merchant banker.

Rob Andrew was England's fly-half for another seven years, off and on. He won seventy-one caps and says he owes a debt of gratitude to Ian McGeechan for turning his career around on the Lions tour of 1989. Geech was his coach again on the 1993 tour. 'I only worked with him for two summers and I wish we'd had longer,' said Andrew, who followed his mentor into coaching. Andrew had eleven eventful years coaching Newcastle before moving in 2006 to the high-powered post of Director of Elite Rugby at the RFU.

Richard Hill, the tempestuous figure in the No. 9 jersey, played his final Test in the World Cup final in 1991. When the game went professional, he quickly turned to full-time coaching, cutting his teeth at Gloucester and Harlequins before taking over at Newport and then spending six years at Bristol, where he remained until 2009.

'I learned a lot from that day at Murrayfield,' he says. 'It was the first time I noticed psychology on the rugby field. The singing of "Flower of Scotland" and the impact of the slow walk on the crowd was masterful, really.' Hilly is now coach of Chalon-sur-Saône in the third division of the French championship.

At thirty-six, Paul Rendall was the oldest man on the field in 1990 and, alas, he was the only England player who never got the chance to make amends for the disappointment. He lost his place in the front row to Jason Leonard the following year and sat on the bench throughout the 1991 Grand Slam season. He won his final cap against Italy in the group stages of the World Cup that autumn. The Judge remains a much-loved character and now coaches Slough Rugby Club.

Jeff Probyn's battles with David Sole continued, spilling over, at times, into a war of words played out in the tabloids. After the 1991 Calcutta Cup, Probyn complained bitterly about some of Sole's scrummaging tactics, saying that if he didn't stop what he was doing the Scot was going to end up breaking an opponent's neck. Sole rubbished Probyn's criticism and retaliated by accusing his opponent of habitual cheating. The following year, in his autobiography, Sole wrote that it was 'a terrible indictment on international referees that Probyn is not pulled up for the things he does. It is blatantly illegal and everybody knows that he does it.' In Probyn's own autobiography, published in 1993, he said that Sole had a psychological block about playing against him.

At his peak, Probyn was considered one of the finest props in the world and the fact that he was never selected for a Lions tour is seen in the English game – and beyond – as a great injustice. His big mate was, and still is, Paul Rendall. Having roomed together for years on international trips, they are now alongside each other in the history books as the oldest and second oldest players to have played for England. The Judge was 37 years and 232 days when he made his last appearance, Probyn was 36 years and 334 days when he bowed out at the end of the Five Nations championship of 1993.

Probyn sold the family furniture business and has been semi-retired since 2002. He does some rugby punditry on TalkSport radio.

Wade Dooley continued to bring his unique brand of menace to the England team for three more seasons, retiring in 1993 at the age of thirty-five with fifty-five caps to his name. He left the police force in 2007 and opted for a genteel life, opening a tea room and catering business in Wrea Green on the Fylde coast.

At the end of 2008, in one of rugby's most humorous examples
of poacher turned gamekeeper, the RFU enlisted Dooley as a
citing officer in their disciplinary department, an appointment
so loaded with irony that it made headlines in the sports pages.
Even Big Wade was laughing.

Paul Ackford outranked Wade Dooley in the police force but
extra stripes on his uniform were no kind of protection from
Dooley's caustic slagging. In the autumn of 1990, England played
the Pumas at Twickenham and Ackford was floored by a punch
from Federico Mendez, the eighteen-year-old prop. In fairness
to Ackford, he never saw the blow coming and stood no chance
of protecting himself.

'His eyes had completely glazed over and he was talking like
a three-year-old,' says Dooley of his old mate. 'He got up off the
floor and his legs had gone. We called him Bambi after that.
And Dunny – after Richard Dunn, the British boxer who kept
getting knocked out. At the dinner afterwards we kept throwing
white napkins at Ackers like we were throwing in the towel.'

The greatest ever England second-row combination lasted
just another season after 1990, Ackford retiring after the 1991
World Cup final. He left the police for a career in the media and
is the rugby correspondent of the *Sunday Telegraph*.

Peter Winterbottom was an England international for eight
turbulent years before the Grand Slam showdown came along.
His international career lasted eleven years and took in fifty-
eight caps, two Grand Slams and two Lions tours. He retired
from playing in 1993. He earns his living in the world of high
finance in London.

As an illustration of how highly he was thought of, Will Carling
tells a story. 'About four or five years ago, Winters texted me and
said, "Buy *The Times* tomorrow". So I said, '"Why?", and he said,
"Just buy it". So I bought it and he'd done a column. He'd picked
his all-time best rugby team based on players he had played with

and against. And I was in the team. Honestly, I couldn't believe it. That's the truth. He was my absolute hero. One of the true England greats. Throughout all those years I wondered what he thought about me as a player, but I was never going to ask him. Now I knew. Winters was the business.'

If Mike Teague had a pound for every time somebody has asked him about his famous knock-on at the scrum at the beginning of the second half he reckons he'd be a multimillionaire by now. Not that it bothers him. There wasn't a whole lot that ruffled Teaguey's feathers when he was playing and he hasn't changed much over the years. 'I know Mooro loses sleep over 1990, but that's him for you. That bloody scrum? If he hadn't hooked the ball back to me at about a hundred-mile an hour then maybe I wouldn't have dropped it. That's my story anyway and I'm sticking to it.'

He owns Teague's Bar, a popular pub on Kingsholm Road in Gloucester, right across the street from the stadium where he made his name.

A month after England lost the Grand Slam, Mick Skinner ventured north again, this time with his dad. 'My father was a long distance lorry driver and when I was growing up I didn't see that much of him,' says Skinner. 'He worked his balls off. The only time I spent with him was fishing. I always said that one day we'd go and fish in the Tweed, this legendary river packed full of salmon.

'We went up in the April. We stayed in a village in the Borders and went in for a drink the first night – me and my old man in our Harlequins jumpers. The place was alive with people. They spotted us and started singing "Flower of Scotland" before we'd taken the first sup of a pint. We responded by singing "God Save The Queen". Takes some chin, that, I can tell you. They could have killed us, but they were brilliant.

'The banter flew back and forth and, next day, me and me dad went on the Tweed and we caught this bloody great salmon. Honestly, it was the nicest thing I ever tasted in me life. I think about what happened in 1990 and I remember the sinking feeling from Murrayfield. But I also picture that lovely Scottish salmon and the bonding I did with my old man in the Borders. Bitter-sweet memories, really.'

Skinner is a computer analyst in London and remains the life and soul of any party. He became known for his ferocious tackling and revelled in the nickname Mick The Munch. A week after the Grand Slam, his No. 6 jersey from Murrayfield was returned to him. He never found out who stole it, but it didn't matter. He kept it as a constant reminder that in rugby, particularly Calcutta Cup rugby, there is no such thing as a certainty.

# CHAPTER 22

# THE IMMORTALS

On the morning of Monday 19 March David Sole, Ian McGeechan and JJ went to London. Nothing better indicated their new-found profile than their appointments in the big city – JJ and Geech were wanted on *The Terry Wogan Show*, Sole was off to meet the prime minister at Downing Street. The irony of ironies was that Will Carling, the Tory Boy of Scottish mythology, the man branded as Margaret Thatcher's captain, had also been invited to see the PM, but had turned down the offer.

Sole and his wife Jayne mingled with a celebrity crowd at Number 10. From the telly there was Cilla Black and the cast of *Coronation Street*. From the world of sport, the British gold medal winners from the Commonwealth Games and cricketing legend Sir Len Hutton. The Thatchers wasted no time in making their way to the Soles.

'Bad luck on Saturday,' said Denis.

'Don't be so stupid,' said Margaret. 'This is David Sole – the Scottish captain.'

'Oh, yes, of course. Congratulations. Very well played.'

'Thank you, Mr Thatcher.'

Geech always said that Sole was years ahead of his time as a player. Sadly for Scotland, he was also years ahead of his time as a retired player, walking away from the game in 1992 with the same determined stride as he had shown in his finest hour at Murrayfield.

He was at his peak when he quit – barely thirty, six years younger than Jeff Probyn was when the Englishman won his final cap. No doubt his young family and his burgeoning business life were part of the reason he gave it up, but there were other forces driving the decision.

Sole may have been a softly spoken leader, but he never shirked an issue and was never less than forceful in what he said. He clashed with the committee of the Scottish Rugby Union on professionalism. It was Sole's belief that the players deserved some kind of financial recognition for all the time they devoted to the game. The committee felt otherwise – and the committee ruled. The more Sole talked about players' rights, the more suspicious they became of him.

It all came to a sorry end. Just before the beginning of the 1992 Five Nations championship, word reached Sole that a senior figure at Murrayfield was bad-mouthing him behind his back. Sole was described by one of the committee's most powerful men as 'a cancer at the heart of Scottish rugby'. Upset and angry, he considered giving up the game there and then. He consulted with Geech and decided to see out the season – and then go.

In February 1992 he announced that his family and his career were his priorities and that he would be retiring from all rugby that summer. After forty-four Tests, Scotland's most famous captain and one of its finest ever players walked away.

He says he has no regrets about his decision and nothing but good memories from his Scotland days – and of one day in particular. 'It always comes up,' he says. 'The Slow Walk. Even twenty years later, people talk about it. On the morning of the game, when Geech made his really moving speech about how Scots all around the world were willing us on, it registered big time. But, as I've discovered in the years since, it was even bigger than any of us could have imagined at the time. I'd have been a quivering wreck in the dressing room had I fully realised what the day meant to people.'

Having spent many years with United Distillers and Diageo, Sole set up his own business coaching company in Edinburgh in 2001. He also does occasional rugby punditry in print and on radio and television.

Margaret Thatcher didn't see out the year 1990 as prime minister. For much of her premiership, the Scots were convinced she wasn't listening to them and that November her own party came to the conclusion that she wasn't listening to their views either. They rebelled and forced her to resign. History records that it was primarily her support for the poll tax that destroyed her. She left Downing Street in tears, but there were different emotions on show in Scotland. The *Daily Record* captured the mood of the country with its gleeful front page headline: 'Jobless At Last'.

John Major replaced her and he wasted little time in binning the poll tax. But for many in Scotland the Tories remained the party of Thatcher. When they lost power to Tony Blair's New Labour in 1997, they were wiped out north of the border, their eleven seats vanishing overnight. In a belated effort to change their image, David Cameron, elected Conservative Party leader in late 2005, apologised for the errors they made in the Thatcher era. 'The imposition of the poll tax was the most egregious,' he said. 'The decision to treat Scotland as a laboratory for experimentation was clumsy and unjust.'

In 2008, Thatcher's daughter, Carol, revealed that her mother had dementia and had been showing signs of mental deterioration for the best part of a decade. Her political legacy is guaranteed for all time, but vast parts of Scotland remain steadfast in their opposition to her premiership and still view her with an unconcealed, and unbreakable, hostility.

Ian McGeechan and his family drove back down to Leeds the day after the game. The southbound A1 was bumper to bumper with jubilant Scots returning to England. Geech was now at the centre of the rugby world, the game's most talked-about coach. Not that he had any of the trappings of fame. Anybody who saw him on the motorway in his battered old Capri must have wondered what he was doing driving such a clapped-out motor.

His other life beckoned once more, but the complications of his teaching job had not gone away. The headmaster of his school was still not happy with the amount of time Geech spent in Scotland coaching rugby and, as the months went by, it became increasingly obvious that a decision between teaching and coaching had to be made. When the ultimatum came from his boss, Geech resigned from his teaching job. 'I told the head, "I'm not giving up Scotland". And that shocked him. He wondered how I was going to make a living. I wondered that myself, to be honest. Two young kids, it could have been a serious error on my part.'

Word got out. The *Scotsman* revealed the news that Geech was now looking for work. Within a fortnight of the article appearing he received nine offers of employment. 'I got an offer from the president of the RFU at Twickenham, who said he could get me a teaching position on the south coast with all the time off I needed. I was choked. In the end, I went with Scottish Life, managed by Malcolm Murray, a great rugby man. Suddenly, I'm on full pay, pension and a new car. The Capri went into a long overdue retirement.'

Geech remained Scotland coach until 1993 before moving on to take charge of Northampton. In 1997 he renewed his partnership with Jim Telfer on the Lions tour. The fly-on-the-wall documentary *Living With Lions* shows how perfectly the two men combined the good cop, bad cop routine that proved so successful for Scotland in 1990.

He returned to Scotland as coach in 2000. Then he moved upstairs as director of rugby from 2003 to 2005 and these were the most contentious and unhappy years of his professional rugby life. Not helped by the relentless politicking behind the

scenes at Murrayfield, the one-time hero soon became unpopular for some of the decisions he made, most notably his appointment of the Australian Matt Williams as Scotland coach. Williams
fared dismally in the post.

When Geech left the SRU, it came as a relief. He returned to
club coaching with Wasps and won a Heineken Cup and a
Premiership title. In 2009, he was head coach for the Lions for
the fourth time, losing a thrilling Test series in South Africa 2–1.
His autobiography was published later the same year.

After so much success in his career, he says one of his greatest
regrets is that his father, Bob, didn't live long enough to see him
play for Scotland.

Gavin Hastings went on to captain Ian McGeechan's Lions in
New Zealand in 1993 and won sixty-one caps. By the time he
retired after the World Cup in 1995, he had broken points records
on all fronts, for Watsonians, Scotland and the Lions. He is now
a sports ambassador for HSBC and is chairman of Edinburgh
Rugby Club.

If Tony Stanger has one regret about his match-winning try it
was that it came at the start of his career rather than the end.
At twenty-one, he says, he didn't really take in the enormity of
what he'd done. He laughs off suggestions from Jim Telfer and
from some of his old teammates that he never grounded the ball
properly that day. Twenty years on, it is still the most famous
try in the history of Scottish rugby.

He stayed in the team until 1998, winning fifty-two caps – the
last of them, coincidentally, a try-scoring appearance against
England at Murrayfield. Having worked with London Irish as
their skills and fitness coach, Stanger moved back to Scotland in
2008 to become talent manager for the Scottish Institute of Sport.

Scott Hastings won his sixty-fifth – and last – cap in 1997, as a
replacement against England at Twickenham. For a period of

time he was the most capped Scottish player ever, something he may have mentioned to his big brother, Gavin, once or twice. He is a marketing consultant and a regular rugby analyst on television.

Sean Lineen may have been a kilted Kiwi, but he chose to settle in Scotland once his international career came to an end in 1992. He got into top-level professional coaching in 2003 as assistant at Glasgow and became head coach three years later, a position he still holds.

Iwan Tukalo kept his lucky crucifix with him for the further two years he played for Scotland. 'It was like a comfort blanket,' he says. He looks back on 1990 and wonders if the atmosphere at Murrayfield that day will ever be repeated. 'The collective will of the people was extraordinary and we may not see its like again. I feel honoured to have been a part of it.'

Tukalo is now group safety manager for Scottish & Southern Energy.

With his bad hair and his bloody nose, Craig Chalmers' day did not get off to a good start, but it had the perfect end. Not only were his kicks at goal critical in the winning of the Slam, but he also took home one of the three balls used that day. He donated it to his club, Melrose.

Chalmers never bought into the theory of the arrogant English. He knew most of them – and liked them. A month after the match, Harlequins came up to play in the Melrose Sevens and Will Carling was with them. 'I thought, "Fair play to you, Will". I'm sure he didn't have to come. But he did. I was having a pint with him at the Greenyards and there were some guys giving him stick. One bloke, in particular, was giving him dog's abuse. I knew the fella and he was being a real dick.

'Carling squares up to him and says, "Right, okay, let's go". The guy says, "What?" Carling goes, "You and me outside, let's fucking settle this here and now". The fella almost shat himself. I was chucklin' away at the bar. There was more to Will than people thought.'

Chalmers was Scotland's fly-half through much of the 1990s and won sixty caps. He continued performing at club level into the new millennium, appearing for Harlequins, Worcester and the Pertemps Bees. He returned to Melrose and is now club coach.

Gary Armstrong became one of Scotland's finest and feistiest players. In 1995, he left the Borders, joined Newcastle as a professional and stayed in the English league for seven years. Jonny Wilkinson, a former teammate, still rates Armstrong as one of the toughest players he's ever encountered. Jim Telfer once said that Armstrong wasn't a 'normal human being' when it came to playing through the pain barrier. Coming from Telfer, that was a hell of a compliment. He played for Scotland for nine seasons after the Grand Slam, ending a tumultuous Test career by captaining his country to the championship in 1999. He returned home to play for the Borders in 2002, eventually retiring in 2004. He now runs his own haulage company and remains an avid supporter of his old club, Jed-Forest.

When Scotland won the Five Nations in 1999, there were just two survivors from 1990 – Gary Armstrong and Paul Burnell. The Unsung, as Burnell was sometimes known in the squad, went about his business quietly. 'I was a good scrummager and I understood my limitations,' he says. 'And to compensate, I probably trained harder than anybody else.' He won fifty-two caps and is now commercial director for Biffa, a waste management company.

Unlike many others in the 1990 Scotland side, Kenny Milne didn't have big career prospects. 'I was in a dead-end job delivering pies.' For him, rugby was it. The be-all and end-all.

Jim Telfer's abuse upset him. At times, it completely crushed him. When Telfer was going around the room pelting the players with flak, some of the boys would wince when it came to Milne's turn. They knew that Del Boy could take it and that Whitey could somehow spin it around and use it as motivation. But Milne? He always seemed more sensitive than the others.

'I hated Creamy at times. The way he belittled you, I didn't think it was necessary. He destroyed my confidence. Don't get me wrong, he was a fantastic coach and I have absolute respect for him, but he could have got more out of me had he handled me differently.'

Milne played international rugby for another five years and finished in 1995 with thirty-nine caps. He has many Telfer stories from his days in the firing line. One favourite stands out. 'It's probably the only time any player ever got one over on him. It was the only time I ever managed to get the better of him, that's for sure.'

The team were at the post-match reception in Dublin in 1990 and Milne had been downing the wine at an alarming rate. 'I'd been sick at the dinner table. I was in a terrible state and then Willie Anderson, the Irish captain, got up to make his speech and he started by saying, "Isn't it nice to see Kenny looking so well", and everybody turned around to look at me. I could feel Creamy's eyes burning a hole through me. So I went up to him afterwards and I said, "Jim, honestly, it's not my fault, the lads know I'm allergic to wine and they're making me drink it".

'Later on, one of the boys heard him saying, "Kenny's not drunk, he's got an allergy to wine". I still don't know how I fooled him. It was the first and last time it ever happened.' Milne is now sales director for a printing company in Edinburgh.

Chris Gray remembers the series of scrums towards the end of the first half of the match as if it were yesterday. He remembers the sights and sounds and smells of those pivotal minutes, remembers the camaraderie of his teammates and the confusion on the faces of their counterparts. He won another dozen caps after 1990, and only twenty-two in all, but the memories of his three years in the team and of the great taskmaster, Telfer, will never fade. As he was in 1990, Gray is still a dentist in Nottingham.

Del Boy was a one-off, a curiosity whom Telfer could never figure out. Cronin would make the long trek up from Bath and Telfer admired him for that. He'd also stroll about as if he didn't care much for rugby, which Telfer could never understand. 'Creamy would call me a lazy bastard and, to be fair, I was. They said the same at Bath. I had my teammate Roger Spurrell on my case. Spurrell was an ex-paratrooper. He supposedly ate a bat once. Or bit the head off a bird. Something weird anyway. So I had Spurrell in England and Creamy in Scotland. A pair of lunatics using my arse for target practice.

'I always did my own thing, regardless. If you look at the graph of my career, it's like a yo-yo. I'd be in the Bath team and then out again. Back in and back out. I went on the sauce when I wanted, didn't train all that hard when I couldn't be bothered and just drifted along. Still managed forty-five caps, though. Not bad, eh?' Cronin went on to play for Bourges in France and then won a league championship with Wasps. He played his last Test, against England, in 1998. He's still ducking and diving in the world of antiques.

Finlay Calder may have been the most intense man Mooro had ever met, but he was also never slow to make fun of himself. He tells a story about being in a Glasgow bar with JJ and Roy Laidlaw when a big bear of a man came over for a chat.

'It's Roy Laidlaw, isn't it?' says the stranger to the Grand Slam-winning scrum-half of 1984. 'What an honour to have you in my local pub. And John Jeffrey – The White Shark! The wife will never believe me.' The man turned to Calder and addressed him with reverence. 'And you, sir, are the hardest man ever to play for Scotland. David Leslie, let me shake you by the hand!'

Leslie, openside flanker on the 1984 team, got a huge kick out of that tale, but Calder, possibly the second hardest man to play for Scotland, enjoyed it just as much. Calder retired from Test rugby after the 1991 World Cup semi-final loss to England. Himself and Mooro remain good mates. Clearly, all those years listening to the hooker lacerating 'Flower of Scotland' have hit the mark because, in 2009, Calder said the old Bannockburn war cry should be ditched as the national anthem. 'It's embarrassing,' said Calder. 'The anti-English stuff has to stop.' Once he'd finished playing, the former captain went on to coach Gala and Edinburgh Academicals. As in 1990, he makes his living as a grain merchant.

For Derek White, the satisfaction of 1990 was enormous, even though he only saw half an hour's action on the big day. Had it not been for his tries in Dublin in their first match of the championship there would have been no history made at Murrayfield, no glory to talk about through the generations. Whitey suffered badly at Jim Telfer's hands, but he never caved in. He stayed in the team until he was thirty-four, winning forty-one caps. Of the unholy trinity in the back row, he was the last to retire.

'I've met Jim lots of times in the years since and we get on fine, now that he's stopped haranguing me. We spoke about it once, after I'd finished playing. He thought he could get the best out of me by treating me that way. Was he right? I don't know. Possibly. I don't think he has any regrets. Jim said he did what he felt he had to do to get Scotland winning. He was ruthless, but, in fairness, he got the job done.' Nowadays, White is a director at Murdoch Asset Management in Hampshire.

John Jeffrey has hardly changed in twenty years. He has the same devilish wit, the same natural warmth, lives in the same house, farms the same land, and, most incredibly of all, has the same waistline. All that Kelso air in his lungs is keeping him young and healthy, he says.

To this day, there are former adversaries who'd be willing to swear on a stack of bibles that, from his first international in 1984 to his last in 1991, JJ was never onside. Others say, with absolute certainty, that in his forty matches for Scotland he set an unbreakable record for the number of unpunished infringements at rucks by one man. When his contemporaries mention these things, they're meant as compliments. For JJ is remembered as one of the most competitive animals rugby has known. He retains an involvement in the game as manager of Scotland's U-20 team and as a devoted supporter of his lifelong club, Kelso.

Rugby remains at the heart of Jim Telfer's life. He loves watching it, talking about it and coaching now as much as he ever did, even if his active involvement only amounts to the tutoring of the Melrose U-18 side. To him, that's as important as anything he's done before. Teaching the next generation the right habits is a task he loves.

'You should see him,' says JJ. 'His presence on the sideline is worth about twelve points to Melrose. He doesn't have to open his mouth. The referee looks over and goes, "Christ, that's Jim Telfer", and gets all nervous. "Offside! Penalty for Melrose!" He's still a very intimidating man to a lot of people who don't know him.'

JJ might be exaggerating about the penalties, but there is no doubting the scale of Telfer's reputation around the world. It's hard-earned and well-deserved. He won two Grand Slams, a Five Nations championship and a Lions series. The power of his oratory was captured brilliantly in the documentary *Living With Lions*. His address to his forwards on the morning of the first Lions Test in South Africa – 'This is your Everest, boys' – has gone into rugby legend. As JJ said: 'Thanks to that documentary, the rest of the world could see for themselves what we'd seen for years; the man is inspirational.'

Telfer gave up his Scotland role in 1991 to concentrate fully on his teaching career, but it wasn't long before he was lured back. The national team was in a major slump when he took back the reins in January 1998, having lost 10 of their previous 12 Test matches including a mortifying 58-point loss to South Africa at Murrayfield.

The new era began with a victory in Dublin and then seven straight losses. Scotland conceded 45 points to Australia in Sydney, 51 points to Fiji in Suva and 51 more to France in Edinburgh. Telfer's team were discounted ahead of the 1999 Five Nations, but, to the bewilderment of the outside world, Scotland won the championship, an against-all-odds success sealed with an astonishing victory in Paris. Scotland scored five times in the space of twenty breathless first-half minutes and won 36–22. It was – and remains – the most points the Scots ever scored against the French.

Later, as the all-powerful director of rugby at the SRU, his take on the way Scotland should proceed in the professional game caused controversy and ill feeling. He had public fallouts with some of his former players – Calder, Sole, Gavin Hastings and even JJ – but these wounds have healed in time. Many of his former players say that Telfer was the most extraordinary rugby man they ever met.

Telfer is sitting in his home in Galashiels, talking about rugby – Scottish rugby, European rugby, world rugby. He's as opinionated about the game as he ever was. He doesn't dwell on the past and says he hates reunions. 'There's been a few – for the Melrose championship-winning team, for the Grand Slam sides of 1984 and 1990 and for the Lions of 1997. I try to avoid them. They're a complete and utter waste of time. Everyone moves on. The common bond has gone. The only thing that united us was a moment in time that's long past. So I stay away if I can.'

You ask him for his greatest memory of 1990 and he sits back in his chair in heavy contemplation. It wasn't David Sole's walk, he says, because he didn't see it. Or Tony Stanger's try, which he still thinks was iffy. It wasn't Scott Hastings' critical tackle on Rory Underwood or the psychological warfare of the scrum series in the corner.

'It was Finlay tapping that penalty and running at England. Finlay was a great bloke. A man amongst men. That was the moment for me. Our boys had worked like beasts on the training ground, they'd performed that very move I don't know how many times. And me screaming at them all the while, 'Get lower! Get tighter!' When they did it on the day, it was precision. It was text book. England were driven back, and the crowd went wilder than I'd ever heard them before. And I felt a shiver. Twenty years later I can close my eyes and still see it; the piece of perfection you dream about, that told me there and then, aye, the boys were going to be all right.'

# ACKNOWLEDGEMENTS

This book could not have been done without the support of the England team. That was the starting point. I was hopeful that the victorious Scots would be willing to talk, but what about the beaten team? Would Will Carling and Brian Moore and their teammates be prepared to speak about such a crushing defeat?

The first phone call I made was to Will, the second to Mooro. The book hinged on them agreeing to speak to me – and they could not have been more helpful had they won by 50 points that day. I'm hugely grateful for all the time they gave me – and for their honesty and wit. They are both immensely likeable.

I'm indebted to Jim Telfer and John Jeffrey, who are also central characters in the story. I did several interviews with Jim at his home in Galashiels and he was fascinating company. I also paid a number of visits to JJ's farm in Kelso. The hospitality was much appreciated.

Thank you also to David Sole and Ian McGeechan, captain and coach. And to Paul Burnell, Craig Chalmers, Damian Cronin, Chris Gray, Gavin Hastings, Scott Hastings, Sean Lineen. Kenny Milne, Tony Stanger, Iwan Tukalo and Derek White.

And in the England camp: Paul Ackford, Geoff Cooke, Wade Dooley, Jerry Guscott, Simon Halliday, Richard Hill, Simon Hodgkinson, Jeff Probyn, Paul 'The Judge' Rendall, Mick

Skinner, Mike Teague, Rory Underwood, Roger Uttley, Peter Winterbottom.

Many others were generous with their time, including David Bishop, the referee on the day, Tom McNab, the Scot in the England camp; and all those who helped me on the politics side, among them: Tam Dalyell, Magnus Linklater, Jim Sillars, David Stewart, Gerald Warner and David Torrance, whose book *We In Scotland: Thatcherism in a Cold Climate* is the definitive study of Margaret Thatcher and her relationship with the Scots.

I spent many hours at the Mitchell Library in Glasgow and would like to thank the staff there for putting up with my many botched attempts at loading the microfilm by myself. I would also like to thank Mike O'Reilly at the Scottish Rugby Union library at Murrayfield. I pored over every newspaper in Scotland and England from the mid 1980s to 1990 and drew on the work of many outstanding rugby writers. I won't list them here for fear of leaving somebody out – but you know who you are.

Also, the help of the following was much appreciated: Stuart Barnes, Graham Bean, Dick Best, Robbie Brown, Brian Campsall, Alan Davies, David Ferguson, Michael Grant, Gordon McKie, Alasdair Reid, John Rutherford, Keith Robertson, Les Snowdon, Ron Sutherland, Paul Morgan, Alan Pearey, Peter O'Reilly, Brendan Fanning, Stephen Jones.

Thanks to Mark Stanton, always a soothing voice on the end of the telephone. And to Richard Bath, who cast his forensic eye over the manuscript. Tristan Jones commissioned the book at the outset and his faith in the project meant an awful lot to me. I also owe a debt of thanks to Matt Phillips, editorial director at Yellow Jersey, and to Juliet Brooke, who edited *The Grudge* and whose support and expertise was a major boost in the final months.

The finest journalist I know also happens to be my brother, Alan. For his enthusiasm, his guidance on structure and for the improvements he made to the copy, I really can't thank him enough. He has written three brilliant rugby books and his first,

*Stand Up and Fight: When Munster Beat the All Blacks,* was the inspiration behind *The Grudge.*

A lifetime of gratitude and love goes to my parents, Tom and Anne. I could be here for an awfully long time thanking you for all you've done for me. Heartfelt thanks also to Jim and Edna Beveridge for being the best in-laws in all the world.

For my wife, Lynn, and our children, Eilidh and Tom, I save the biggest thank you. Without your incredible support, I would never have got to the end. I cherish the note Eilidh left on my desk at one point: 'Daddy, when you are finished the book, can we have a present?' It's got no pictures to colour in or pop-ups of Harry Potter, but, hey, it's finished. And I dedicate it to the three of you – with much love.

# SELECTED BIBLIOGRAPHY

## BOOKS

Andrew, Rob, *A Game and a Half: An Autobiography.* Coronet Books, 1994

Armstrong, Gary, and Derek Douglas, *Jethart's Here! The Gary Armstrong Story.* Mainstream Publishing, 1995

Bills, Peter, *Carling: A Man Apart.* Witherby, 1993

Blake, Peter, and Andrew John, *The World According to Margaret Thatcher.* Michael O'Mara Books, 2003

Campbell, John, *Margaret Thatcher, Vol. 1: The Grocer's Daughter.* Jonathan Cape, 2000

Campbell, John, *Margaret Thatcher, Vol. 2: The Iron Lady.* Jonathan Cape, 2003

Carling, Will, *Captain's Diary 1989–1991.* Pan Books, 1991

Carling, Will, *My Autobiography.* Coronet Books, 1998

Cleary, Mick, *The Carling Years: England Rugby 1988–96.* Victor Gollancz, 1996

Connor, Jeff, *Giants of Scottish Rugby.* Mainstream Publishing, 2000

Devine, T. M., *The Scottish Nation 1700–2000.* Penguin Books, 1999

Dooley, Wade, with Gerry Greenberg, *The Tower and the*

*Glory: The Wade Dooley Story*. Mainstream Publishing, 1992

Guscott, Jeremy, *The Autobiography*. Headline, 2001

Guscott, Jeremy, with Stephen Jones, *At the Centre: The Autobiography*. Pavilion Books, 1996

Hastings, Gavin, with Clem Thomas, *High Balls and Happy Hours: An Autobiography*. Mainstream Publishing, 1994

Hastings, Scott, and Derek Douglas, *Great Scott!* Mainstream Publishing, 1996

Kemp, Arnold, *The Hollow Drum: Scotland since the War*. Mainstream Publishing, 1993

Marr, Andrew, *The Battle for Scotland*. Penguin Books, 1992

McGeechan, Ian, with David Sole, Gavin Hastings, Ian Robertson and Mick Cleary, *Scotland's Grand Slam 1990*. Stanley Paul, 1990

Moore, Brian, with Stephen Jones, *Brian Moore: The Autobiography*. Partridge Press, 1995

Probyn, Jeff, and Barry Newcombe, *Upfront: The Jeff Probyn Story*. Mainstream Publishing, 1993

Raban, Jonathan, *God, Man, & Mrs Thatcher*. Chatto & Windus, 1989

Sole, David, with Derek Douglas, *Heart and Sole: A Rugby Life*. Headline, 1992

Telfer, Jim, with David Ferguson, *Looking Back . . . For Once*. Mainstream Publishing, 2005

Thatcher, Margaret, *The Downing Street Years*. HarperCollins, 1993

Thatcher, Margaret, *The Path to Power*. HarperCollins, 1995

Torrance, David, *'We in Scotland': Thatcherism in a Cold Climate*. Birlinn, 2009

## ADDITIONAL SOURCES

*Daily Record*, *Daily Telegraph*, *Edinburgh Evening News*, *Glasgow Herald*, *Guardian*, *Independent*, *Observer*, *Rugby World & Post*, *Rugby News*, *Scotsman*, *Scotland on Sunday*, *Sunday Telegraph*, *Sunday Times*, *The Times*.

# APPENDIX

## THE 1990 FIVE NATIONS CHAMPIONSHIP

**20 January, Twickenham: England** (7) **23–0** (0) **Ireland**
**England**: S. Hodgkinson (Nottingham), R. Underwood (Leicester
& RAF), W. Carling (Harlequins, captain), J. Guscott (Bath),
M. Bailey (Wasps), R. Andrew (Wasps), R. Hill (Bath), P. Rendall
(Wasps), B. Moore (Nottingham), J. Probyn (Wasps), W. Dooley
(Preston Grasshoppers), P. Ackford (Harlequins), M. Skinner
(Harlequins), P. Winterbottom (Harlequins), D. Egerton (Bath)
**Tries:** Probyn, Egerton, Underwood, Guscott
**Conversions:** Hodgkinson (2)
**Penalties:** Hodgkinson
**Ireland:** K. Murphy (Cork Constitution), M. Kiernan (Dolphin),
B. Mullin (Blackrock), D. Irwin (Instonians), K. Crossan
(Instonians), P. Russell (Instonians), F. Aherne (Lansdowne),
D. Fitzgerald (Lansdowne), S. Smith (Ballymena), G. Halpin
(Wanderers), N. Francis (Blackrock), W. Anderson (Dungannon,
captain), P. Matthews (Wanderers), P. O'Hara (Sunday's Well),
N. Mannion (Corinthians)
**Replacement**: J. McDonald (Malone) for S. Smith, 33mins


**3 February, Lansdowne Road: Ireland** (7) **10–13** (0) **Scotland**
**Ireland:** K. Murphy (Cork Constitution), M. Kiernan (Dolphin),

B. Mullin (Blackrock), D. Irwin (Instonians), K. Crossan (Instonians), B. Smith (Oxford University), F. Aherne (Lansdowne), J. Fitzgerald (Young Munster), J. McDonald (Malone), D. Fitzgerald (Lansdowne), P. O'Hara (Sunday's Well), D. Lenihan (Cork Constitution), W. Anderson (Dungannon, captain), P. Matthews (Wanderers), N. Mannion (Corinthians)
**Try:** Fitzgerald
**Penalties:** Kiernan (2)
**Replacement:** P. Collins (London Irish) for P. O'Hara, 38mins
**Scotland:** G. Hastings (London Scottish), T. Stanger (Hawick), S. Hastings (Watsonians), S. Lineen (Boroughmuir), I. Tukalo (Selkirk), C. Chalmers (Melrose), G. Armstrong (Jed-Forest), D. Sole (Edinburgh Academicals, captain), Kenny Milne (Heriot's) P. Burnell (London Scottish), C. Gray (Nottingham), D. Cronin (Bath), J. Jeffrey (Kelso), F. Calder (Stewart's Melville), D. White (London Scottish)
**Tries:** White (2)
**Conversion:** Chalmers
**Penalty:** Chalmers

**3 February, Parc des Princes: France** (0) **7–26** (13) **England**
**France:** S. Blanco (Biarritz), M. Andrieu (Nimes), P. Sella (Agen), D. Charvet (Toulouse), P. Lagisquet (Bayonne), F. Mesnel (Racing Club), P. Berbizier (Agen, captain), P. Ondarts (Biarritz), L. Armary (Lourdes), J. P. Garuet (Lourdes), T. Devergie (Nimes), D. Erbani (Agen), E. Champ (Toulon), L. Rodriguez (Dax), O. Roumat (Dax)
**Try:** Lagisquet
**Penalty:** Charvet
**Replacement:** P. Marocco (Montferrand) for L. Armary, 61mins
**England:** S. Hodgkinson (Nottingham), R. Underwood (Leicester & RAF), W. Carling (Harlequins, captain), J. Guscott (Bath), M. Bailey (Wasps), R. Andrew (Wasps), R. Hill (Bath), P. Rendall (Wasps), B. Moore (Nottingham), J. Probyn (Wasps), W. Dooley (Preston Grasshoppers), P. Ackford (Harlequins), M. Skinner (Harlequins), P. Winterbottom (Harlequins), M. Teague (Gloucester)
**Tries:** Underwood, Guscott, Carling
**Conversion:** Hodgkinson
**Penalties:** Hodgkinson (4)

**17 February, Murrayfield: Scotland** (3) **21–0** (0) **France**
**Scotland:** G. Hastings (London Scottish), T. Stanger (Hawick),
S. Hastings (Watsonians), S. Lineen (Boroughmuir), I. Tukalo
(Selkirk), C. Chalmers (Melrose), G. Armstrong (Jed-Forest),
D. Sole (Edinburgh Academicals), Kenny Milne (Heriot's),
P. Burnell (London Scottish), C. Gray (Nottingham), D. Cronin
(Bath), J. Jeffrey (Kelso), F. Calder (Stewart's Melville),
D. White (London Scottish)
**Tries:** Calder, Tukalo
**Conversions:** Chalmers (2)
**Penalties:** Chalmers (2), G. Hastings
**France:** S. Blanco (Biarritz), P. Hontas (Biarritz), P. Sella (Agen),
F. Mesnel (Racing Club), P. Lagisquet (Bayonne), D. Camberabero
(Beziers), H. Sanz (Narbonne), M. Pujolle (Nice), L. Armary
(Lourdes), P. Ondarts (Biarritz), T. Devergie (Nimes), O. Roumat
(Dax), J. M. Lhermet (Montferrand), A. Carminati (Beziers),
L. Rodriguez (Dax, captain)
**Red card:** Carminati, 49mins

**17 February, Twickenham: England** (16) **34–6** (0) **Wales**
**England:** S. Hodgkinson (Nottingham), S. Halliday (Bath),
W. Carling (Harlequins, captain), J. Guscott (Bath),
R. Underwood (Leicester & RAF), R. Andrew (Wasps), R. Hill
(Bath), P. Rendall (Wasps), B. Moore (Nottingham), J. Probyn
(Wasps), W. Dooley (Preston Grasshoppers), P. Ackford
(Harlequins), M. Skinner (Harlequins), P. Winterbottom
(Harlequins), M. Teague (Gloucester)
**Tries:** Carling, Underwood (2), Hill
**Conversions:** Hodgkinson (3)
**Penalties:** Hodgkinson (4)
**Wales:** P. Thorburn (Neath), M. Titley (Swansea), M. Ring
(Cardiff), M. Hall (Cardiff), A. Emyr (Swansea), D. Evans (Cardiff),
R. Jones (Swansea, captain), M. Griffiths (Cardiff), K. Phillips
(Neath), L. Delaney (Llanelli), A. Allen (Newbridge), G. Llewellyn
(Neath), P. Davies (Llanelli), R. Collins (Cardiff), M. Jones (Neath)
**Try:** Davies
**Conversion:** Thorburn

**3 March, Cardiff Arms Park: Wales** (3) **9–13** (10) **Scotland**
**Wales:** P. Thorburn (Neath), M. Hall (Cardiff), M. Ring (Cardiff),
A. Bateman (Neath), A. Emyr (Swansea), D. Evans (Cardiff),
R. Jones (Swansea, captain), B. Williams (Neath), K. Phillips
(Neath), J. Pugh (Neath), P. Davies (Llanelli), G. Llewellyn
(Neath), M. Perego (Llanelli), R. Collins (Cardiff), M. Jones (Neath)
**Try:** Jones
**Conversion:** Thorburn
**Penalty:** Thorburn
**Scotland:** G. Hastings (London Scottish), T. Stanger (Hawick),
S. Hastings (Watsonians), S. Lineen (Boroughmuir), I. Tukalo
(Selkirk), C. Chalmers (Melrose), G. Armstrong (Jed-Forest), D. Sole
(Edinburgh Academicals, captain), Kenny Milne (Heriot's), P. Burnell
(London Scottish), C. Gray (Nottingham), D. Cronin (Bath), J. Jeffrey
(Kelso), F. Calder (Stewart's Melville), D. White (London Scottish)
**Try:** Cronin
**Penalties:** Chalmers (3)

**17 March, Murrayfield: Scotland** (9) **13–7** (4) **England**
**Scotland:** G. Hastings (London Scottish), T. Stanger (Hawick),
S. Hastings (Watsonians), S. Lineen (Boroughmuir), I. Tukalo
(Selkirk), C. Chalmers (Melrose), G. Armstrong (Jed-Forest),
D. Sole (Edinburgh Academicals, captain), Kenny Milne (Heriot's),
P. Burnell (London Scottish), C. Gray (Nottingham), D. Cronin
(Bath), J. Jeffrey (Kelso), F. Calder (Stewart's Melville), D. White
(London Scottish)
**Try:** Stanger
**Penalties:** Chalmers (3)
**Replacement:** D. Turnbull (Hawick) for D. White, 30mins
**England:** S. Hodgkinson (Nottingham), S. Halliday (Bath),
W. Carling (Harlequins, captain), J. Guscott (Bath), R. Underwood
(Leicester & RAF), R. Andrew (Wasps), R. Hill (Bath), P. Rendall
(Wasps), B. Moore (Nottingham), J. Probyn (Wasps), W. Dooley
(Preston Grasshoppers), P. Ackford (Harlequins), M. Skinner
(Harlequins), P. Winterbottom (Harlequins) M. Teague (Gloucester)
**Try:** Guscott
**Penalty:** Hodgkinson
**Replacement:** M. Bailey (Wasps) for J. Guscott, 64mins

# INDEX